mumok

AVANT-GARDE AND LIBERATION

EDITED BY CHRISTIAN KRAVAGNA AND
MUMOK – MUSEUM MODERNER KUNST STIFTUNG LUDWIG WIEN

CONTEMPORARY ART AND DECOLONIAL MODERNISM

VERLAG DER BUCHHANDLUNG
WALTHER UND FRANZ KÖNIG, COLOGNE

IN MEMORY OF RADCLIFFE BAILEY, VIVAN SUNDARAM
AND EMMA WOLUKAU-WANAMBWA, WHO PASSED AWAY IN 2023
DURING THE PREPARATIONS FOR THIS EXHIBITION.

KAROLA KRAUS, MATTHIAS MICHALKA

FOREWORD

As an institutional link between past and present, a museum not only struggles constitutively with questions of historicity, with ways to preserve and adequately represent historical knowledge while also considering new insights and criticism in this regard; it is also itself part of the constant reevaluations, omissions, and shifts in focus that underlie its specific substantive work.

Although the collection of mumok—Museum moderner Kunst Stiftung Ludwig Wien focuses on artistic developments that took place in the nineteen-sixties and were dedicated to coming to terms with changes and conflicts in politics and society, for a long time its collection and exhibition policy nonetheless reproduced those very historical hegemonies and exclusions against which resistance has grown since the twentieth century, both politically and artistically and both inside and outside Western societies. Resistance has in particular taken the form of postcolonial revisions aiming at adequate consideration of the Global South, thus tempering the Eurocentric perspective.

Although isolated attempts were made to include artists from Africa, Asia, and Latin America in the decades after the museum was founded in 1962, and increased attention was devoted to developments in Eastern Europe after the fall of the Iron Curtain, a self-critical shift in perspective and systematic inclusion of the Global South did not come about until the beginning of the twenty-first century. At the invitation of mumok, Christian Kravagna, Professor of Postcolonial Studies at the Academy of Fine Arts Vienna, conceived twenty years ago an acquisition concept programmatically titled *Beyond NATO Art* that was designed to counter the dominance of Western art in the collection, linking acquisitions to questions of colonialism, migration, and globalization. Among the more than twenty new artists whose works were integrated into the collection at that time were Yto Barrada and Vivan Sundaram, who are of central importance to the exhibition *Avant-Garde and Liberation*. With occasional solo exhibitions, cinema screenings, conferences, acquisitions, and donations, mumok continues to pursue this initiative to expand the collection. And yet we are very much aware that artists of color and non-Western perspectives and developments are still far from being adequately represented in our collection and in our program.

Even though a single exhibition cannot compensate for our structural deficits and omissions, *Avant-Garde and Liberation* serves us as a constructive and forward-looking model for how to deal with the challenges of globalization and our one-sided Western conditioning. Instead of merely trying to play a game of catch-up in acknowledgment of a new awareness of diversity issues by showing works by previously neglected artists from Africa, Asia, and the "Black Atlantic," *Avant-Garde and Liberation* plumbs the very foundations of inequality and its effects on society while proposing ways to overcome it. The exhibition shows how artists worldwide are responding to contemporary forms of racism, exploitation, and oppression by making pointed reference to the history of decolonial liberation efforts.

What comes to light here is the vital importance that reactivating history has for artists of the Global South today, and this corresponds to the basic mission of any museum. For Walter Benjamin, it was the historian's task to stop "telling the sequence of events like the beads of a rosary. Instead, he grasps the constellation which his own era has formed with a definite earlier one."[1] Stories about the past thus become stories about the present, and "history is the subject of a structure whose site is not homogenous, empty time, but time filled by the presence of the now."[2] There could hardly be a more apt description of the methodology pursued in *Avant-Garde and Liberation* and the exhibition's exemplary function for mumok's handling of issues of marginalization and exclusion.

We are delighted that this groundbreaking exhibition and publication could be realized despite difficult conditions. Accordingly, many people deserve our thanks for the success of this project. Our deepest gratitude goes to the participating artists Mathieu Kleyebe Abonnenc, Omar Ba, Yto Barrada, Mohamed Bourouissa, Diedrick Brackens, Serge Attukwei Clottey, william cordova, Atul Dodiya, Robert Gabris, Jojo Gronostay, Leslie Hewitt, Iman Issa, Janine Jembere, patricia kaersenhout, Belinda Kazeem-Kamiński, Zoe Leonard, Vincent Meessen, The Otolith Group, Fahamu Pecou, Cauleen Smith, and Moffat Takadiwa for their invaluable support in the development and realization of the exhibition and the conception of the catalogue. We very much regret that

Radcliffe Bailey and Vivan Sundaram will no longer be able to attend the exhibition, although both artists were intensely involved in the preparations. Our special thanks to Vivan Sundaram's widow, Geeta Kapur, who made it possible for us to present his expansive installation *One and the Many* in Vienna and to integrate it into our collection.

We would also like to express our appreciation to the many institutional and private lenders who made their works available to us, namely the Artworkers Retirement Society; Backslash Gallery, Paris; Livia Benavides 80M2, Lima; Lonti Ebers; Shireen and Kurush Jungalwala Collection, Mumbai; Kiran Nadar Museum of Art New Delhi; Elisabeth und Filip de Keersmaecker; Christiane Leister; Miyoung Lee and Jiwon Simpkins; Elena Markwalder; Galerie Marcelle Alix, Paris; Mennour, Paris; Michael C. Carlos Museum, Atlanta; Morán Morán, Los Angeles / Mexiko; Nicodim Gallery, Los Angeles; Perrotin, Paris; Judit Reszegi; Rodeo Gallery, London / Piraeus; Sfeir-Semler Gallery, Beirut / Hamburg; Jack Shainman Gallery, New York; Sikkema Jenkins & Co, New York; Simchowitz Gallery, Los Angeles; The Estate of Maud Sulter; Galerie Templon, New York / Paris / Brussels, and Wonnerth Dejaco, Vienna.

Wilfried Kühn and Wassily Walter from Kuehn Malvezzi Architects developed empathetic exhibition architecture that does justice to the complexity of the presentation, for which we owe them a great debt of gratitude.

Clemens Jahn has our sincere thanks for designing the catalogue with such sensitivity.

We would also like to thank the authors for their informative essays. Against the backdrop of theoretical reflections on temporality in current anti-racist movements, Christian Kravagna discusses in his introductory essay the various forms in which artists have taken recourse to decolonial modernity. Kravagna argues for a new understanding of the avant-garde that overcomes a narrow Eurocentric reading to encompass the radical potential for change displayed by global modernisms.

In their conversation, Nana Adusei-Poku and Christian Kravagna discuss the background behind a "politics of time" in the wake of historical liberation movements. Adusei-Poku, who organized the highly acclaimed exhibition *Black Melancholia* in 2022, refers to the problematic entanglement of a linear concept of time based on progress narratives with European notions of modernism and the avant-garde, speaking about alternative historical time concepts that made it possible to set mechanisms of liberation in motion.

In her essay, Saloni Mathur deals specifically with modernism in India, describing the decolonization movements there and their extraordinary significance for contemporary Indian art. Artists today draw on historical places, events, and figures such as Rabindranath Tagore and Mahatma Gandhi, whose iconic status is located in a realm "between history and myth," as motifs for addressing anew the intertwining of modernism with the decolonization processes in India.

Lina Ramadan's essay focuses on the motif of return in the works of North African artists Yto Barrada, Mohamed Bourouissa, and Iman Issa, especially in terms of language and speech (including whispering). Ramadan analyzes how language is frequently robbed of its original context of meaning in their works as a way to undermine the underlying power relations. Form, representation, and historical references become the revenants of a "diasporic revolution."

Zeigam Azizov's essay likewise addresses the inseparability of the concept of time from the ideas of liberation embraced by European modernism but introduces yet a further aspect, namely the crisis of externalization. The crisis of visualizing what is external to oneself ultimately means a crisis of art itself, insofar as art presents a way of making elements of the external world visible. Time, understood as a non-linear, transhistorical phenomenon, is externalized by way of dialogue, and only a dialogical passage through time, like that accomplished by liberation movements, makes it tangible.

We take this opportunity to recognize the entire staff at mumok, who worked with great enthusiasm to make this project a reality. Project manager Claudia Dohr in particular contributed significantly to the success of the exhibition with her incredible dedication and careful professional coordination. A major role was played as well by Ines Gebetsroither and Nina Krick in terms of their editorial support for the publication and expert production management, for which they deserve our sincere thanks. We would also like to thank Birgit Schretzmayr for her energetic support. Our deepest thanks as well to the staff of the mumok collection under the direction of Marie-Therese Hochwartner, to the conservation department headed by Tina Hierl, in particular Karin Steiner, and to the entire art education team led by Julia Hürner. Katharina Murschetz and Katharina Kober deserve recognition for their press and public relations work, as do Martina Kuso and her team Elisabeth Dopsch, Isabella Pedevilla, Malina Schartmüller, and Lisa Sycha for their marketing efforts. We owe the smooth exhibition setup to the support of the Technical and Operations Department headed by Oliver Kern, especially Tina Fabijanic and her team. For the professional organization of the fundraising and sponsorship activities, along with the accompanying events, our warm thanks go to Karin Kirste and her colleague Cornelia Stellwag, as well as to Sandra Adam, Simone

Arnold, Victoria Mascha, and Barbara Panny. And to all museum employees not named here, our sincere thanks for your hard work and dedication.

Our deepest thanks go to Christian Kravagna, who from the very start committed his time and attention to this exhibition and publication with loving devotion and incredible precision. It is thanks to his expertise based on long years of research in the fields of postcolonial studies, global modernisms, migration, the politics of representation, and institutional critique, together with the resulting network, that works never before seen in Austria can now be presented to the public and important voices can be heard in this publication. Karola Kraus would also like to express her special thanks to Matthias Michalka, who supported this project with great dedication from the outset and has been at Christian Kravagna's side at all times to offer help and advice.

We would like to thank the mumok Board, the Institut français d'Autriche, the Mondriaan Fund, the Hotel Josefine in Vienna, and the Academy of Fine Arts Vienna for their financial support, without which the realization of this ambitious project would not have been possible.

1   Walter Benjamin, "Theses on the Philosophy of History," in Benjamin, Illuminations, ed. Hannah Arendt, transl. Harry Zohn (New York: Shocken Books, 1969), p. 261.
2   Ibid., p. 263.

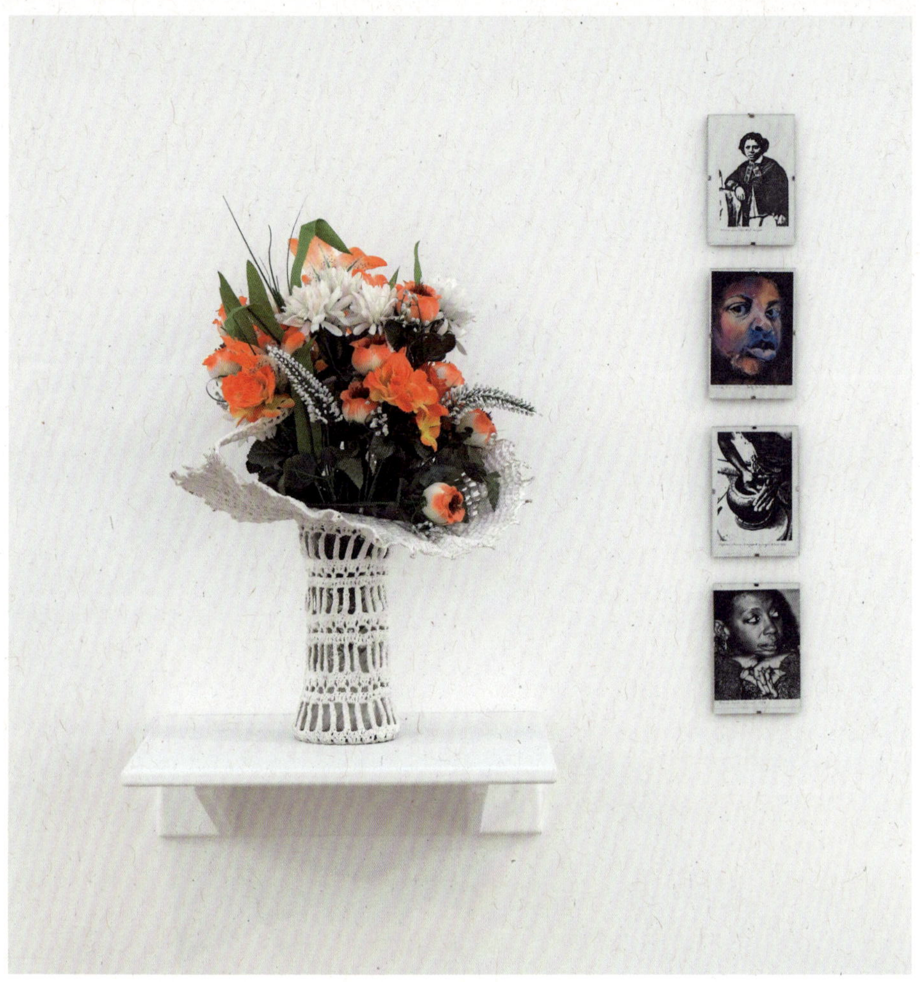

Marlene Smith
Art History, 1987
Installation view, *The 1980s: Today's Beginnings?*,
Van Abbemuseum, Eindhoven, 2016

CHRISTIAN KRAVAGNA

AVANT-GARDE AND LIBERATION

Art history is about reconnecting with what, and who, went before, inquiring into questions of genealogy. Art history is the alternative narrative, the search for other, suppressed truths, and a form of resistance to the violence of cultural exclusion. *Art History* is the title of a fascinating work by the British artist Marlene Smith from 1987. In it she argues for the necessity of a history of Black women's arts that were afforded no place in the galleries, museums, universities, and publications of their time. The sugar-water-starched crochet work wrapped around a vase holding a bouquet of plastic flowers celebrates how the artist's mother decorated her private space with hand-crafted pieces. The four images next to it put into context historical and contemporary women artists from the Black Arts Movement that Smith co-founded in Britain: a portrait photograph of nineteenth-century African American sculptor Edmonia Lewis, a reproduction of a painted self-portrait by British artist Simone Alexander, a photograph taken by Ingrid Pollard of Kenyan-British ceramicist Magdalene Odundo's pottery-making hands, and a close-up of a woman's face by British artist Brenda Agard. It is not only the historical depth of *Art History* that makes it remarkable—reaching all the way back to one of the first known Black women artists, known primarily for works dealing with liberation from slavery—but also the sheer breadth of media covered by the references. The media range from sculpture and painting to photography and onward to ceramics. Marlene Smith's art history thus defies cultural hierarchies to showcase the diversity of Black women's aesthetic practices. Overall, the arrangement of the floral decorations and the framed small-format photographs is more reminiscent of domestic furnishings and family pictures than what is classically found in an art exhibition space. The varied forms of expression and the transitions between private and public, between the aesthetics of everyday life, craft, and art indicate that this revision of art history is to be understood as part of a broader emancipatory movement devoted primarily to changing the life circumstances and prospects of groups that have been rendered invisible both socially and in cultural history. With *Art History*, Marlene Smith produced a work against the backdrop of the racist British society of the nineteen-eighties that mobilized resistance to the exclusionary white art world while incorporating two essential missions of any liberation movement—to bring together the dedicated forces of the present and to tie them into a history of previous struggles. A work such as *Art History*, made over thirty years ago and groundbreaking for its time, is today already itself a historical reference. It can serve as a model for the challenge of mounting an exhibition about the significance of liberation-minded twentieth-century avant-gardes for artists of the present day.

Avant-Garde and Liberation features works by twenty-four artists that respond to current political threats to freedom and survival by drawing on concepts, projects, and achievements of decolonial modernism. Covering a wide range of working methods, media, and aesthetics, this exhibition opens up a forum for engaging with the legacy of radical artistic and intellectual endeavors in the historical context of decolonization. The exhibition does not set out to trace a history of modernism in this context. This task has recently been taken up by other projects.[1] We thus do not present the art of decolonial modernism but rather demonstrate its far-reaching impact on critical contemporary art. This show surveys the present-day topicality of the liberationist spirit of those twentieth-century avant-gardes. It examines the legacy of the avant-garde through the prism of the art of today in its coming to terms with the setbacks that the project of liberation and justice is currently experiencing at the hands of neo-fascist, fundamentalist, and nationalist politics in the twenty-first century.

The project of decolonization has no beginning and no end. Anti-colonial movements are as old as colonialism. They achieved their first major triumphs with the revolution in Haiti (1791–1804) and the abolition of slavery and experienced the greatest consolidated progress with the political independence of many colonies in the decades following the Second World War. As Frantz Fanon and Ngũgĩ wa Thiong'o, as well as the authors from the Indian Subaltern Studies Group, have shown, the processes of decolonization of international relations, economic conditions, educational institutions, culture, and historiography are protracted and still not complete today.[2] The fact that the Ghanaian politician Kwame Nkrumah published a book on neocolonialism as early as 1965, just a few years after his country's independence, illustrates the problematic nature of any linear account of colonialism, anti-colonial

movements, decolonization, and neocolonial relations.[3]

When we speak of decolonial modernism in the context of this exhibition, we mean modernisms that have made an artistic contribution to the liberation movements of the colonized world and the anti-racism movements in the Western world. The artistic references to decolonial modernism span a period from the early twentieth century to the nineteen-seventies. But some of the allusions reach as far back as the anti-colonial revolution in Haiti, for example Radcliffe Bailey's sculpture *Untitled* (2010) **(p. 62)**, devoted to the revolutionary leaders Toussaint Louverture and Jean-Jacques Dessalines. Other works look back to indigenous resistance to Spanish rule in South America, as in william cordova's installation *this one's 4U (pa' nosotros)* (2008–15) **(pp. 74–75)**, which brings together Túpac Amaru II from eighteenth-century Peru and his namesake, rapper Tupac Amaru Shakur. Such transhistorical encounters between artists and activists of the present and the past are typical of the complex politics of time in the works on view in the exhibition. The essays in this catalogue explore this aspect in more detail. Saloni Mathur, for example, discusses the "strange temporalities" in certain works that relate to Indian modernism. In a conversation with Nana Adusei-Poku, we discuss the concept of "hetero-temporality" that she has proposed for certain works of art from the African diaspora. Lina Ramadan talks about "a past centered today centered tomorrow" in her essay on artists from North Africa. And Zeigam Azizov reflects from a philosophical perspective on how decolonization in and of itself undermines the notions of time established by Western modernist thought.

In geographical terms, the works on display refer back to historical movements in South Asia, the Middle East, Africa, the Americas, and Europe. In India, contemporary artists such as

Vivan Sundaram and Atul Dodiya are responding to the current Hindu nationalist threat to the secular state and to social cohesion. They draw here, for example, on the cosmopolitan educational projects of Rabindranath Tagore, the radical art produced by the sculptor Ramkinkar Baij in the nineteen-thirties, and Gandhi's art of nonviolent resistance. African artists including Omar Ba and Moffat Takadiwa are reengaging with anti-colonial intellectuals such as Cheikh Anta Diop and musicians such as Thomas Mapfumo, whose projects stood for African liberation in the sixties, much like the contemporary avant-garde architecture in Accra or Abidjan, which Jojo Gronostay takes a fresh look at. In North Africa, artists including Mohamed Bourouissa and Yto Barrada are updating for today the ideas of anti-colonial theorists such as Frantz Fanon, as well as the sculptural work of Saloua Raouda Choucair. In response to systemic racism and anti-Black violence in the USA, African American artists such as Fahamu Pecou, Leslie Hewitt, and Cauleen Smith are reactivating the legacy of the Harlem Renaissance, Pan-Africanism, and the Black Power era. And in European societies that are in the process of militarizing their immigration policies and where nationalism is shifting to the political center, artists like Mathieu Abonnenc and patricia kaersenhout are reconstructing the anti-colonial film aesthetic of directors such as Sarah Maldoror and the Black feminism of authors like Jeanne and Paulette Nardal.

THE CRISIS AND THE AVANT-GARDE

A stack of books, freestanding, about one meter high. Fifty-three copies of the same book, first editions of James Baldwin's *The Fire Next Time*, published in 1963. The number of books corresponds to the years that elapsed between the publication of Baldwin's reckoning with American racism and the making of Zoe Leonard's sculpture *Tipping Point* (2016). The structure of the work with its vertical layering of books is simple and yet creates a complex object prompting reflection on time, history, and conjunctures of violence. The sculpture stands for 2016 just as it stands for 1963. It represents the half century in between and addresses our present-day deliberations on the need to take recourse to Baldwin in view of the racial violence of our times. How do the social conditions in the years in which the two works were created relate?

Baldwin warned in his book of the total catastrophe that would result from ignoring radical inequality in the culture of white supremacy. "God gave Noah the rainbow sign / No more water, the fire next time," goes the "slave song" that inspired the book's title. "They have destroyed and are destroying hundreds of thousands of lives and do not know it and do not want to know it," Baldwin writes of his white compatriots.[4] Leonard's stacking of the books can be understood as an analogy for the incessantly repeated warning. "The serial aspect of the sculpture is only legible through another repetition," writes Darby English, "the repetition defining a crisis engendered by police killings of innocent and unarmed black citizens."[5] Baldwin wrote the two texts brought together in the book during the height of the Civil Rights Movement and to mark the 100th anniversary of the legal abolition of slavery by Abraham Lincoln's Emancipation Proclamation in 1863. *The Fire Next Time* is a critical appraisal of the great liberation project for which Black and white abolitionists laid the groundwork in the nineteenth century and which achieved its first great success with the abolition of slavery. One hundred years later, however, the Civil Rights Movement still had to fight for desegregation and voting rights and was menaced by the violence of white terror. "You know, and I know, that the country is celebrating one hundred years of freedom one hundred years too soon," Baldwin wrote to his nephew James.[6] The boy was only fourteen

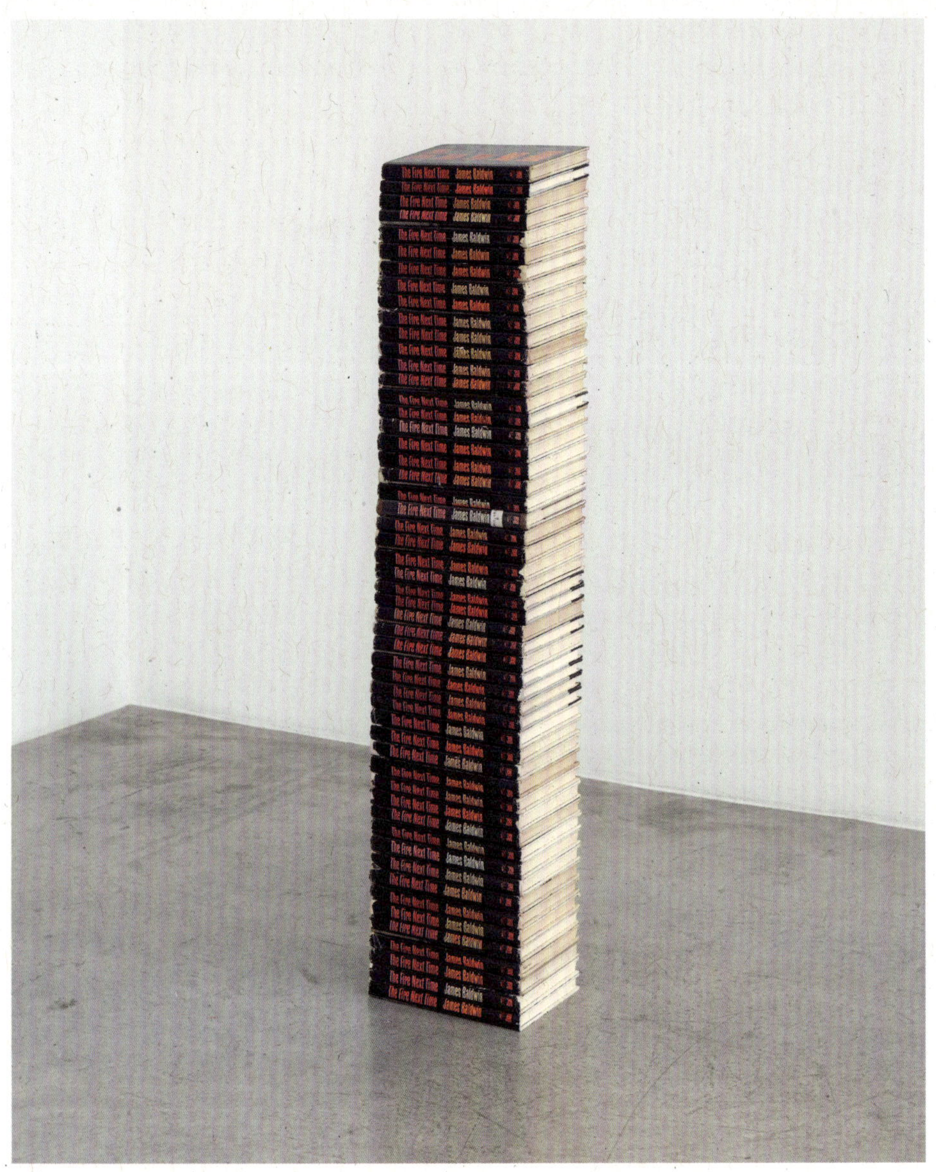

Zoe Leonard
Tipping Point, 2016

years old when his uncle started preparing him for the destructiveness of American racism by advising vigilance and preaching love as the antidote to inhumanity. In 2012 Trayvon Martin was seventeen years old when he was shot and killed by a neighborhood watchman. Tamir Rice was only twelve years old when he was shot dead by police in 2014, and Michael Brown was eighteen when he fell victim to a white police officer's gunfire that same year. Baldwin looks to the future in an attempt to protect his nephew from society's anti-Black violence. Fifty years later, many who are facing that same violence today are looking back at the history of deadly racism. The visual culture of Black Lives Matter is replete with references to the iconography of the Civil Rights Movement, and the current killings of Black people by representatives of institutional racism can be related to the lynchings during the white terror against the anti-racist movement in the nineteen-fifties and -sixties. Of all the artistic and intellectual figures of that era, Baldwin is among those cited most often today. Zoe Leonard's *Tipping Point* is a pointed articulation of the explosive nature of Baldwin's radical thinking on danger and on Black resilience. It is a reflection of the numerous attempts in the years between Trayvon Martin (2012) and George Floyd (2020) to understand the current crisis via recourse to Baldwin.[7]

In response to the wave of killings of young Black people prompted by institutional racism, writer Jesmyn Ward published in 2016 an anthology of poems and essays on the current situation, a book about "the fire of rage and despair and fierce, protective love currently sweeping through the streets and campuses of America."[8] She titled her book *The Fire This Time: A New Generation Speaks about Race*. "In desperation, I sought James Baldwin," Ward writes.[9] Faced with an existential threat, the memory of her predecessor flashes before her eyes. The fire of love rooted in rage is burning *now*, because white America did not take Baldwin's warning of the "next time" seriously. The current state of emergency and the challenge it poses to thought, feeling, and resistant action can only be understood through the lens of the earlier state of emergency, and especially in light of Baldwin's response—a refusal to allow racist violence and the rage it unleashes to turn into self-destruction. Jesmyn Ward intended to divide her book into sections pertaining to the past and others looking toward the future. But only three of the texts refer explicitly to the future, while most dealt with the past and present: "And that told me … how inextricably interwoven the past is in the present, how heavily that past bears on the future; we cannot talk about black lives mattering or police brutality without reckoning with the very foundation of this country."[10]

Eddie Glaude published his book *Begin Again: James Baldwin's America and Its Urgent Lessons for Our Own* in 2020. He, too, describes a looping movement of thought in time that demands a critical understanding of the present: "This book moves backward and forward, vacillating between past and present as I think *with* Baldwin about this troubled period in American history."[11] For Glaude, this thinking along with Baldwin in the context of the crisis of Trump-era USA means grappling with the ghosts of history that haunt both Baldwin's time and our present day. "Thus, the book moves about: gesturing to the past, abruptly turning to the present, drawing on Baldwin's biography and close readings of his essays, and ending with my thoughts about our current morass."[12] Ta-Nehisi Coates undertakes another kind of updating of Baldwin's letter to his nephew in his 2015 book *Between the World and Me*.[13] The book is a letter to the author's fifteen-year-old son in which Coates confronts the American history of violence against Black people, the role of the police, and the physical experience of racism with white repression of history. Baldwin formulated white America's relationship to history by saying: "They are, in effect, still trapped in a history which they do not understand; and until they understand it, they cannot be released from it."[14] A measure of hope for change is still present when he writes to his nephew: "We can make America what America must become."[15] Such hope is no longer present in what Coates has to say. He took the title of his book from a 1935 poem by Richard Wright, thus referencing along with Baldwin another radical African American author of the twentieth century. In Wright's poem, "icy walls of fear" surround the narrator, who has happened upon the eerie traces of a lynching scene. The feeling of powerlessness mixed with anxiety that his own son might fall victim to state-sanctioned violence stands "between the world and me." What Jesmyn Ward, Eddie Glaude, and Ta-Nehisi Coates express in their books, and what Zoe Leonard brings to life for us with her sculpture, are the complex temporal dimensions that frame any attempt to come to terms with the current crisis, whether theoretical, artistic, or activist. The question we pose in this exhibition concerns the forms and figures of temporality in those contemporary art practices whose confrontation with acute threats to freedom are fed by the memory of the liberationist concepts of decolonial modernism. Just as Jesmyn Ward seeks out James Baldwin in a moment of despair, so do the artists in this exhibition think back on other avant-gardes of liberation in the midst of the crisis they are experiencing during their own lifetime. They seek out and consult Frantz Fanon and Cheikh Anta Diop, Sarah Maldoror and Faith Ringgold, Rabindranath Tagore and Ramkinkar Baij, Mahalia Jackson and Thomas Mapfumo, Zora Neale Hurston and Langston Hughes, among others.

THE SPIRITS OF LIBERATION

What does it actually mean to invoke a historical figure of liberation in a moment of danger and despair? The paragraph that Jesmyn Ward ends with "I sought Baldwin" begins with speechlessness in the face of the incomprehensible and a search for a way to express this feeling: "I needed words."[16] The desire for "kinship in this struggle" leads Ward to Baldwin. To comprehend what is happening in 2016 seems impossible without looking back at 1963. This is not necessarily a matter of causal justifications or of demonstrating continuities. Instead, it is first of all an attempt to transform helplessness into agency, in this case converting speechlessness into a book that can in turn help others to find words. For this purpose, one needs this kinship, those who went before, the tradition, the lines of descent—"you come from a long line of great poets," Baldwin writes to his nephew—which can be sought out in the moment of menace and whose struggles can be invoked when they have to be taken up again under new conditions. Further on we will discover the terms that artists use to describe these (elective) affinities. But let us first keep in mind that the ghosts of history cited by Eddie Glaude and others must not be understood solely as evil spirits of the past that still haunt the present. We must think as well of the appearance of ghosts as it was described in Jacques Derrida's *Specters of Marx*, as the conjuring of the specter/the spirits of a past struggle, as "a certain emancipatory and *messianic* affirmation, a certain experience of the promise."[17]

Avant-Garde and Liberation brings the spirits of liberation to the fore, that is, the movements and protagonists of decolonial modernism that are invoked today when it comes to combating current threats to freedom, life, and justice. A work by Janine Jembere illustrates the effort to summon the past in the literal sense as a moment of inspiration—the reception of the spirit. Her photographic series *Channelling (Vienna)* (2023) portrays ten artists from the Vienna scene who, eyes closed, make contact with a figure from a twentieth-century lib-

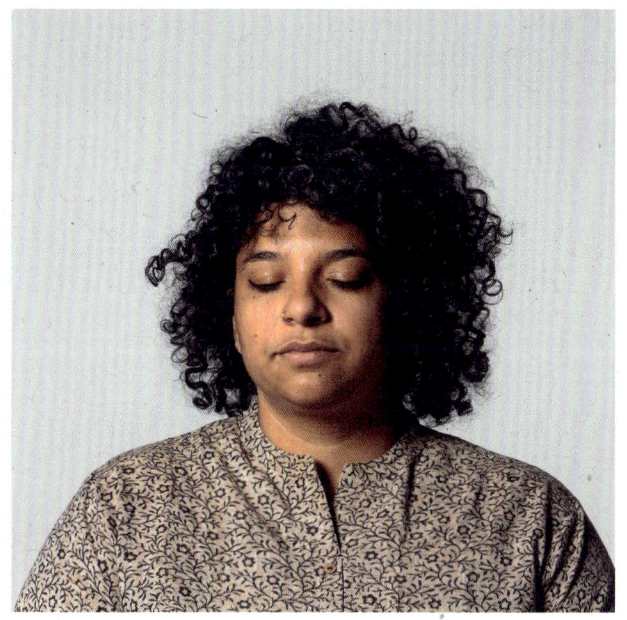
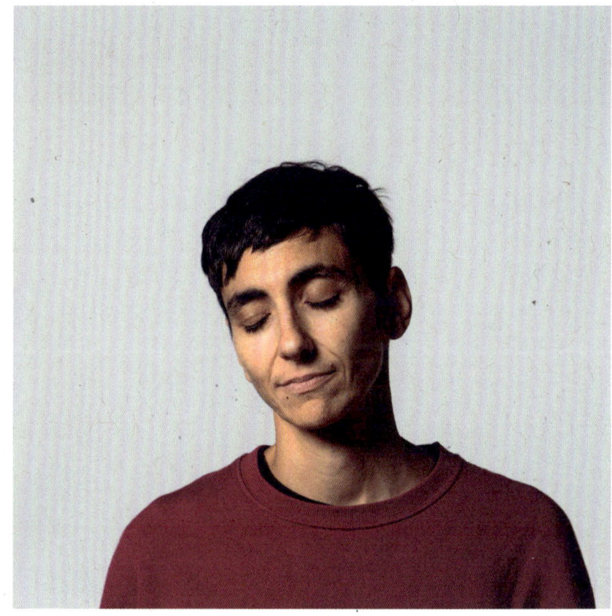

Janine Jembere
Channelling (Vienna), 2023

eration movement, whether the Black feminist avant-garde—*Abiona Esther Ojo channelling Faith Ringgold*— or the avant-garde of anti-colonial film—*Janine Jembere channelling Sarah Maldoror*. The portrait of the presence of a local community is created in the moment of connection with the ancestors in spirit, whose work the portrayed artists are carrying on. In relation to a work like this, we can also speak of the dreams of the politics of liberation, as invoked for example by Robin D. G. Kelley in his book *Freedom Dreams*: "My main point is that we must tap the well of our own collective imaginations, that we do what earlier generations have done: dream."[18] Jembere's work is one of the most recent in *Avant-Garde and Liberation*. The way she treats the intertwining of historical channeling and present-day connection in the local community shows a remarkable kinship not only to Marlene Smith's *Art History* but also to *Hysteria* (1991) by Maud Sulter, the oldest work in our exhibition. Sulter staged in *Hysteria* a complex photographic drama around the historical figure of American sculptor Edmonia Lewis. The players in this drama about the creativity and self-assertion of a Black woman artist in the late nineteenth century are Sulter herself in the role of Lewis and British artist friends including Bernardine Evaristo and Lubaina Himid in other roles.[19]

LIFE DOES NOT CONTAIN THE PAST TENSE

James Baldwin was one of the most committed intellectuals of the African American liberation movement in the sixties and seventies. His forthright words on the toxic constitution of an American society built on slavery and racism had a major impact. As an artist, however, Baldwin was equally aware of the importance of close observation and study of the details.[20] In a text accompanying an exhibition by the painter Beauford Delaney in Paris, Baldwin recounts the school of seeing he underwent in the course of his close relationship with the artist over many years. On walks through New York with his older friend, "in poverty and uncertainty," Baldwin learned from Delaney how to really pay attention to the things all around him—"a brown leaf on the black asphalt, oil moving like mercury in the black water of the gutter." He learns a kind of seeing that is

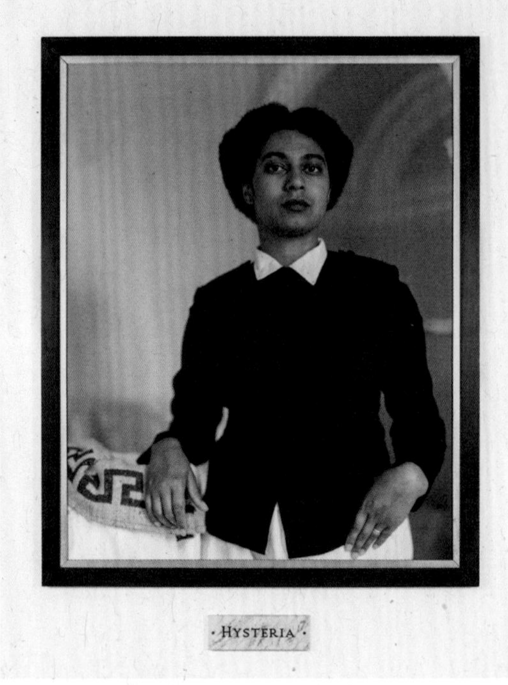

Maud Sulter
Hysteria, 1991

not a one-time act of noticing that something is there but rather a process of understanding, not least of understanding his own shifts in perception. Delaney "is *seeing* all the time."[21] Baldwin realizes that one can rely neither on what has been learned nor on memory. He has the insight "that life does not contain the past tense: the sunset one saw yesterday, the leaf that burned, or the rain that fell, have not been seen unless one is prepared to see them every day."[22] If we take another look at Baldwin's books in Zoe Leonard's *Tipping Point* with these thoughts in mind, we can see the sculpture from yet another angle. Although each book is part of the same edition, the spines and the cut of each copy look quite different. The books bear the traces of time and use by their readers. Each individual copy has its own history, and the social life of the object is linked to the biographies of its users. Who has read the individual books over the past fifty-three years? What did they each mean to their readers? What experiences and social circumstances did those readers associate with Baldwin's diagnosis

from their vantage point in the eighties and nineties, and what about the early twenty-first century? Piling *The Fire Next Time* up so high that the stack verges on tipping over can be understood as a sign of endurance, of (the limits of) patience, with ever-new "editions" being added to the struggle for freedom, equal rights, and recognition. Tyler Schmidt interprets Baldwin's thoughts on the temporality of seeing along these lines: "When he states that 'memory is a traitor and that life does not contain the past tense' ..., Baldwin cues us into his approach to history, specifically America's persistent oppressions and racial violence."[23] Learning how to see from his painter friend, the writer and activist develops from this experience a political conception of historicity— "Delaney's call to see 'anew,' to narrate a history that is always girded in an unfolding 'now,' unsettled Baldwin's writing practices."[24]

Here, the impossibility of distinguishing the political author from the artist becomes apparent. Baldwin's example is relevant to the approach taken in this exhibition, in which pictorial seeing is just as important as political seeing. The artworks in *Avant-Garde and Liberation* demand to be looked at with both eyes. With an eye for the light and the colors and the forms, the techniques and materials, the structures and rhythms. And also an eye for the motif, the narration, the reference, the concept, and the proposal.[25] Take, for example, the paintings by Serge Attukwei Clottey. They show young Black men in somewhat stiff poses that remind us of classic portrait photography. Clottey is interested in how Africans represent themselves, both in today's social media, from which he often draws his motifs, and in the era of decolonization of African societies after the mid-twentieth century. While the artist addresses issues of ecology and resource distribution as well as the circulation of commodities, waste, and artworks in his "Afro-gallonist" works, which are created by recycling the yellow plastic gallon containers commonly used in Ghana, his paintings revolve around the performance of identity and the cultures of fashion and styling in media appearances by Africans. Clottey's images refer back to the first generation of African studio photographers such as Seydou Keïta and Malick Sidibé in Mali, who in the fifties and sixties enabled their clients to choose from a selection of dignified image templates for modern African subjects. These pictures not only formed a counterpoint to colonial photography but also offered a way to imagine the future prospects of African societies.

If we look at Clottey's paintings with the eye for detail that Baldwin demands, we notice not only the oil paint as medium but also the use of duct tape. This is the kind of tape used by the Austrian police officers who suffocated Nigerian asylum seeker Marcus Omofuma during a deportation flight in 1999. Without explicitly depicting an instance of lethal state violence like this one, Clottey, who did an artist residency in Vienna in 2013, uses duct tape to underlay his images of self-determination—almost invisibly—with the ubiquity of racist violence. The Ghanaian artist based his painting *James Baldwin* (2020–21) on a portrait of the writer made by US photographer Richard Avedon in the early sixties, the period when he wrote his texts on racist America and painterly seeing. But in Clottey's remake, Baldwin seems to become an African, because the artist has filled the largely empty space in Avedon's historical portrait with clippings from African fashion magazines. Elsewhere as well, Clottey's portraiture subtly interweaves African, American, and European strands of colonial violence with the techniques of liberation found in photography and literature.

The fact that Serge Clottey commemorates Marcus Omofuma from an African perspective is important for an exhibition taking place in Vienna. The best-known but by no means only case of racist state violence in Austria was also a catalyst for increased self-organization by the Black community, and it stands for the fact that, despite the different historical foundations of racism in the USA and Central Europe, there are certain structural similarities. This is also evidenced by the works of Robert Gabris, which are predicated on a Central European experience of racist and sexist discrimination but in their methodological implementation follow practices inaugurated by US art of the Black Power era. In the group of works titled *Insectopia* (2020) **(pp. 82–83)**, Gabris addresses how racist colonial science lives on in contemporary regimes of categorizing and stereotyping human beings. In the performance, the artist turns himself into an insect that can be dissected, prepared, and exhibited. The queer Roma body is subjected to a symbolic biological classification. This preparation as a "specimen" refers at the same time to the compulsion to represent a certain identity, just as the artist feels forced to do in institutional and curatorial relationships. Gabris works with imprints of his body that are shifted into the realm of zoological illustration through delicate drawn corrections. These body prints express the push and pull between direct expression as a liberating force and the boundaries forcibly imposed by society on self-realization. The artist was inspired in his work by the body prints that David Hammons made during the era of the Black Arts Movement in the late sixties and seventies. *Insectopia* also calls to mind, however, the accusation made by Senegalese director Ousmane Sembène in a 1965 conversation with the anthropologist Jean Rouch: "What I hold against you and the Africanists is that you look at us as if we were insects."[26]

If life knows no past tense, and a new chapter must be added to the history of racial persecution and liberation struggles in this current moment of danger, then this understanding recalls the concept of history that Walter Benjamin developed in the face of the rise of fascist terror in Europe: "To articulate the past historically does not mean to recognize it 'the way it really was.' ... It means to seize hold of a memory as it flashes up at a moment of danger."[27] Benjamin opposes a conception of history that locates it in homogeneous and empty time, and speaks of the necessity, at a certain moment of crisis and upheaval, to turn to a "past charged with the time of the now,"[28] that is, to a historical moment full of relevance for today. To do so, the continuum of history must be blasted open. The historian "grasps the constellation which his own era has formed with a definite earlier one."[29] Benjamin attributes an awareness of this relationship between present and past to "the revolutionary classes at the moment of their action."[30] The Jewish Marxist philosopher living in the fascist thirties and the Black writer witnessing the civil rights activism of the sixties independently arrive at similar insights concerning the relationship between history and the present. Benjamin himself provides an explanation for such affinities when he writes: "The tradition of the oppressed teaches us that the 'state of emergency' in which we live is not the exception but the rule."[31] This insight can be gleaned from various traditions of the oppressed, in Benjamin's case especially the Jewish and proletarian experience, in Baldwin's the Black and queer experience. In our exhibition, these nonlinear and discontinuous notions of time and action are revealed in artists' targeted recourse to historical moments of liberation that today—in the "state of emergency" or "moment of danger"—are taking on new meaning.

LIMITS OF THE WESTERN AVANT-GARDE DEBATE

The notion of avant-garde in the context of an exhibition on the current relevance of decolonial modernisms needs some explaining, because the avant-garde discourse remains to this day largely Eurocentric. In the context of the anti-colonial and anti-racist movements of the twentieth century, we understand avant-garde as a constellation of political, intellectual, and artistic projects and practices that aimed to overcome colonial domination, racial discrimination, and mental and cultural colonization. In our context, avant-garde does not simply denote a particularly advanced form of artistic expression in relation to other contemporaneous cultural articulations. Instead, when we speak of avant-garde in decolonial modernism, the advanced forms of its artistic, literary, theoretical, and activist praxis are always also part of a politics of liberation. This liberationist streak is dedicated to transforming the power relations that emerged from the colonial structures of modernism toward social justice and equality. However, we cannot simply speak of *the* decolonial avant-garde as a given entity. Saloni Mathur reminds us of this problem in her essay for this catalogue **(pp. 141– 149)**. Referring to the artists represented in the

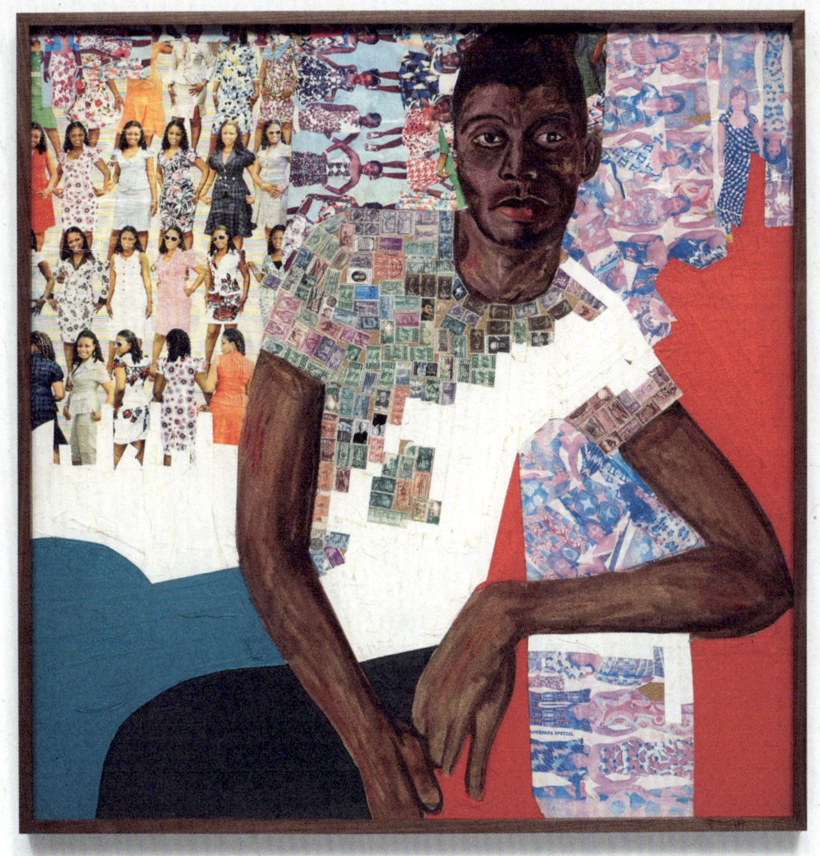

Serge Attukwei Clottey
James Baldwin, 2020–21

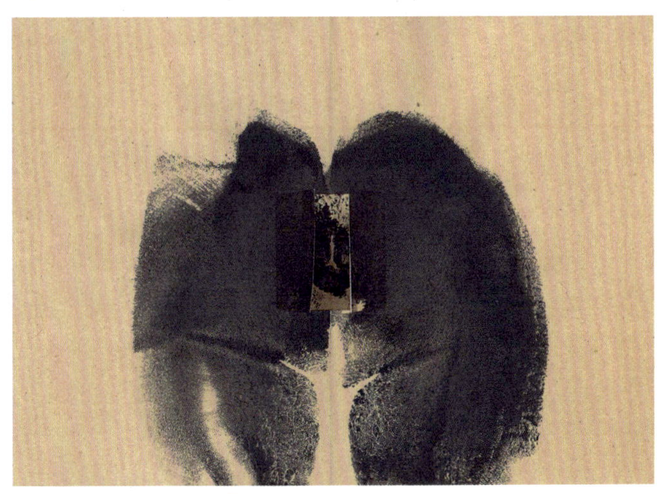

Robert Gabris
Insectology in My Body, 2020

exhibition who invoke Indian modernism in the context of the independence movement, Mathur writes that Vivan Sundaram, Atul Dodiya, and The Otolith Group "do not passively inherit an aesthetic tradition presumed to preexist as the 'decolonial avant-garde.' They actively seek the experimental agency of the past and reactivate this agency for a more socially just future."[32] Other artists whose work is on view proceed similarly concerning different manifestations of decolonial modernism. None of these artists has merely inherited something. "Inheritance is never a *given*, it is always a *task*."[33] To tackle this task requires a "self-conscious effort to *actively mine* the decolonial past and its imaginative resources to fuel the needs of the present and future."[34]

The concept of the avant-garde is controversial. Art historian Paul Wood speaks of a "radically unstable concept,"[35] and cultural scholar Anne Friedberg diagnoses a "profound and lasting conflation of what is considered 'modernism' and what is considered the 'avant-garde.'"[36] Nevertheless, we have reached a certain agreement in Western art history about which twentieth-century movements are to be considered avant-garde. A comparable consensus does not exist for non-European modern art. The twentieth-century avant-garde discourse largely excluded non-Western and non-white modernisms. In Eurocentric thinking, there is no room for the idea of a non-European avant-garde. The Western concept of the avant-garde is instead saturated with Euromodern ideas of progress and the linear concepts of time underlying them, which in turn were developed in distinction to the societies and cultures of the colonized world. In the course of the anti-colonial movements and the critique of the colonial worldview, alternative notions of temporality have been proposed that correspond to the life worlds of colonized people who find themselves situated somewhere between the violently imposed Western capitalist time

regime and the notions of time of their own cultural tradition. Even though the paradigm of catching up and making up for lost time may have played a role in the national modernization projects of the post-colonies, merely claiming a spot in the Western avant-garde "canon" was never an option for the critical discussion of decolonial modernisms. The recognition of other avant-gardes calls instead for a wholesale revision of the Eurocentric paradigms of the avant-garde discourse.

The central reference work in the avant-garde discourse to this day is still Peter Bürger's *Theory of the Avant-Garde*. Published in 1974, the Marxist literary scholar's book has been widely criticized, and yet it remains a pivotal point of orientation in the debate. In a 2005 book discussing the avant-garde and neo-avant-garde, the editor writes: "And still today Bürger's book is the inevitable starting point for every alternative prospect of the avant-garde's nature and the place that the avant-garde holds within twentieth century cultural history."[37] Bürger's *Theory of the Avant-Garde* delivers a narrative of the emergence of the avant-garde, its revolutionary ambitions, and its historical failure with all the consequences for critical approaches to art in the postwar decades. The argumentation is based on a fundamental distinction between historical avant-garde and neo-avant-garde. The historical avant-garde developed on the basis of the institution of art as established in nineteenth-century bourgeois society. With the autonomy of art and the ideology of *l'art pour l'art*, art distanced itself from the praxis of life and the class conflicts of modern society. In the art of this society, problems of form prevailed over problems of content. Even when political content did appear in art, it was neutralized by the autonomy of the social subsystem of the art world. The historical avant-garde, which Bürger primarily sees as comprising Surrealism, Dadaism, and Russian Formalism, got its start as a self-critique of (the function of) art; it "reveals the nexus between autonomy and the absence of any consequences."[38] The avant-garde launched its attack on the institution of art with the aim to transform art into life praxis—a *new* life praxis whose values as derived from art, such as freedom and aesthetic experience, contradicted the predominant purposeful rationalism of capitalist modernity. With its radical intentions, the historical avant-garde failed in its efforts to make art part of everyday life. Still, the avant-garde attacks on art did have strong implications for art itself and the concept of the artwork (readymade, montage, chance, fragmentation). According to Bürger, neo-avant-garde art in the postwar period (Happening, Fluxus, Pop Art) succeeded in integrating the revolutionary means of the historical avant-garde into the autonomy of art. "The neo-avant-garde institutionalizes the *avant-garde as art* and thus negates genuinely avant-gardist intentions."[39]

In his review of the 1984 English translation of Bürger's book, Benjamin Buchloh notes that he finds it "absurd" to reduce the diversity of twentieth-century avant-garde practices, as Bürger did, to *one* central concern—the abolition of the false autonomy of art. The Dadaist John Hartfield would certainly have been pursuing other concerns in 1939 than the dissolution of an institution of art that was divorced from life praxis. Buchloh criticizes Bürger's extensive ignorance of contemporary art and its critique of institutions which is partly related to his own concept of the avant-garde. Bürger's blanket dismissal of the neo-avant-gardes of the postwar period likewise resulted from this ignorance, according to Buchloh. Bürger's interpretation of the social role played by art in maintaining the status quo of bourgeois society is for Buchloh another factor that limits his perspective. The fact that the avant-garde's radical attacks on the bourgeois autonomy of art were interrupted cannot mean

that such concerns should be abandoned forever. For our post-Eurocentric context, an interesting point of Buchloh's argument is a political comparison he uses to reject Bürger's assertion that, after the dissolution of the institution of art failed, all subsequent aesthetic practices would be of equal value: "One has only to consider the argument in terms of other ideological struggles to reveal its absurdity (e.g., since most struggles for self-determination in Latin American countries are aborted, colonialist and imperialist policies are historically just as valid as the politics of liberation)."[40]

In 1994 Hal Foster criticized Bürger's generalization of the affirmative character of the neo-avant-garde as well as the linear understanding of time on which he based his narrative of the historical avant-garde as radical critique, its failure, and its repetition as an empty gesture in the neo-avant-garde. Bürger's version of events remained rooted in a historicist model of original versus repetition, Foster claimed, the same model to which Clement Greenberg's progress-oriented theory of modernism is committed. This mindset arguably caused Bürger to take the avant-garde rhetoric of radical rupture, revolution, and the transformation of art into life praxis too literally. According to Foster, avant-garde artists such as Marcel Duchamp were less interested in pursuing such romantic ideas than in putting the conventions of art and its practice to the test. And this was precisely the approach that neo-avant-garde artists (from Daniel Buren and Michael Asher to Andrea Fraser and Fred Wilson) took further by actually pursuing a critical institutional analysis, including a critique of the appropriation of avant-garde art by the institutions. "Rather than cancel the historical avant-garde, the neo-avant-garde enacts its project for the first time—a first time that, again, is theoretically endless."[41] Contrary to the linear scheme of originality and repetition, of before and after in the sense of cause and effect, Foster works with the psycho-analytical concept of *Nachträglichkeit*, or "deferred action," which recognizes a "reconstructed past" and an "anticipated future" and assumes that it is only through repetition or deferred action that the first time actually becomes comprehensible in retrospect. In this understanding, the neo-avant-garde reacts to the historical avant-garde, while the latter in turn has an effect on the former.

Foster's chronopolitical correction of Bürger's model is important for a better understanding of the relationship between contemporary art and modernism or the avant-garde. Nevertheless, its references remain exclusively European and US-American, so that it must be followed by a geopolitical correction—a "deliberate deflection," as Geeta Kapur puts it. In the early nineties, Griselda Pollock was one of the first European art historians to add a geographical dimension to the avant-garde debate by considering—with a focus on Paul Gauguin—the artistic detour via the colony and the construction of the exoticized woman as a reservoir of innovation for the white male avant-garde of the late nineteenth century. However, Pollock's necessary expansion of the horizon to non-European terrain remains limited to the radius of action and the imagination of the European artist.[42]

Rosalind Krauss, another important voice in the Western avant-garde debate, does not take Bürger's theory into account.[43] Her concept of the avant-garde is much broader, and the period she considers ranges from the nineteenth century to the postwar decades. Krauss analyzes the discourses of modernism and the avant-garde—largely equated here—in relation to their cult of the original, the ideology of the absolute new beginning, and the creative liberation from any dependencies or repetition. For all the differences in how the avant-garde

artists present themselves, what remains constant is the invocation of the zero point of creation, the discourse on originality (and the repression of copying and repetition). The idea of rebirth, of the purity of experience and free creation, the metaphor of the candid gaze of the child and the uniqueness of the creative act define the self-image of the avant-garde artist, even if the impression of spontaneity is carefully staged, as in Monet's painting, for example. "The discourse of originality ... represses and discredits the complementary discourse of the copy. Both the avant-garde and modernism depend on this repression," writes Krauss.[44] Her reading of the avant-garde as being obsessed with originality unfolded against the backdrop of a postmodern group of artists in the late seventies who became known as the Pictures Generation after Douglas Crimp's exhibition of that name. In Sherrie Levine's copies of Edward Weston's photographs, Krauss recognized an explicit deconstruction of the modernist concept of originality. Krauss makes it clear that a critical analysis of the basic assumptions of modernism/the avant-garde is only possible in retrospect and through the lens of the paradigm of the copy or reproduction, as in Levine's art. "It is thus from a strange new perspective that we look back on the modernist origin and watch it splintering into endless replication."[45]

Krauss refers critically to the other strand of the avant-garde discussion (alongside Bürger), which goes back to Clement Greenberg, who introduced the term to US art criticism. Before the Second World War, the term avant-garde was hardly ever used for art but instead mainly to describe revolutionary political parties. Lenin's Communist Party saw itself as the "avant-garde of the proletariat." In 1939 Greenberg published the essay "Avant-Garde and Kitsch" in the left-wing *Partisan Review*, which discussed (with Leon Trotsky and others) the revolutionary role of art in times of fascism and

Stalinism and published articles on the question of the cultural and literary avant-garde. For Greenberg, the avant-garde was an instrument in the struggle for the survival of culture in bourgeois society. It presented a remedy against the stagnation of academicism, providing the kind of strength that keeps culture moving and thus guarantees it a high standard. The avant-garde achieved this through its anti-bourgeois impulses and its relative autonomy—"art for art's sake"—vis-à-vis politics and the dominant ideology. Griselda Pollock and Fred Orton summarize Greenberg's position: "The aim of the *avant-garde* was to preserve, direct and advance culture. ... The *avant-garde* functions by defining and pursuing the proper concerns of art."[46] The liberation from themes and objects in modernist painting thus resulted in a concentration on the medium itself and in abstraction. For Greenberg, the opposite of this is kitsch, that is, the industrially produced and easy-to-digest mass culture that was elevated to official culture by the totalitarian systems. At this moment of crisis in bourgeois capitalist society, avant-garde culture had to ally itself with the revolutionary forces, if only for the sake of its own survival, and turn towards socialism. As Pollock and Orton write, the central mission of the avant-garde in Greenberg's understanding was to rescue sophisticated art: "The major concern of the *avant-garde* is the preservation of art, and its exclusive responsibility is to the values of art."[47] For Greenberg, the avant-garde is therefore interested in exactly the opposite of what Bürger argues in his theory. Its aim is not to attack the institution of art and transform art into life praxis but to protect innovative and self-critical art from the destructive forces of the consumer industry and totalitarianism.

DECOLONIAL AVANT-GARDE AND THE CHRONOPOLITICS OF MODERNISM

Both "schools" of Western avant-garde theory are only of limited use for a discussion of the avant-garde in the horizon of global modernism. This is because in most of the societies in colonized or recently independent countries there can be as little talk of a bourgeois institution of art that needs to be attacked or defended as there can be of the autonomy of art. In such societies, it has often been necessary instead to first develop institutional and discursive structures of art production. The university and art school founded by Rabindranath Tagore in Shantiniketan near Kolkata in 1921 are the best example of this. The Otolith Group portray Shantiniketan in their film *O Horizon* (2018) as a "structure of decolonization" that is currently threatened by the politics of Hindu nationalism. From their point of view, it is necessary today to activate the potential of a decolonial future for Tagore's project as against the "forward-looking backwardness" of fundamentalism. The same can be said of Latin America, as Lori Cole notes: "Even in the early twentieth century, the artistic communities that I examine in sites like Cuba and Argentina were not concerned with attacking art as an institution; they worked to construct literary and artistic canons rather than to refute or undermine them."[48] Accordingly, as elsewhere, a rhetoric of new beginnings prevailed among the anti-colonial avant-garde in Cuba. In contrast to the radical break with tradition in Europe, however, this avant-garde presented a way to search for an identity for *arte americano* that would draw on indigenous and Afro-Cuban sources while still participating in the international network. Where radical and revolutionary artistic positions form in South Asia, Africa, or Latin America, they rarely take aim at the institution of art. They are directed instead against other instances and institutions: against colonial rule and neocolonial dependency, against the postcolonial persistence of exploitative conditions at the hands of national elites, against the dominance of a European idea of culture, and, last but not least, against the

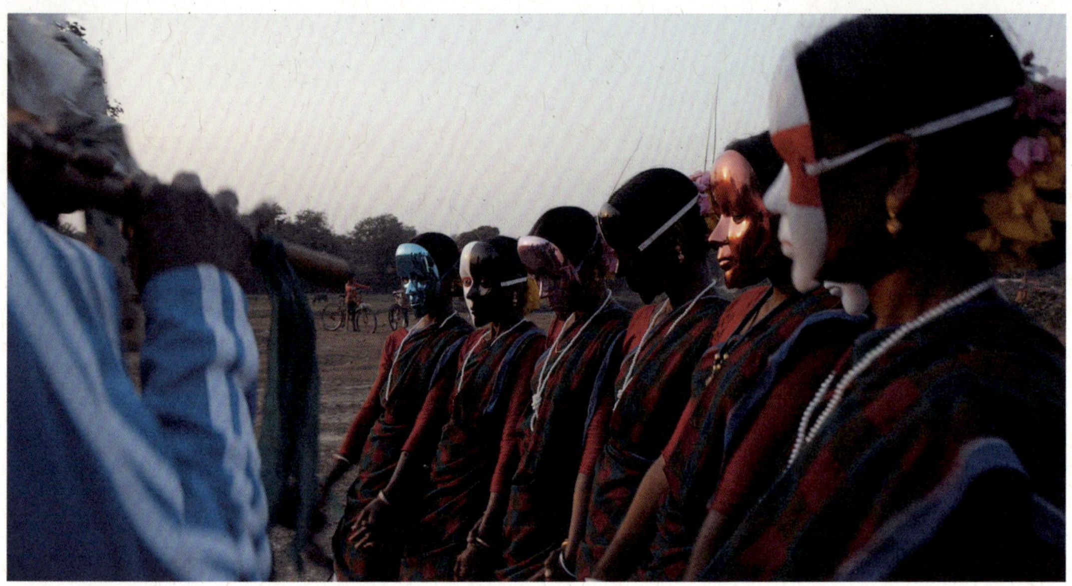

The Otolith Group
O Horizon, 2018

imposition of universalized parameters of Western thought in philosophy, science, and art. Aimé Césaire's reckoning with the European fetish of reason is exemplary of this mission: "Reason, I crown you evening wind / Your name voice of order? / To me the whip's corolla."[49] A concept that had a liberating effect for many in "enlightened" Europe was experienced by the colonized in the form of violent oppression.

Equally problematic is the relationship between the periodization of the Western avant-gardes and the historical realities of the development of avant-garde movements in the (formerly) colonized world. The distinction established between historical avant-garde and neo-avant-garde does not apply here. To name just one example: At the time when Peter Bürger's swan song to the (neo-)avant-garde was published, the Laboratoire Agit'Art was founded in Senegal, the first artistic movement to oppose the institutionalization of art within the framework of Léopold Sédar Senghor's politics of Négritude. While in one place (Europe) the failure of the avant-garde is being declared, elsewhere (West Africa), an avant-garde of decolonial awakening is just being formed. The anti-insti-

tutional orientation of this grouping around Issa Samb and their program of reconnecting art to the social urban space via a new interpretation of African theater correspond more to the characteristics of the historical avant-garde in Bürger's model. Bürger wrote his theory of the failure of the artistic avant-garde under the impression of the breakdown of the revolutionary aspirations of the student movement of the sixties. Vincent Meessen's film *Juste un mouvement* (2021) offers us a postcolonial view of the links between avant-garde and revolution during those years. Taking as his springboard Jean-Luc Godard's film *La Chinoise* (1967), in which Omar Blondin Diop plays the African member of a group of Maoist students, Meessen follows Diop's revolutionary activities in Senegal in the early seventies and the ties between the Marxist, who died in the Gorée prison at the age of twenty-six, and the country's artistic avant-garde. Together with artists and activists, the film reflects on the relevance of historical movements for contemporary efforts towards decolonization and democratization in Senegal.

The crisis that some authors describe the avant-garde was experiencing in the "long 'depression'

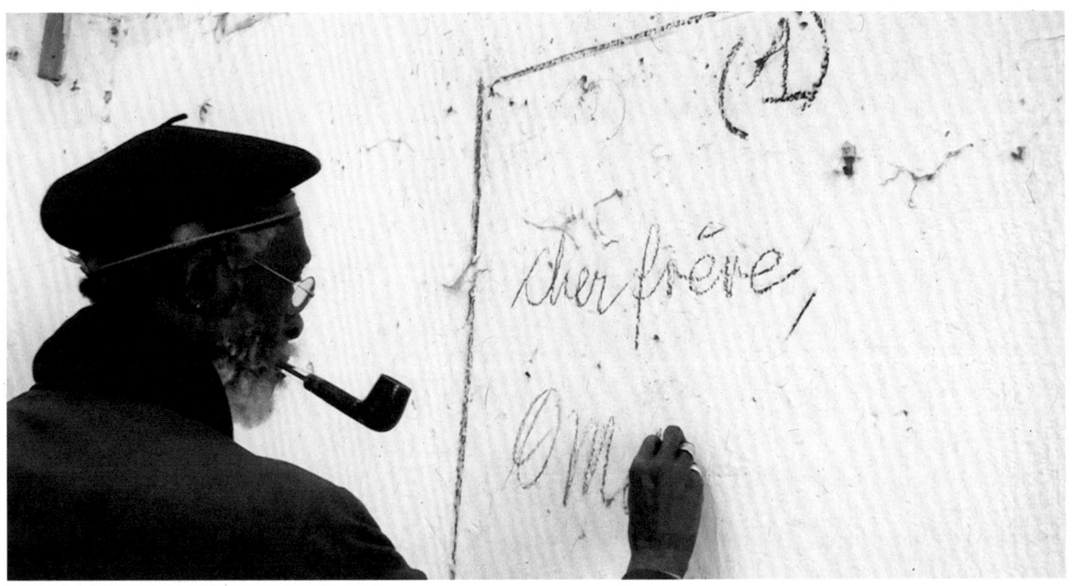

Vincent Meessen
Juste un mouvement, 2021

that lasted from the '30s until the end of the 'reconstruction' in the mid-'50s" was not shared by artists outside Europe.[50] This period "did not offer the space, let alone the incentive, for radical artistic experimentation," writes Dietrich Scheunemann.[51] The necessity of a "topographic turn"[52] in the discourse on the avant-garde becomes obvious here, because the period in which the European avant-garde experienced this apparent "depression" was in fact one of the most fruitful phases for the global avant-garde—we need only think of Wifredo Lam, Aimé Césaire, and Suzanne Césaire in the Caribbean, the Art et Liberté group in Egypt, or the Progressive Artists' Group in India. Our exhibition highlights the present-day relevance of these anti-colonial avant-gardes of the thirties and forties. In his painting *Return to My Native…* (2012), Fahamu Pecou refers back to Aimé Césaire's *Cahier d'un retour au pays natal* (1939) and the formative phase of the philosophy of Négritude in the Black Atlantic. patricia kaersenhout deals with the often marginalized role of women in this cultural and political milieu from the perspective of Black feminism. Her film *Le retour des femmes colibris* (2022) features Suzanne Césaire

and the Nardal sisters, who proposed the concept of *internationalisme noir* and published the magazine *Revue du Monde Noir*. The bilingual journal, which in the thirties offered Black authors from English-speaking and French-speaking countries a common platform, is also referenced in Fahamu Pecou's painting *A.W.N. (Artist with Négritude)* (2012) **(p. 119)**. Georges Henein, the Egyptian Surrealist and co-founder of Art et Liberté in Cairo, is in turn one of the historical figures portrayed in Iman Issa's *Proxies, with a Life of Their Own* (2020–22) **(pp. 92–95)**. And Vivan Sundaram recalls one of the most radical sculptural works of Indian modernism with his interpretation of Ramkinkar Baij's *Santhal Family* (1938).

There are many members of the decolonial avant-garde who cannot be accommodated in the development logic of Western avant-garde theory with its distinction between historical avant-gardes and neo-avant-gardes. Their time frame is a different one, because the political realities under which art is produced also differ dramatically, both in the colonized societies and for the racially discriminated groups in Europe and the USA. For the artists and

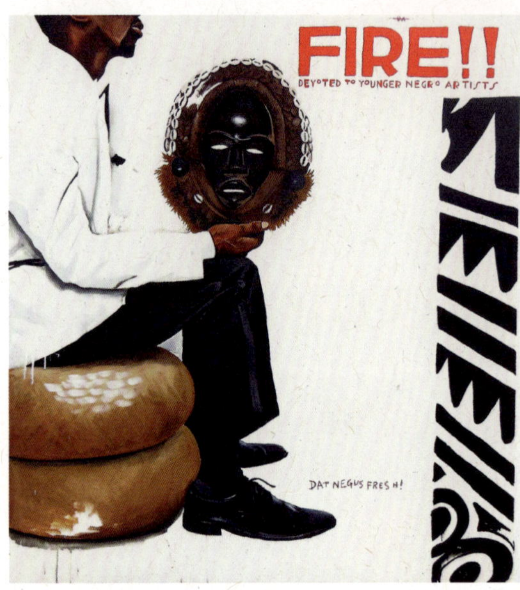

Fahamu Pecou
Return to My Native..., 2012

intellectuals producing work under such conditions, the idea of a continuity of artistic freedom interrupted for two decades by fascism and Stalinism makes little sense. Foreign rule, forced labor, and humiliation have been the reality for these people both before and after the terror regimes in Europe. As Benjamin recognized, a state of emergency is not the exception but the rule for the oppressed. Although the Second World War had an impact on almost all societies in one form or another, other historical caesuras, such as the colonies' gaining of independence and the civil rights struggles, were of greater significance for the experience of freedom or bondage, of self-determination or terror. And yet, divergent historical constellations, cultural frameworks, and political and artistic agendas cannot belie the fact that numerous connections nonetheless existed between Western and non-European avant-gardes. The artists cited above are prime examples with their close contacts to European modernists, many of whom had fled totalitarian systems in Europe to sojourn in Asia, Africa, and the Americas during this time. The European avant-gardes likewise evince an urge for liberation—from the constraints of bourgeois society and common sense, from the instrumental rationale of capitalist modernity, and, of course, from the outdated conventions of the arts. With regard to the artistic means applied—form, color, line—we can also speak here of liberation from the compulsion to represent something. The anti-academicism and non-conformism demonstrated by the European avant-gardes were attitudes often deemed useful by decolonial avant-gardes seeking to overcome European domination in order to liberate the collective subject of those who had been colonized. Accordingly, Aimé Césaire writes of his encounter with Surrealism:

Surrealism had provided me with what I had been confusedly searching for. I have accepted it joyfully because in it I have found more of a confirmation than a revelation. It was a weapon that exploded the French language. It shook up absolutely everything. This was very important because the traditional forms—burdensome, overused forms—were crushing me. ... Surrealism interested me to the extent that it was a liberating factor.[53]

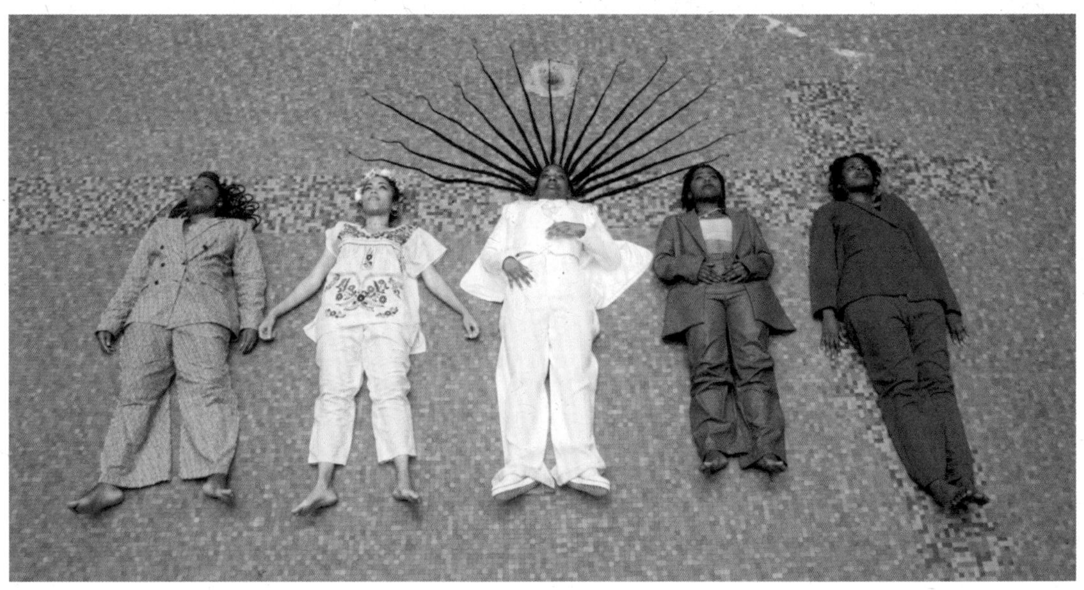

patricia kaersenhout
Le retour des femmes colibris, 2022

Among the European avant-gardes, Surrealism was arguably the current that most influenced the development of some of the decolonial avant-gardes. The poetic revolution of consciousness and the political role played by the dream and the unconscious met up here with anti-colonial efforts at liberation from colonial thought patterns and the terror of Western rationalism. Beyond its artistic concerns, Surrealism was the only European artistic movement whose followers were committed to the fight against colonialism.[54] Robin D. G. Kelley confirms a "deep affinity between black life and culture and surrealism."[55] He emphasizes the inspiration the Surrealists supplied not only to Black artists but also to the anti-colonial struggles. The Surrealist revolution of consciousness, which allowed for a completely new approach to language and images, combined with the Marxist revolution of material (production) relations, opened up new possibilities for Caribbean artists and intellectuals, while their work in turn offered the European Surrealists new ideas and motifs. Referring to the Caribbean avant-garde, Kelley writes:

They have found in surrealism confirmation of what they already know—for them it is more an act of recognition than a revolutionary discovery. As we have already seen, Aimé Césaire insisted that surrealism brought him back to African culture. ... Wifredo Lam said he was drawn to surrealism because he already knew the power of the unconscious, having grown up in the Africanized spirit world of Santeria.[56]

Decolonial avant-gardes localized and made concrete the prospect of liberation, inevitably calling into question in the process the hegemonic position of Europe's radical political and aesthetic movements. Elizabeth Harney discusses the limits of the Western avant-garde discourse in relation to African art, drawing on the reflections of Indian theorist Geeta Kapur, among others. Harney first raises the question of whether theories dealing with the avant-garde are perhaps too closely linked to European notions of art, autonomy, and progress to be useful for an analysis of experimental arts in other regional contexts. But she also reminds us that "many artists across the globe have repeatedly engaged in the histories, tenets, and problematics of the avant-garde as it has been modeled, discussed, or even discredited in the West."[57] Harney finds in Geeta Kapur's response to Hal Foster's arguments about the legitimacy of the postwar neo-avant-gardes "an entry point to histories and understandings of avant-gardism 'elsewhere.'"[58] In her book *When Was Modernism*, published in 2000, Kapur criticizes Foster's ignorance of non-Western concepts of plural modernisms and alternative avant-gardes and argues for adding a "deliberate deflection" in terms of time and politics to Foster's correction of Bürger's historicism. It is after all essential for the non-European avant-garde that it "dismantles the burdensome aspect of western art, including its endemic vanguardism."[59] Kapur develops her avant-garde concept from the Latin American use of the term—something she encountered in Cuba at the Havana Biennale in 1989 and which was avoided in India for a long time—and also from her engagement with contemporary struggles for social justice in Indian society. She posits that the avant-garde in Asia or Africa would have to view the avant-garde model itself as a form of institutionalization: "Once they are unstrung from the logic of a Euro-American master-discourse on 'advanced art,' third-world vanguards can be seen to be connected with their own *histories* and mark that disjuncture first and foremost."[60] Kapur is referring to the artists and activists engaged in anti-colonial struggles, whose radical consciousness has substantially altered the principle of the avant-garde as defined by Western art of the twentieth century: "While the history of the avant-garde gives us a *template* for radical disruptions, it is important to keep alive questions of material practice: It follows that situational politics—the very site for avant-garde initiatives—should be rescued from subsumption in the global imaginary."[61]

Kapur identifies here a point that is of great importance for our exhibition. If we want to discuss the concept of the avant-garde more globally and free it from its Eurocentric provincialism, we must avoid globalizing its established parameters. Rachel Weiss names the other salient point for this exhibition—topicality: "Kapur's current insistence that it is the ambition of the avant-garde—that anachronistic presence—rather than the historical form of it, that remains available to us now as a potent node of possibility."[62] Kapur thus leaves behind the eternal rhetoric of the death, exhaustion, and failure of the avant-garde. The widely divergent local historical conditions for a radical critical practice promising the prospect of social change stand in the way of any general endgame discourse. With her emphasis on the *ambition* of the avant-garde offering us today a means to make a connection, the art critic agrees with Robin D. G. Kelley's argument that we too often measure social movements by whether they were "successful" or not. Judged by this standard, almost every radical movement is doomed to fail: "And yet it is precisely these alternative visions and dreams that inspire new generations to continue to struggle for change."[63] As far as the Indian avant-garde of the early and mid-twentieth century is concerned, the works of Vivan Sundaram, Atul Dodiya, and The Otolith Group on view in *Avant-Garde and Liberation* compellingly demonstrate the validity of Kapur's argument.

Elizabeth Harney for her part recognizes the twofold relationship in the practice of the Laboratoire Agit'Art in Dakar, which was formed in 1973 as a critical response to the École de Dakar founded on the basis of Senghor's cultural policy of Négritude. Issa Samb and the Laboratoire took a clear stance against the dominance of European formats and standards in Senegalese painting—the same canon that Senghor promoted as creating identity and which can be traced back to neo-colonial dependencies. At the same time, they drew on Georgi W. Plekhanov's theories on art and society ("Art and Social Life," 1912) and Antonin Artaud's revolutionary physical theater. Harney sees these processes of translating European concepts and projects into a specific African context as a "local adaptation of selective global sources."[64] She associates these borrowings with the material practice of *récupération*, the artistic recovery and recycling of industrially produced utilitarian objects and natural materials.

Kapur, Harney, and others thus aim to underpin the avant-garde discourse in the postcolonial era from a Southern perspective, taking into account concrete local struggles against oppression and inequality. Saloni Mathur summarizes this endeavor: "At the heart of the proposition is Kapur's call to 'continue with the term avant-garde,' to imbue it with 'dense and diverse (cultural) annotation,' and to give 'valence and purpose to the key avant-garde dialectic,' namely, the imbrication between art and life across the widest possible political scale."[65] The avant-garde concept, with its central dialectic of art and life, thus remains an important tool for understanding the contribution of the arts to the aforementioned struggles.

THE AVANT-GARDE AND HISTORY

What unites the Western avant-garde concepts is the importance of the new and its positive connotation. In many cases, art operated in line with the progressive thinking of modern capitalism and its principle of competition: "Each of the historical avant-gardes adhered to the principle of their own exceptionality, leaving no possibility for any other to be first and foremost, to be in the vanguard as well."[66] According to Rosalind Krauss, the artistic avant-gardes were not only concerned with producing something new that had never been seen before in order to gain a position of uniqueness; they proclaimed something even more fundamental: "More than a rejection or

dissolution of the past, avant-garde originality is conceived as a literal origin, a beginning from ground zero, a birth."[67]

What does this radical rejection of history and tradition, together with the ideology of an absolute new beginning, mean for artistic movements in colonized regions, and also for Black modernism in Europe and North America? Partha Mitter has dealt extensively with the discourse of belatedness and imitation in Western art history as applied to non-European modernisms. His call to decentralize the concept of modernism is informed in part by a critique of the "pathology of influence" derived from the Eurocentric cultural geography of center versus periphery.[68] Homi Bhabha described the original delay of the colonized world in terms of the discourse of modernism using the term "time lag." "Homi Bhabha's notion of writing out of the colonial time-lag is useful to consider here: When so-called 'primitive' peoples always come late to modernity, how can they ever catch up? Their belatedness in relation to modernity is inscribed within the very discourse of modernity."[69] May Joseph refers to the "perceived cultural time lag between the European avant-garde movements and 'Third World' modernisms"—the alleged absence of innovations in Africa and Asia, compared to Dadaism, Futurism, and Surrealism in Europe. She reminds us of the "delusional idea of teleological progression, whose end logic lay in the gas chambers of Auschwitz," as analyzed by Theodor Adorno and Max Horkheimer in the *Dialectic of Enlightenment*. This "epistemological knot" of linear progress, which also dominates the discourse on the avant-garde, has a colonial background. In terms of the necessary geographical localization of modernity, Joseph therefore speaks of a "global network of arrivals and departures, thefts and exchanges, influences and rejections, circulations and still points."[70]

This positioning within the power structures of contemporary colonial politics already means that what the European avant-gardes claimed for themselves cannot apply to the non-European and Black avant-gardes of the twentieth century. While the Western avant-gardes radically broke with the past and opened their minds unconditionally to the future, casting aside old values and standards and traditions of every kind, such a negative dismissal of history makes no sense when it comes to artistic renewal for societies and social groups that were fundamentally denied their own history or a historical consciousness under the sway of the colonial ideology of modernity. The art of decolonial modernism found itself confronted with social ties that had been torn apart by slavery, colonialism, and expulsion, by the material destruction of cultural heritage, and by the racist distortion of local history by colonial sciences, arts, and institutions. The Nigerian writer Chinua Achebe spoke of the close connection between the task of restoring an African identity and the retelling of history: "The twentieth century for all its many faults did witness a significant beginning, in Africa and elsewhere in the so-called Third World, of the process of 're-storying' peoples who had been knocked silent by the trauma of all kinds of dispossession."[71] For Achebe, "restoring" African self-awareness and "re-storying" the colonial experience and the traumatic history of enslavement becomes a single process of emancipation of the colonized peoples.

In the conversation with Nana Adusei-Poku in this catalogue, we discuss this radically differ-ent point of departure for European versus decolonial avant-gardes and recall the historian Arturo (Arthur) Schomburg, who, against the backdrop of the New Negro Movement of the interwar period, spoke of the necessity of excavating the buried Black past.[72] Historical themes in fact had a high priority among African American avant-garde painters such as Aaron Douglas, Jacob Lawrence, Loïs Mailou Jones, and Hale Woodruff, in stark contrast to their contemporaries in the European avant-gardes.[73] Their cycles tracing Black history (and art history) from its African roots and the era of slavery to the anti-colonial movements of emancipation and the Great Migration contributed—in line with Achebe's thoughts—to the formation of a new, self-determined identity and to the struggle for cultural recognition and political rights.[74] In the Mexican avant-garde of the revolutionary period, the historical perspective on the colonial past and indigenous cultures is simi-larly significant.[75] For Wifredo Lam and Lydia Cabrera, living at the time of Cuban decolo-nization in the postwar period, the stories and symbolic worlds of Afro-Cuban tradition were important points of reference,[76] while mod-ernist artists in India drew on traditions of Mughal painting and folk art,[77] and in Nigeria, postcolonial modernists of the Zaria Art Society as well as others referred to local traditions of Uli drawing, conjoining them under the con-cept of "natural synthesis" with design ele-ments borrowed from European avant-gardes.[78]

These are just a few examples indicating the complex understanding of time, history, and tradition among the decolonial avant-gardes in contrast to the progressivism of the white avant-gardes in Europe and North America. For the Western avant-garde, the focus on the new and on change in the immediate future was linked to breaking with history, a process of leaving behind and overcoming traditions. The decolonial avant-garde is just as focused on renewal, change, and liberation. And yet this focus is inextricably bound up with an urge to reclaim history and reconnect with the cultural heritage of ancestors. Liberation here does not mean liberation from the past but from a violently imposed foreign order, including forced integration into the hegemonic Western understanding of time and progress. Cultural history was not the ballast from which they sought to free themselves but rather colonial dispossession and subjugation, which also included the expropriation of culture and the distortion of history. A "beginning from ground zero" was not on the agenda.

MAKING CONTACT

Liberation is the act of overcoming oppression. Where it starts and what it presupposes is the subject of debate. Some artists address the body, consciousness, and language as elementary sites of colonial oppression and therefore also fundamental terrain for decolonial resistance. Atul Dodiya's images (pp. 78–81) of the legacy of the Indian independence movement shed light on Gandhi's physical self-liberation and the psychic automatism of Tagore's drawings. In *Untitled, K. T. C. I.* (2022) (pp. 104–107), Belinda Kazeem-Kamiński refers to Augusto Boal's *Theatre of the Oppressed*, whose central theme is performative liberation from the oppressor in one's own head. "Killing the cop inside" is a prerequisite for political liberation from institutions of oppression. In his works incorporating elements of computer keyboards, Moffat Takadiwa attacks the power of the colonial English language in Africa (pp. 136–139). He draws here on the decolonial linguistic criticism of the writer Ngũgĩ wa Thiong'o and his rehabilitation of the pre-colonial language and indigenous theater traditions in Kenya, as well as on the comparable return to regional language in the music of Thomas Mapfumo in Zimbabwe. "The computer keys are like libraries and are like writing instruments. They meant quite a lot to me and I destroyed them. Physically. And I unplugged the keys, and then we used them to fabricate my own language."[79] The fact that Ngũgĩ's book *Decolonising the Mind* takes up concepts from Boal's *Theatre of the Oppressed*[80] points to the many instances of cross-fertilization among decolonial modernisms, some of which are highlighted in our exhibition.

We speak of liberation movements even if they have not (yet) achieved their goal. The term encompasses more than just the successful process. It also includes the imagination of liberation, as a political program or aesthetic articulation, as well as the development of procedures and instruments to realize the anticipated freedom. Often, the unfinished, halted, and suppressed processes of liberation are what later become a point of reference for new struggles.[81] william cordova takes up in his work *this one's 4U (pa' nosotros)* techniques and tactics of Third Cinema and connects the anti-colonial resistance in South America with the Black Power knowledge of hip-hop, speaking in this context of "discontinued movements." One of the subjects that interests him is how artists have carried on certain struggles that political activists have been compelled to cease or interrupt.[82] "Why do we think that forever equates with success? How do we measure success?" asks Cauleen Smith, whose film *Sojourner* (2018) brings together historical figures and Black liberation projects in the USA—from the abolitionist and women's rights activist Sojourner Truth to the musician Alice Coltrane, and from the feminist Combahee River Collective to sculptor Noah Purifoy. They all "created pathways toward liberation, autonomy, and self-determination. These figures embody models for radical generosity."[83] In this spirit, we speak not of freedom but of liberation when we look at the works in this exhibition.[84]

The transistor radios that the young women in *Sojourner* carry with them on their way through the sculptural landscape of the desert at sunrise supply one of the most wonderful metaphors for the communication between contemporary artists and representatives of the avant-gardes of liberation. As if the antennas of these devices were making contact with the spirit of the ancestors, we hear the Afro-futuristic sound and spiritual texts of Coltrane

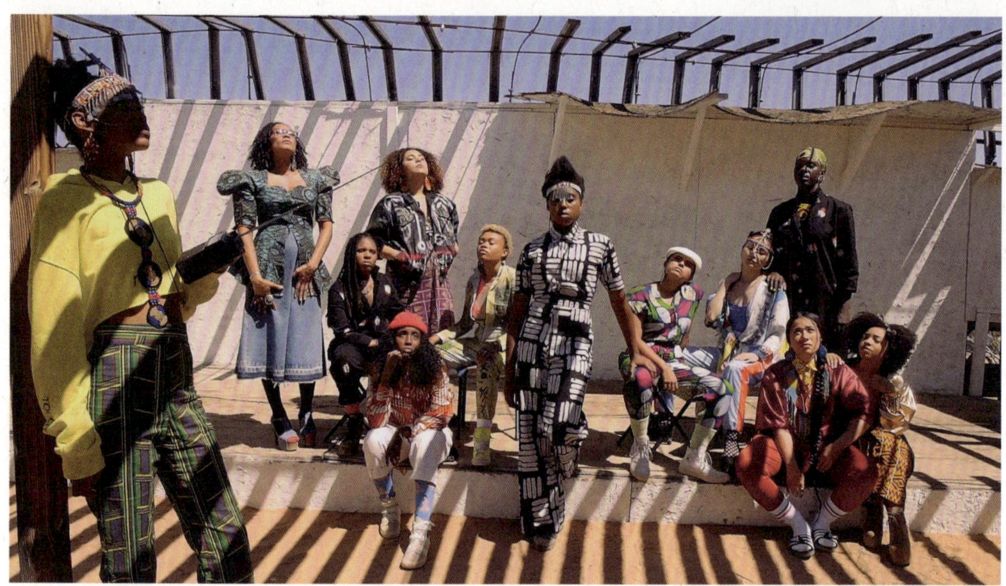

Cauleen Smith
Sojourner, 2018

as well as fragments from the publication *Combahee River Collective Statement* from 1977. The motif of the receiver invites us to reflect on the media and the telecommunication channels that enable artists today to establish a timeless connection with the activists of decolonial liberation, and also on the names by which they address these precursors. At the beginning of this text, we spoke based on the artwork *Art History* by Marlene Smith of the artistic focus on the relationships and (elective) affinities between Black artists of the nineteen-eighties and the early days of modern Black art. This frame of reference is still important for many artists today. Janine Jembere, for example, stages "channeling" situations when she connects herself and her fellow performers with the "ancestors in spirit" whose work they are carrying on. william cordova speaks of "family members" when he refers to politically and artistically related musicians, artists, and film directors.[85] Belinda Kazeem-Kamiński uses the word *Heim-Suchung*, a German term for "haunting" that can also mean "looking for a home."[86] Diedrick Brackens speaks of "ancestors" when he cites the queer and Black artists of the past whose works inspire him.

He describes communication with them as "conjuring" and "talking to ghosts."[87] But contemporaries can also be precursors. "Faith Ringgold makes me possible," says Brackens. The youngest artist in our exhibition sees this contemporary, who also belongs to James Baldwin's generation, as "a kind of artistic foremother" and refers to Ringgold's decades of work on artistic and feminist lines of descent.[88] Her quilts, such as *Le Café des Artistes* (1994), are influential forerunners of the more recent recourse to the avant-garde in contemporary art. The artist reflects on the milieus of Black and white modernism in Paris and New York and queries the contacts between them. It is in the circle of historical avant-garde artists—Paul Gauguin and Vincent van Gogh, Aaron Douglas and Romare Bearden, Elizabeth Catlett and Edmonia Lewis—that Ringgold's fictional protagonist presents her "Colored Woman's Manifesto of Art and Politics." She criticizes therein the colonial expropriation of African art and the exoticist sexism in male-dominated European modernism: "Paris artists are shaping the culture of the world with their ideas. But modern art is much bigger than Western Europe or Paris. I am here, (in Paris).

I am there (in Africa) too. That is why I am issuing a Colored Woman's Manifesto of Art and Politics."[89]

In the nineteen-twenties, Alain Locke called on African American artists to draw on the artistic heritage of their African ancestors as a source of inspiration for an authentic Black art of modernism.[90] In other parts of the world, too, avant-garde movements in the context of decolonization pursued concepts of reconnecting with a heritage buried by colonialism in order to reactivate it within the horizon of global modernism. Today, it is the aesthetic and political endeavors of the decolonial avant-gardes of the twentieth century that form the "legacy of the ancestors" that is invoked when instruments of resistance against current threats are to be developed and new prospects offered for liberation.

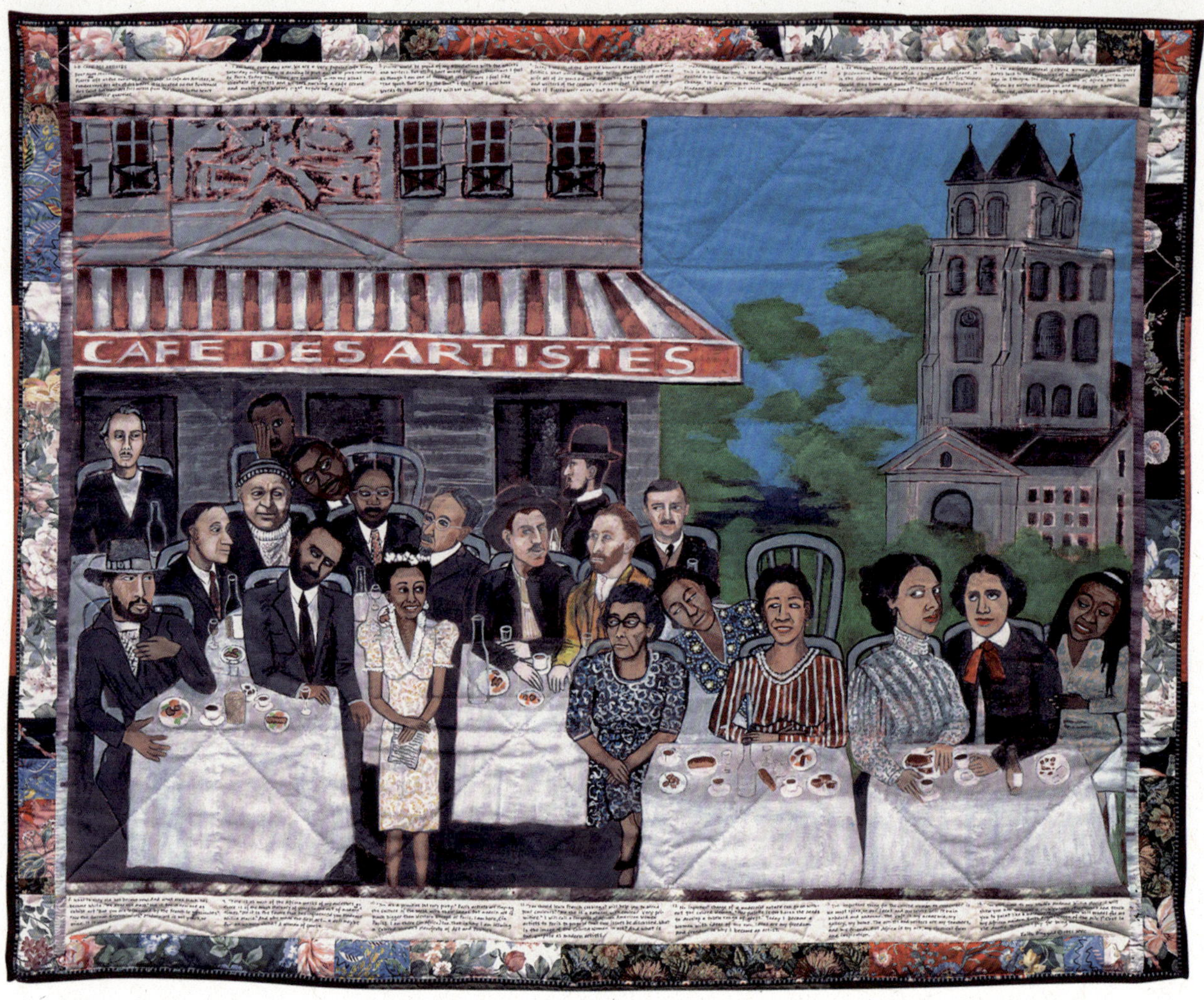

Faith Ringgold
Le Café des Artistes (The French Collection, Part II: #11), 1994

1 Just to name a few examples: *Afro Modern: Journeys through the Black Atlantic*, Tate Liverpool, 2010; *Art et Liberté: Rupture, War and Surrealism in Egypt (1938–1948)*, Centre Pompidou, 2016; *Soul of a Nation: Art in the Age of Black Power*, Tate Modern, 2017; *Taking Shape: Abstraction from the Arab World, 1950s–1980s*, Gray Art Gallery, New York University, 2020; *The Casablanca Art School: Platforms and Patterns for a Postcolonial Avant-Garde 1962–1987*, Tate St Ives, 2023.

2 Frantz Fanon, *The Wretched of the Earth* (New York: Grove Press, 1963); Ngũgĩ wa Thiong'o, *Decolonising the Mind: The Politics of Language in African Literature* (Oxford: James Currey, 1986); Ranajit Guha and Gayatri Chakravorty Spivak, eds., *Selected Subaltern Studies* (New York and Oxford: Oxford University Press, 1988).

3 Kwame Nkrumah, *Neo-Colonialism: The Last Stage of Imperialism* (New York: International Publishers, 1965).

4 James Baldwin, "My Dungeon Shook: Letter to My Nephew on the One Hundredth Anniversary of the Emancipation," in Baldwin, *Collected Essays*, ed. Toni Morrison (New York: The Library of America, 1998), p. 292.

5 Darby English, *To Describe a Life: Notes from the Intersection of Art and Race Terror* (New Haven and London: Yale University Press, 2019), p. 15.

6 Baldwin, p. 295.

7 These include Raoul Peck's film *I Am Not Your Negro* (2017), which is based on Baldwin's manuscript about his murdered friends Malcolm X, Medgar Evers, and Dr. Martin Luther King Jr, and Barry Jenkins's film adaptation of Baldwin's novel *If Beale Street Could Talk* (2018).

8 Jesmyn Ward, ed., *The Fire This Time: A New Generation Speaks about Race* (New York: Scribner, 2016), p. 8.

9 Ibid., p. 7.

10 Ibid., p. 9.

11 Eddie S. Glaude Jr., *Begin Again: James Baldwin's America and Its Urgent Lessons for Our Own* (New York: Crown, 2020), p. xviii.

12 Ibid., p. xxvii.

13 Ta-Nehisi Coates, *Between the World and Me* (Melbourne: The Text Publishing Company, 2015).

14 Baldwin, p. 294.

15 Ibid.

16 Ward, p. 6.

17 Jacques Derrida, *Specters of Marx: The State of the Debt, the Work of Mourning, and the New International* (New York: Routledge, 1994), p. 111.

18 Robin D. G. Kelley, *Freedom Dreams: The Black Radical Imagination* (Boston: Beacon Press, 2002), p. xii.

19 Bernardine Evaristo posted an apt remark on the topicality of Maud Sulter, who died young: "She would be in her element right now, as society catches up with us." Evaristo on Instagram, May 8, 2021, https://www.instagram.com/p/COnwNcQLX95/?img_index=1.

20 Hilton Als pointed out how the current references to Baldwin as a political critic threaten to push Baldwin the artist into the background. Coralie Kraft, "Hilton Als on Giving James Baldwin Back His Body," *The New Yorker*, January 16, 2019, https://www.newyorker.com/culture/photo-booth/hilton-als-on-giving-james-baldwin-back-his-body.

21 James Baldwin, "Introduction to Exhibition of Beauford Delaney Opening December 4, 1964 at the Gallery Lambert," in *Beauford Delaney: A Retrospective*, exh. cat. The Studio Museum in Harlem, New York (New York, 1978), unpaginated.

22 Ibid.

23 Tyler T. Schmidt, "Lessons in Light: Beauford Delaney's and James Baldwin's 'Unnameable Objects,'" in *Of Latitudes Unknown: James Baldwin's Radical Imagination*, ed. Alice Mikal Craven, William E. Dow, and Yoko Nakamura (New York and London: Bloomsbury, 2019), p. 53.

24 Ibid.

25 "The best art is political and you ought to be able to make it unquestionably political and irrevocably beautiful at the same time," writes Toni Morrison in "Rootedness: The Ancestor as Foundation," in *I Am Because We Are: Readings in Africana Philosophy*, ed. Fred Lee Hord and Jonathan Scott Lee (Amherst: University of Massachusetts Press, 2016), p. 403.

26 "A Historic Confrontation between Jean Rouch and Ousmane Sembène in 1965: 'You Look at Us as if We Were Insects,'" in *The Short Century: Independence and Liberation Movements in Africa, 1945–1994*, ed. Okwui Enwezor (Munich: Prestel, 2001), p. 440.

27 Walter Benjamin, "Theses on the Philosophy of History," in Benjamin, *Illuminations*, ed. Hannah Arendt, transl. Harry Zohn (New York: Shocken Books, 1969), p. 255.

28 Ibid., p. 261.

29 Ibid., p. 263.

30 Ibid., p. 261.

31 Ibid., p. 257.

32 Saloni Mathur, "Strange Temporalities: Indian Modernism in Contemporary Art," p. 147 in this catalogue.

33 Derrida, p. 67.

34 Mathur, p. 143.

35 Paul Wood, "Modernism and the Idea of the Avant-Garde," in *A Companion to Art Theory*, ed. Paul Smith and Carolyn Wilde (Oxford: Blackwell, 2002), p. 215.

36 Anne Friedberg, *Window Shopping: Cinema and the Postmodern* (Berkeley et al.: University of California Press, 1994), p. 163.

37 Dietrich Scheunemann, ed., *Avant-Garde/Neo-Avant-Garde* (Amsterdam and New York: Rodopi, 2005), p. 9.

38 Peter Bürger, *Theory of the Avant-Garde* (Minneapolis: University of Minnesota Press, 1984), p. 22.

39 Ibid., p. 58.

40 Benjamin Buchloh, "Theorizing the Avant-Garde," *Art in America*, November 1984, p. 21.

41 Hal Foster, "What's Neo about the Neo-Avant-Garde?" *October* 70 (Fall 1994), p. 20.

42 Griselda Pollock, *Avant-Garde Gambits, 1888–1893: Gender and the Color of Art History* (London: Thames and Hudson, 1992).

43 The English translation of *Theory of the Avant-Garde* did not appear until 1984.

44 Rosalind E. Krauss, *The Originality of the Avant-Garde and Other Modernist Myths* (Cambridge, MA, and London: MIT Press, 1985), p. 168.

45 Ibid., p. 170.

46 Fred Orton and Griselda Pollock, "Avant-Gardes and Partisans Reviewed," in Orton and Pollock, *Avant-Gardes and Partisans Reviewed* (Manchester: Manchester University Press, 1996), p. 154.

47 Ibid., p. 158.

48 Lori Cole, *Surveying the Avant-Garde: Questions on Modernism, Art, and the Americas in Transatlantic Magazines* (University Park: The Pennsylvania State University Press, 2018), p. 21.

49 Aimé Césaire, *Notebook of a Return to the Native Land*, transl. and ed. Clayton Eshleman and Annette Smith (Middletown, CT: Wesleyan University Press, 2001), p. 17.

50 Jean-François Lyotard, "The Sublime and the Avant-Garde," *Artforum* 22, no. 8 (April 1984), p. 41.

51 Dietrich Scheunemann, "From Collage to the Multiple: On the Genealogy of Avant-Garde and Neo-Avant-Garde," in Scheunemann, *Avant-Garde/Neo-Avant-Garde*, p. 35.

52 Per Bäckström and Benedikt Hjartarson, eds., *Decentring the Avant-Garde* (Amsterdam and New York: Rodopi, 2014).

53 René Depestre, "An Interview with Aimé Césaire" (1967), in Aimé Césaire, *Discourse on Colonialism* (New York: The Monthly Review Press, 2000), p. 83.

54 Jody Blake, "The Truth about the Colonies, 1931: Art indigène in Service of the Revolution," *Oxford Art Journal* 25, no. 1, 2002, pp. 35–58.

55 Kelley, p. 158.

56 Ibid., pp. 184–185.

57 Elizabeth Harney, "Postcolonial Agitations: Avant-Gardism in Dakar and London," *New Literary History* 41, no. 4 (2010), p. 739.

58 Ibid., p. 740.

59 Geeta Kapur, *When Was Modernism: Essays on Contemporary Cultural Practice in India* (New Delhi: Tulika Books, 2000), p. 374.

60 Ibid., p. 376.

61 Geeta Kapur, "Proposition Avant-Garde: A View from the South," *Art Journal* 77, no. 1 (Spring 2018), p. 88.

62 Rachel Weiss, "Some Thoughts after Kapur and Mathur," *Art Journal* 77, no. 1 (Spring 2018), p. 99.

63 Kelley, p. ix.

64 Harney, p. 745. In some cases, this question of selective borrowing was critically discussed much earlier and in the immediate context of decolonial movements, for example in Stella Kramrisch's essays in the nineteen-twenties on the forms of appropriation of Cubism in the work of Gaganendranath Tagore. See Christian Kravagna,

"Über das Geistige in der Kunstgeschichte: Stella Kramrisch in der transkulturellen Moderne," *Regards croisés* 11 (2021), pp. 69–81 ("Du spirituel dans l'histoire de l'art: Stella Kramrisch dans la modernité transculturelle," pp. 82–94).

65 Saloni Mathur, "A Response to Kapur's 'Proposition Avant-Garde,'" *Art Journal* 77, no. 1 (Spring 2018), p. 90.

66 Konstantin Dudakov-Kashuro, "Revising the Aporias of the Avant-Garde," in Bäckström and Hjartarson, p. 307.

67 Krauss, p. 157.

68 Partha Mitter, *The Triumph of Modernism: India's Artists and the Avant-Garde, 1922–1947* (London: Reaktion Books, 2007) and Mitter, "Decentering Modernism," *The Art Bulletin* 90, no. 4 (2008), pp. 531–548.

69 Laura Winkiel, "Postcolonial Avant-Gardes and the World System of Modernity/Coloniality," in Bäckström and Hjartarson, p. 99.

70 May Joseph, "Globalization, Modernity, and the Avant-Garde," in Saloni Mathur, ed., *The Migrant's Time: Rethinking Art History and Diaspora* (Williamstown and New Haven: Sterling and Francine Clark Art Institute and Yale University Press, 2011), p. 44.

71 Chinua Achebe, *Home and Exile* (New York: Anchor Books, 2000), p. 79.

72 Arthur Schomburg, "The Negro Digs Up His Past," in *The New Negro: Voices of the Harlem Renaissance*, ed. Alain Locke (New York: Touchstone, 1997), pp. 231–237.

73 Richard J. Powell, Jock Reynolds, et al., *To Conserve a Legacy: American Art from Historically Black Colleges and Universities* (Cambridge, MA: MIT Press, 1999).

74 Christian Kravagna, "Painting the Global History of Art: Hale Woodruff's *The Art of the Negro*," in Kravagna, *Transmodern: An Art History of Contact, 1920–60* (Manchester: Manchester University Press, 2022), pp. 221–253.

75 David Craven, *Art and Revolution in Latin America, 1910–1990* (New Haven and London: Yale University Press, 2002).

76 Lowery Stokes Sims, *Wifredo Lam and the International Avant-Garde, 1923–1982* (Austin: University of Texas Press, 2002).

77 Mitter, *The Triumph of Modernism*.

78 Chika Okeke-Agulu, *Postcolonial Modernism: Art and Decolonization in Twentieth-Century Nigeria* (Durham, NC, and London: Duke University Press, 2015).

79 Adora Mba, "Moffat Takadiwa: The shy guy whose art speaks volumes," *True Africa*, March 31, 2017, https://true africa.co/article/moffat-takadiwa-shy-guy-whose-art-speaks-volumes/.

80 Ngũgĩ, p. 59.

81 Rinaldo Walcott coined the term "long emancipation" for Black life under postcolonial conditions and the aftermath of slavery: "One must note that at every moment Black peoples have sought, for themselves, to assert what freedom might mean and look like, those desires and acts toward freedom have been violently interdicted. It is this ongoing interdiction of a potential Black freedom that I have termed *the long emancipation*." Rinaldo Walcott, *The Long Emancipation: Moving toward Black Freedom* (Durham, NC, and London: Duke University Press, 2021), p. 1.

82 william cordova, personal communication with the author, July 8, 2022.

83 Stephanie Lacava, "'This Planet is Our Spaceship': An Interview with Cauleen Smith," *The New York Review*, November 28, 2020, https://moran-morangallery.com/this-planet-is-our-spaceship-an-interview-with-cauleen-smith/.

84 The artistic references in *Avant-Garde and Liberation* call to mind historical moments of liberation that can be described along with Walcott as "glimpses of Black freedom." Walcott, p. 2.

85 william cordova, personal communication with the author, July 8, 2022.

86 Belinda Kazeem-Kamiński in conversation with Anne Faucheret, in *Belinda Kazeem-Kamiński* (Vienna: Kunsthalle Wien, 2021), p. 46. The artist refers there to Nicola Lauré al-Samarai, "*Inspirited Topography*: Über/Lebensräume, Heim-Suchungen und die Verortung der Erfahrung in Schwarzen deutschen Kultur- und Wissenstraditionen," in *Mythen, Masken und Subjekte: Kritische Weißseinsforschung in Deutschland*, ed. Maureen Maisha Eggers, Grada Kilomba, Peggy Piesche, et al. (Münster: Unrast Verlag, 2005), pp. 118–134.

87 Diedrick Brackens, personal communication with the author, July 6, 2022.

88 Diedrick Brackens, "The Soft Library of Faith," in *Faith Ringgold: American People*, exh. cat. New Museum, New York (London: Phaidon, 2022), p. 163.

89 Quoted from the border text of the quilt *Le Café des Artistes*.

90 Alain Locke, "The Legacy of the Ancestral Arts," in Locke, pp. 254–267.

A FUTURITY EMBEDDED IN A PAST THAT ALLOWED FOR AN OTHERWISE TO EMERGE

CHRISTIAN KRAVAGNA – Nana, I would like to talk with you about the chronopolitics of liberation. You have done important work on the politics of time with a focus on contemporary art based on the Black experience. My work on the exhibition *Avant-Garde and Liberation* began with the observation of a certain urgency in contemporary art of recourse to historical avant-gardes and liberation movements. Of course, I'm not thinking of contemporary art in general but about critical art that reflects crisis phenomena—current forms of racism, neocolonialism, neofascism, fundamentalism, etc. Originally, the working title of the show was *The Crisis and the Avant-garde*, before the pandemic hijacked the concept of crisis. It seems that a sense of threat, an analysis of danger, for the individual and the community necessitates a historical perspective on progressive movements in art and politics. The past—certain pasts—seems to play an important role in reflecting on the present with a perspective of enabling a different future. In your book *Taking Stakes in the Unknown*,[1] you work with the notion of "hetero-temporality," which I found helpful to better understand my own observations. How did you develop this notion? What questions did you think this temporal concept could answer?

NANA ADUSEI-POKU – This is a fantastic question, Christian, because the politics of the time and the difficulty in thinking about Blackness as linear have been a consistent subject in my curatorial and academic work. I arrived at hetero-temporality through Leslie Hewitt's photo series *Riffs on Realtime* (2006–09), in which she created layers of different materials, often snapshots on top of a magazine page or a note, or a snapshot on top of a book and then on a carpet. These works reference Josef Albers's series *Homage to the Square* and an engagement with Henri Bergson's concept of real time. I tried to make sense of the multiplicities of the Black experience that was described by Henri Louis Gates Jr. in the context of post-Blackness.[2] Hewitt's work allows us to see through its layering the synchronicity of some people being and feeling liberated and others still living under the condition of direct colonial control. I have expanded this in the framework of what I call "Black melancholia," which forces us to stay in the present whilst acknowledging how the past is part of our future and how each of these temporalities is deeply affected by anti-Blackness. I don't necessarily think that the framework of hetero-temporality or the temporal dimension of Black melancholia are giving us answers: what they both do is decenter the Western concept of linear time and with it the notion of progress. I think that acknowledges that there is such a thing called change. However, that does not necessarily mean progress, as in towards a liberated existence in which anti-Blackness, and with it gratuitous violence, doesn't affect our lives and

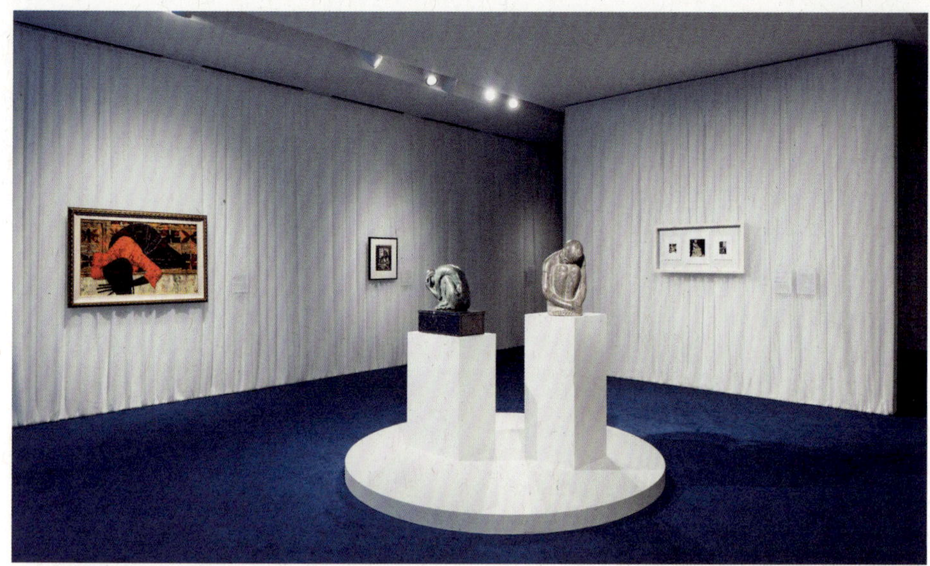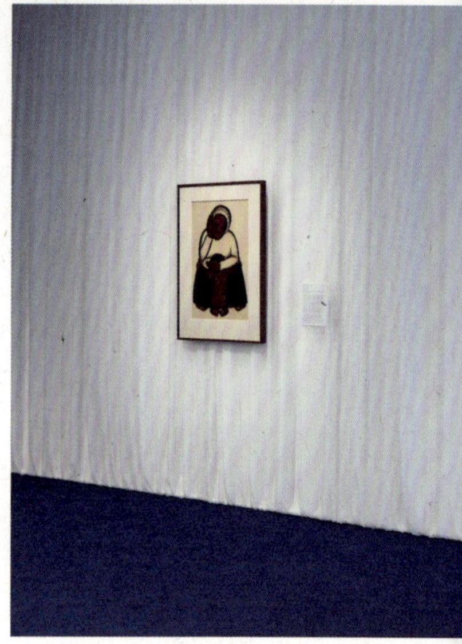

Installation views from *Black Melancholia*,
Hessel Museum of Art, Center for Curatorial Studies,
Bard College, Annandale-on-Hudson, NY, 2022

future lives anymore. Thinking time in this way is a powerful thinking tool and demands for a development of different methodologies.

CHRISTIAN KRAVAGNA – What you are saying about difference in the experience of time under racial conditions in late modernity reminds me of Simon Gikandi's account of radically discrepant experiences in the formative phases of modernity.[3] While the dissolving of the rigid social order spurred social mobility and the liberation of the European subject, for colonized and enslaved people becoming a part of modernity meant the end of freedom. Being aware of such contradictions of colonial modernity has an impact on concepts like the avant-garde, which I am working with for this exhibition. There is hardly any other concept in art that embodies the temporal concept of Euromodernism—the linear, progressive model of time which you addressed above—like that of the avant-garde. The idea of leaving behind all tradition, of cutting all ties with the past to start radically from scratch, wouldn't make much sense for modern artists who belonged to communities whose histories were buried or erased by colonial violence. For Black and non-European vanguard artists, it seemed crucial to dig up their past—in the sense of Arturo Schomburg—to create a foundation for the aesthetic and political designs of a liberating future. This also applies to some of the artists in your exhibition *Black Melancholia*, such as Augusta Savage, Selma Burke, and Charles White. It's such a pity I couldn't see your show last year. I have seen beautiful pictures, however, and I was intrigued by the way you installed the historic and contemporary artworks. In the framework of your time-political considerations, I would love to hear more about your thoughts on the relation between the works of the early modern and the living artists and about the allusion (the white curtains) to the exhibition design of the first documenta in 1955, probably the most prominent exhibition to claim a new beginning for modernism after its persecution by the Nazis.

NANA ADUSEI-POKU – I think your assessment is spot on; yes, African Diasporic artists had from the outset a notion of looking back and forward at the same time. This is particularly true for

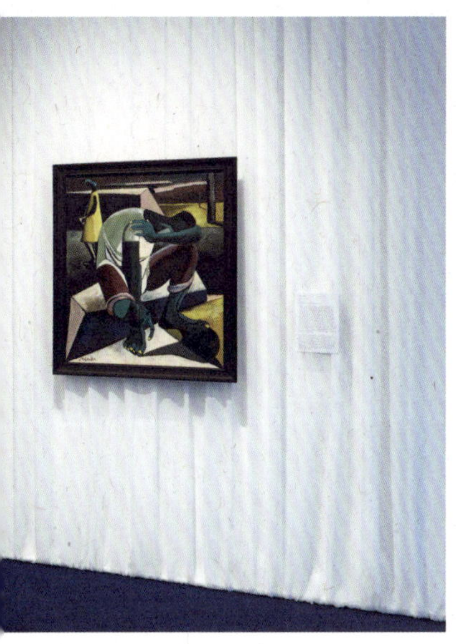 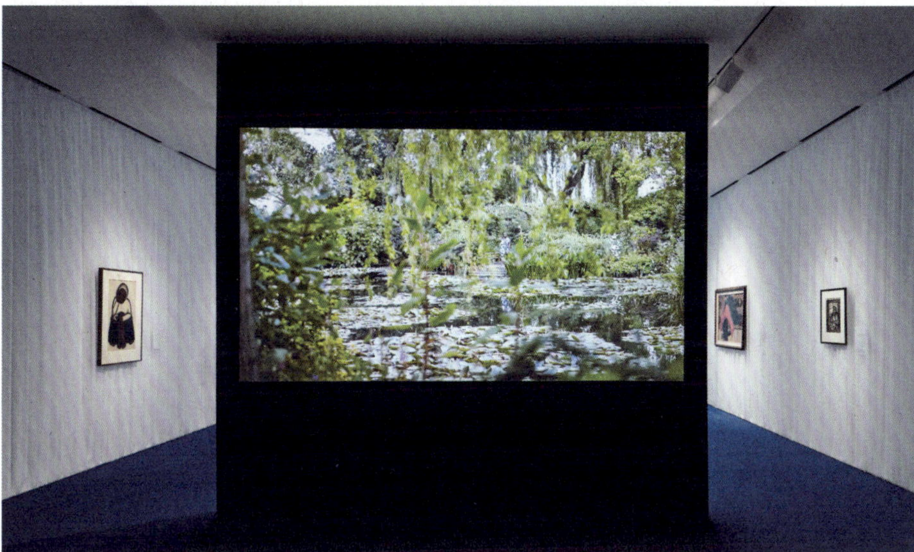

artists of the Harlem Renaissance like Savage or Burke, who were part of *Black Melancholia*. You also mention Arturo Schomburg (who was the son of a white German immigrant and a freeborn Black woman and born in the US Territory of Puerto Rico), who invested in archiving Black culture in the same way as Alain Locke gave the cultural developments of the early twentieth century a theoretical framework with what he called the "New Negro" and with it the New Negro Renaissance. I think it is interesting that the choice fell on Renaissance, which in itself holds a kind of revival or renewed interest in and valuing of something historic. This interest in aesthetics and forms from the African continent hence became central. Artists prior to that like Henry Ossawa Tanner (1859–1937), Robert Duncanson (1821–1872), Edward Bannister (1828–1901), or Edmonia Lewis (1844–1907) did not engage with African forms and rather followed the aesthetic ideals of the French Academy and other European styles.[4] Hence, what Locke and the artists of the Harlem Renaissance proposed was a narrative that was connected to a futurity that can only be embedded in a past that allowed for an Otherwise to emerge. It is

nevertheless important to emphasize that all the ideas about "racial uplift" and progress narratives (as i.e. in the works of Aaron Douglas) that are echoed all the way into the Obama era with the slogans around "change" were nevertheless based, in a sense, on a linearity that had to be produced by Black people.

I think it is worth looking at European avant-garde movements that utilized African forms, Otherness, and Blackness as intrinsic factors to not only push formal developments but also integrate a sense of futurity. I am bringing this up because the forms that were chosen were hence often in dialogue with each other but from very different standpoints and subject positions.

I deliberately played with time in the *Black Melancholia* exhibition because of the circular and repetitive nature of melancholy as an experience in the face of anti-Blackness and gratuitous violence. That violence is as much part of the past as it will be in our future; this understanding hence made it possible to tap into the sadness that Rashid Johnson's work *Black and Blue* evoked as it did the despair that Selma

Burke expressed in the sculpture of the same title. So, instead of just starting off with a historical perspective, the works in the opening room were presented as just as much part of the present as the past. It was a gesture to also pay attention to the fact that the notion of Black melancholia has been overlooked in these artists' works; for example, Rose Piper's painting *Grievin' Hearted* (n.d.) and Sargent Johnson's charcoal drawing *Mother and Child* (1932) reference Dürer's posture-as-portrait in *Melencolia I* (1513/14). I love exhibition histories and think we need to curatorially also utilize that history. The reference to the first documenta was supposed to do both: insinuate a historical break, just as the curtains in the Fridericianum do,[5] and highlight that Black artists were not part of this "reintroduction" of modern art in the German context on a global platform despite their vibrant work. Exhibitions or how art is made public is so foundational for art-historical developments and our methods.

CHRISTIAN KRAVAGNA – What you said about these artists and thinkers also holds true for your own work. You recently edited an important volume on historic Black art exhibitions, *Reshaping the Field: Arts of the African Diasporas on Display*.[6] There have been other publications on the topic, but your volume seems decidedly international in its approach. What specific conditions and urgencies of the present have shaped your perspective on the exhibition histories of the arts of the African Diaspora?

NANA ADUSEI-POKU – Indeed, there have been a few publications about Black exhibitions and their histories, such as Bridget Cooks's *Exhibiting Blackness*[7] and Mabel Wilson's *Negro Building*,[8] which both focused on exhibitions in the United States. However, these are monographs, and there hasn't been an anthology yet that is looking at Black exhibition histories with a wider historical and diasporic arc. I am myself a product of different Black Diasporas at this point; and I am not from the United States, which gives me a much wider perspective and desire to think of the Black or African Diaspora as as large and diverse as possible with a need not to have one perspective dominate the other. Even though often cited against each other, Brent Hayes Edwards[9] and Paul Gilroy[10] both emphasize that the Black Diaspora is a space of cultural exchange and multiplicity. I wanted to emphasize with *Reshaping the Field* historical through-lines in terms of themes as well as a spotlight on differences. My aim with this publication is also to bring current research and researchers in conversation with each other and to generate prospective interest in the subject, which has clearly been overlooked.

CHRISTIAN KRAVAGNA – This broader notion of African Diaspora(s) resonates with an experience I had during the preparation of *Avant-Garde and Liberation*. In my conversations with Black artists from the United States who are participating in this exhibition, they often expressed their delight about the opportunity to share reflections on non-white avant-gardes together with artists from Africa, Asia, and Europe. I myself, in turn, am looking forward to juxtaposing artistic references to historical figures such as Paulette and Jeanne Nardal or Suzanne and Aimé Césaire in works by African American painter Fahamu Pecou and Dutch artist patricia kaersenhout, among others. The Nardal sisters and the Césaires were themselves representatives of a Black modernism that bridged several continents, languages, and cultures. This brings us back to the politics of time in colonial modernity, including the problematic concept of the avant-garde, which I would like to discuss in this exhibition. Because of their different trajectories, non-Western modernisms were often said to be lagging behind. May Joseph describes "the perceived cultural time lag between the European avant-garde movements and 'Third World' modernisms" as a result of an "epistemic bind" caused by Western modernity's "delusional idea of teleological progression."[11] In your book *Taking Stakes in the Unknown* you employ the concept of "racial time" introduced by the historian Michael Hanchard and "defined as the inequalities of temporality that result from power relations between racially dominant and subordinate groups."[12] I consider this a very promising approach for a better understanding of the complex entanglements of different modernisms. Can you explain your understanding of this concept's potential for our understanding of modern and contemporary art which often still seems caught in the epistemic bind mentioned before?

NANA ADUSEI-POKU — First, I want to stress that your exhibition truly promises to be generative of discursive connections that have not been explored in this way before, and I am excited to see its impact on art-historical and potentially artistic productions. I agree with you that the "teleological progression" narrative is so persistent that it hinders seeing the cross connections that you are interested in putting in dialogue. I am, however, still undecided whether the frameworks of multiple modernities as proposed by S. N. Eisenstadt, Partha Chatterjee, or James Smethurst[13] are the way to think about this. To think of modernity in multiplicity and through notions of difference makes sense, but I am still struggling to think of these different frameworks together with the "conditions of modernity" thought as the set of sociohistorical political events that are still ongoing and that affected us globally. Exhibitions like *The New Vanguard*, for example, feed into the notion of consistent innovation without much historical reflection, which curatorially creates more erasure rather than critical reflection. The reason why I am stressing this is

because Michael Hanchard makes it very clear in his text "Afro-Modernity" that time has been a tool for both liberation and oppression. His claim is that "only under conditions of modernity could people defined as African utilize the very mechanisms of their subordination for their liberation."[14] To curatorially declare every three to five years a "new vanguard" can hence be understood as a continuation of a narrative of Black excellence which marginalizes the many traditions in which Black art is rooted. Thinking with Hanchard's notion of modernity as a process has been more productive because it allows agency to make historical processes visible through art as well as allowing us to think the present historically. Erasure has been one of the most effective tools of colonialism and slavery, which is why I consider it mandatory to not think of Black art as consistently trying to detach itself but rather to see much more anchoring in historical consciousness. This is, of course, also connected to the absence of Black art as part of the art-historical canon, but I don't want to open that Pandora's Box here. I hope I answered your question?

CHRISTIAN KRAVAGNA — Absolutely. There is probably not much to gain from the rhetoric of neo-neo-vanguardism, which sometimes seems to mimic the capitalist logic of innovation and tends to ignore long and varied histories of struggles. Your example of *The New Vanguard* resonates with a case that I have been critically engaged with, the problematic discourse of "global contemporary art" that celebrates the globality of art after 1989 and thereby erases the global (or rather transcultural) dimensions of modernism in Asia, Latin America, and the African Diaspora since its beginnings in the early twentieth century. Concepts of linear time and progress have caused too much harm in the past to be relied upon today in contexts of liberation and justice. When you spoke about Hanchard's

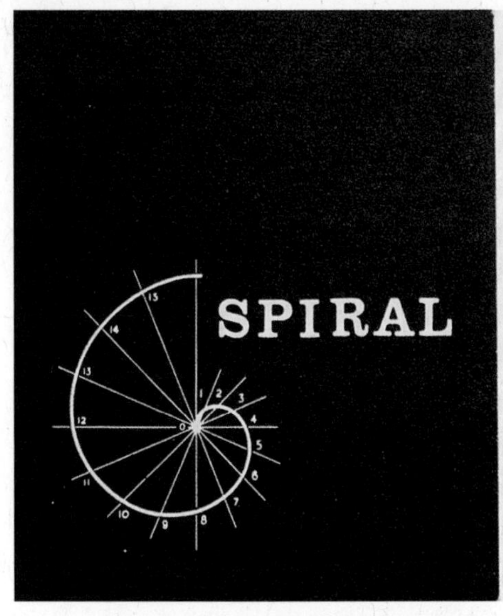

Spiral, *First Group Showing (works in black & white),*
catalogue cover of the artist group's first exhibition in 1965
at 147 Christopher Street, New York (exhibition flyer)

concept but also your own notion of hetero-temporality, a figure of time and motion came to my mind: the spiral—as it was used by the artist group Spiral in the nineteen-sixties, which was founded in response to the March on Washington and included Romare Bearden, Hale Woodruff, and Emma Amos, among others. The spiral turns upwards, opens outwards and backwards, to turn upwards again, encompassing the aesthetic, the social, and the political, in the case of the Spiral group, that was built—in a moment of crisis—on a critical dialogue over the different legacies of abstraction and figuration, the individual and the collective. In a way, the spiral offers a model of conceptualizing non-linear ideas of time and action that have some characteristics of circular time but also of the Sankofa motive. I don't know if this makes any sense to you, but I would love to hear your thoughts on figures like these in relation to your work as an art historian and curator, since you are critical of the multiple-modernities model, which is based on the principle of cultural addition, but also of the presentism of projects like *The New Vanguard.*

NANA ADUSEI-POKU – I am so glad you are equally troubled by the framework of global contemporary art. To answer your question: I try not to show work in a linear manner. A work from Edward Mitchell Bannister from 1884 was paired with a Tyler Mitchell piece from 2020, and yet *Black Melancholia* started with artists from the beginning of the twentieth century, but more because of a formal question regarding the posture of melancholy and not so much because of their temporal proximity or linearity. I try to pay more attention to affect in the space through light, sound, spacing, floor treatment, and color, so that an exhibition speaks to the body in a transformative way.

I am curious if you feel comfortable sharing what your curatorial approach is in regard to time. Are there other curatorial tools that you apply in this exhibition to support your argument about time, modernism, and critical theory? Are there works that you want to particularly highlight?

CHRISTIAN KRAVAGNA – The first thought that occurred to me in response to your question relates to a significant difference between our

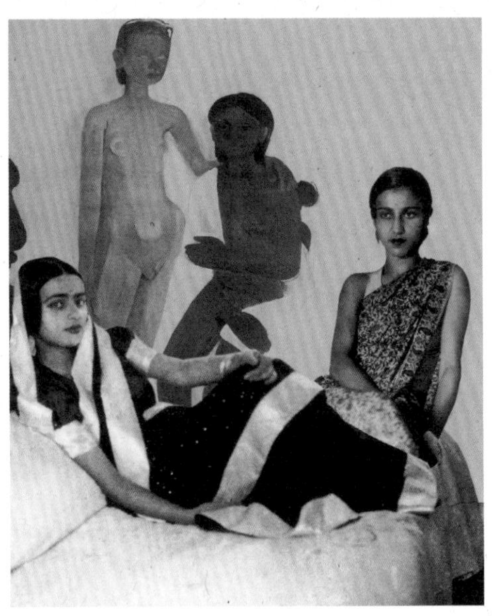

Vivan Sundaram
Re-take of Amrita, photo 8, 2001–02

exhibitions. While you, as a curator, create a dialogue between a painting from the nineteenth century and a work from 2020, in my exhibition I have artworks that already combine the present and historical practice. I am fascinated by your curatorial accentuations by means of spatial design, light, and color. If I am very restrained with such interventions, it has to do with the different questions of our projects. With *Black Melancholia* you direct attention to a state of mind in its political dimension. In contrast, my focus is on artistic processes of updating historical arts and movements of liberation. In my exhibition, it is the artists themselves who connect history and today.

If you ask me about specific works, I would like to mention Vivan Sundaram, who passed away in March 2023 during the preparations for our exhibition, which makes me very sad. Vivan was one of the artists who are responsible for *Avant-Garde and Liberation* without knowing it. I showed his series on the Indian modernist painter Amrita Sher-Gil in my exhibition *Routes* in 2002. On a visit to New Delhi, I realized how much his work on Amrita, and other works by Vivan remembering Indian avant-garde artists are part of the secular cultural scene's current struggle against the anti-democratic violence of the Hindu nationalist movement. Perhaps it was through Vivan that I really understood what Walter Benjamin said about the image of the past in the moment of danger. I show Vivan's work together with Atul Dodiya's paintings on Mahatma Gandhi and Rabindranath Tagore, next to The Otolith Group's film on Tagore's World University in Santiniketan, hoping for mutual illumination regarding the topicality of the Indian avant-garde and the possibilities of its actualization in the face of crisis. Political concepts of temporality, as you have developed them in your book and exhibition, are of eminent importance for the understanding of *Avant-Garde and Liberation*. I am therefore grateful for the conversation.

1   Nana Adusei-Poku, *Taking Stakes in the Unknown: Tracing Post-Black Art* (Bielefeld: transcript, 2021).
2   Touré, *Who's Afraid of Post-Blackness?* (New York et al.: Free Press, 2011), p. 5.
3   Simon Gikandi, *Slavery and the Culture of Taste* (Princeton and Oxford: Princeton University Press, 2011).
4   Nevertheless, is it not quite true that African Americans completely lost their aesthetic traditions or interest in African subjects. See, among others, Huey Copeland, "Making Black Feminist Art Histories," *American Art* 31, no. 2 (Summer 2017), pp. 27–29, and Sharon F. Patton, *African-American Art* (Oxford and New York: Oxford University Press, 1998).
5   Charlotte Klonk, *Spaces of Experience: Art Gallery Interiors from 1800–2000* (New Haven: Yale University Press, 2009), p. 176.
6   Nana Adusei-Poku, ed., *Reshaping the Field: Arts of the African Diasporas on Display* (London: Afterall, 2022).
7   Bridget R. Cooks, *Exhibiting Blackness: African Americans and the American Art Museum* (Amherst: University of Massachusetts Press, 2011).
8   Mabel O. Wilson, *Negro Building: Black Americans in the World of Fairs and Museums* (Berkeley, Los Angeles, and London: University of California Press, 2012).
9   Brent Hayes Edwards, *The Practice of Diaspora: Literature, Translation, and the Rise of Black Internationalism* (Cambridge, MA, and London: Harvard University Press, 2003).
10 Paul Gilroy, *The Black Atlantic: Modernity and Double Consciousness* (London and New York: Verso, 1993).
11 May Joseph, "Globalization, Modernity, and the Avant-Garde," in Saloni Mathur, ed., *The Migrant's Time: Rethinking Art History and Diaspora* (Williamstown and New Haven: Sterling and Francine Clark Art Institute/Yale University Press, 2011), p. 44.
12 Michael Hanchard, "Afro-Modernity: Temporality, Politics, and the African Diaspora," *Public Culture* 11, no. 1 (January 1999), p. 253.
13 Partha Chatterjee, *Our Modernity*, SEPHIS CODESRIA lecture no. 1 (Dakar: SEPHIS, 1997); S. N. Eisenstadt, "*Multiple Modernities*," *Daedalus* 129, no. 1 (Winter 2000); James Edward Smethurst, *The African American Roots of Modernism: From Reconstruction to the Harlem Renaissance*, The John Hope Franklin Series in African American History and Culture (Chapel Hill: University of North Carolina Press, 2011).
14 Hanchard, p. 246.

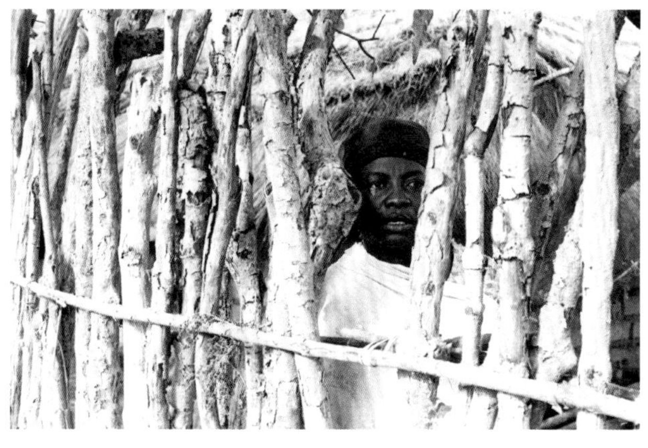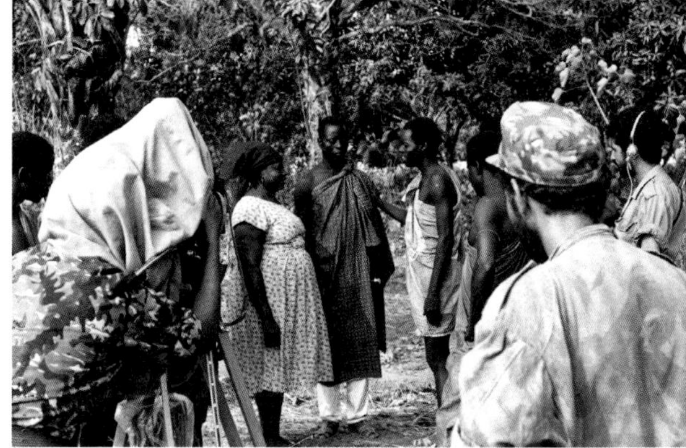

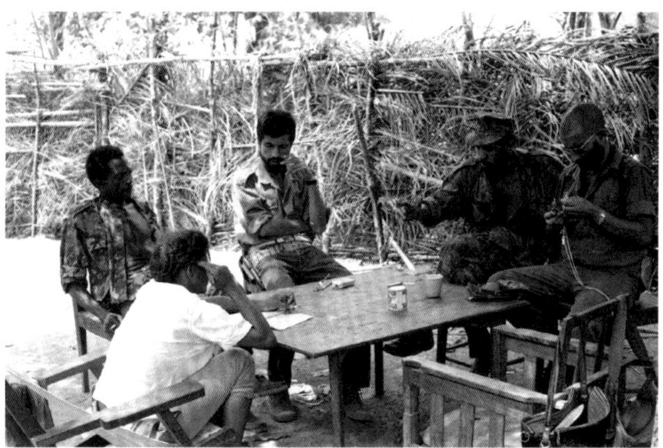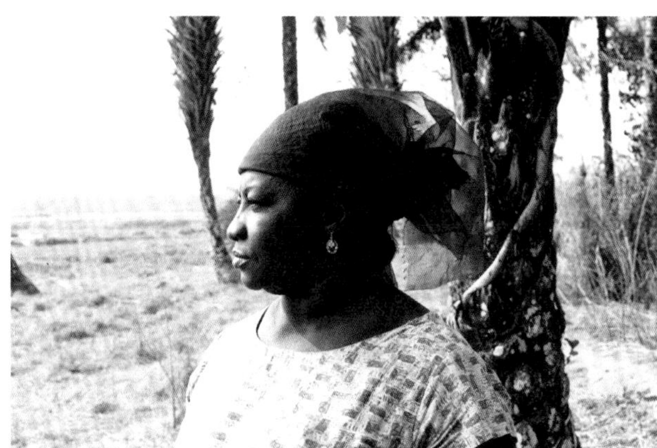

1

MATHIEU KLEYEBE ABONNENC
FOREWORD TO GUNS FOR BANTA
2009–11

Mathieu Kleyebe Abonnenc's work reconstructs the unfinished film *Guns for Banta* (1970) by Sarah Maldoror, the legendary French director from Guadeloupe. The film told the story of the struggle and death at a young age of Awa, a country girl who joins the African Party for the Independence of Guinea and Cape Verde and fights for the liberation of Guinea-Bissau. Maldoror's film was commissioned by the Algerian government, but a conflict between the director and the client prevented it from ever being completed. The only material evidence of its existence consists of photos taken by war photographers on the film set. Abonnenc's work seeks to restore the collective memory of Maldoror's unfinished film, whose main goal was to portray the involvement of women and children in the struggle for independence. The photos are complemented by a voiceover conversation between Abonnenc, the director, and the latter's ex-partner, Angolan writer Mário Pinto de Andrade.

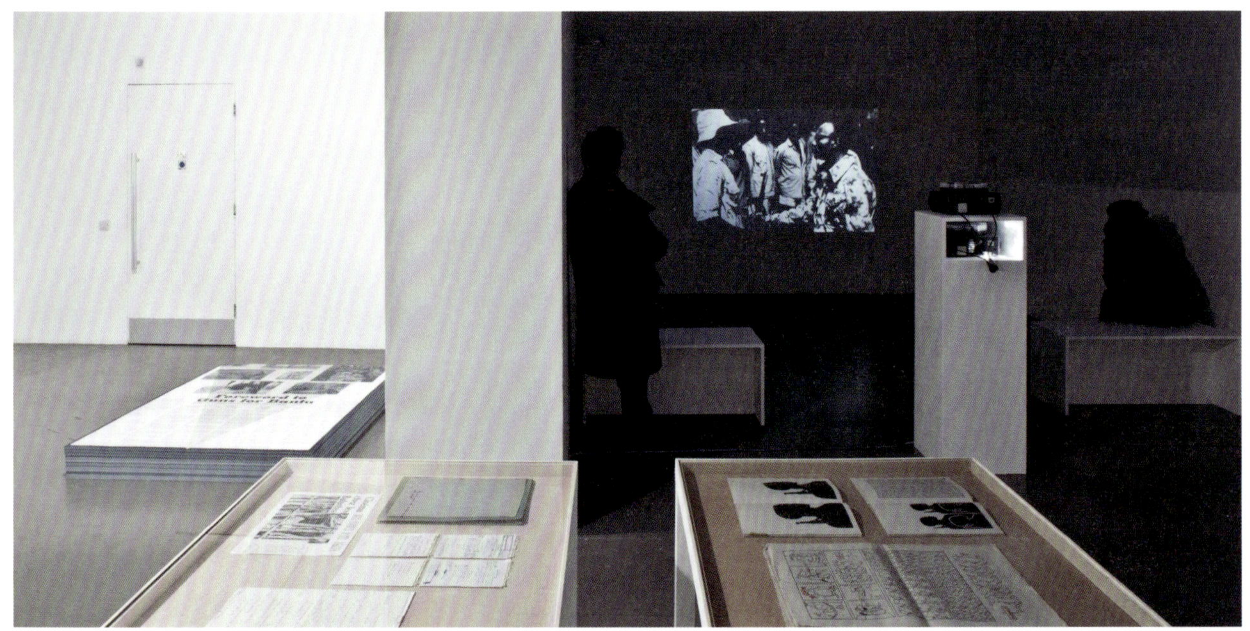

1

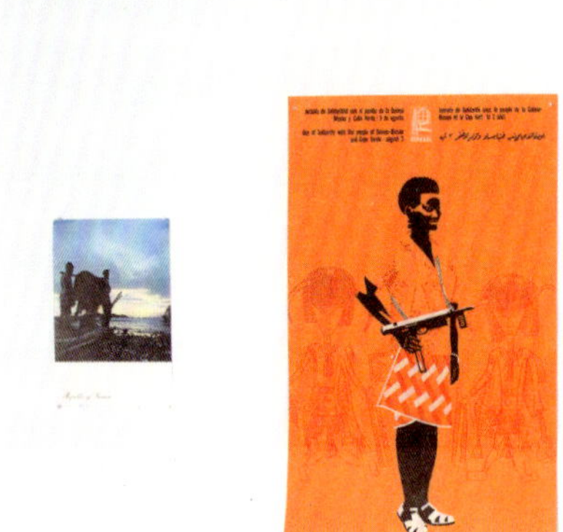

2

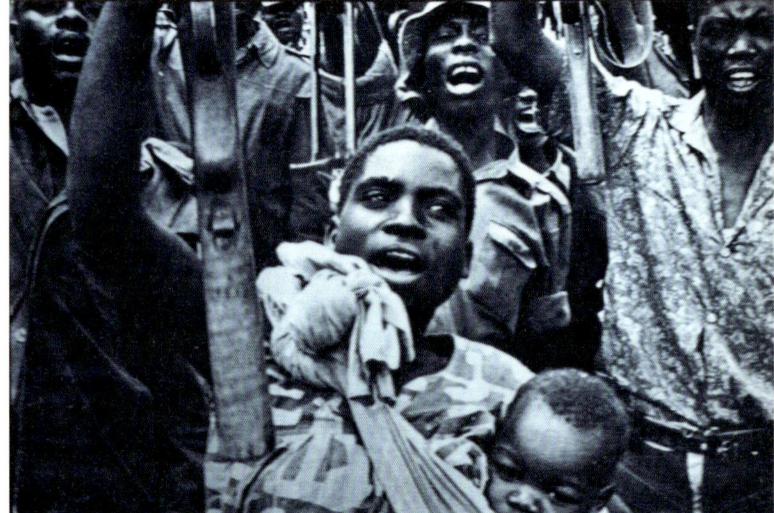

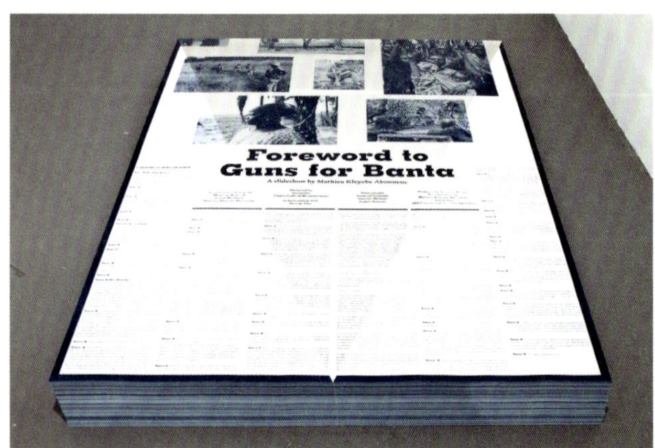

3

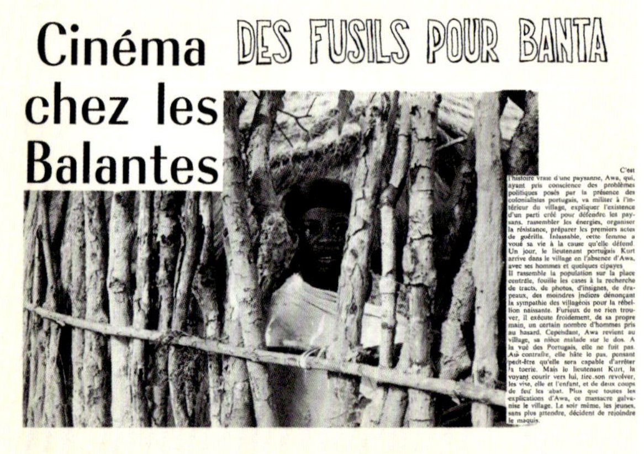

Cinéma chez les Balantes
DES FUSILS POUR BANTA
C'est l'histoire vraie d'une paysanne, Awa, qui, ayant pris conscience des problèmes politiques posés par la présence des colonialistes portugais, va militer à l'intérieur du village, expliquer l'existence d'un parti créé pour défendre les paysans, rassembler les énergies, organiser la résistance, préparer les premiers actes de guérilla. Infatigable, cette femme a voué sa vie à la cause qu'elle défend. Un jour, le lieutenant portugais Kurt arrive dans le village en l'absence d'Awa, avec ses hommes et quelques cipayes. Il rassemble la population sur la place centrale, fouille les cases à la recherche de tracts, de photos, d'insignes, de drapeaux, des moindres indices dénonçant la sympathie des villageois pour la rébellion naissante. Furieux de ne rien trouver, il exécute froidement, de sa propre main, un certain nombre d'hommes pris au hasard. Cependant, Awa revient au village, sa nièce malade sur le dos. A la vue des Portugais, elle ne fuit pas. Au contraire, elle hâte le pas, pensant peut-être qu'elle sera capable d'arrêter la tuerie. Mais le lieutenant Kurt, la voyant courir vers lui, tire son revolver, les vise, elle et l'enfant, et de deux coups de feu les abat. Plus que toutes les explications d'Awa, ce massacre galvanise le village. Le soir même, les jeunes, sans plus attendre, décident de rejoindre le maquis.

4

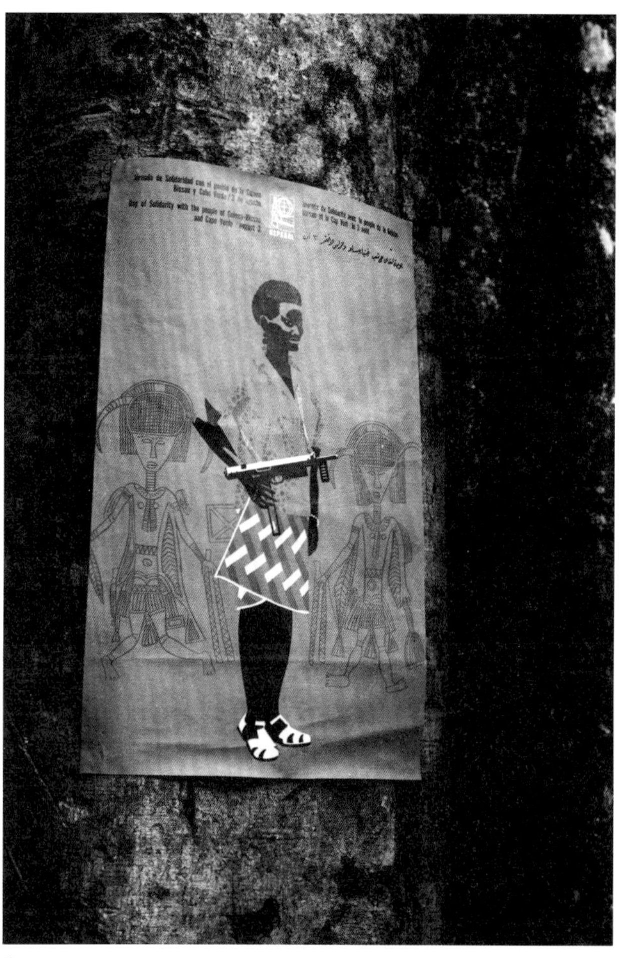

5

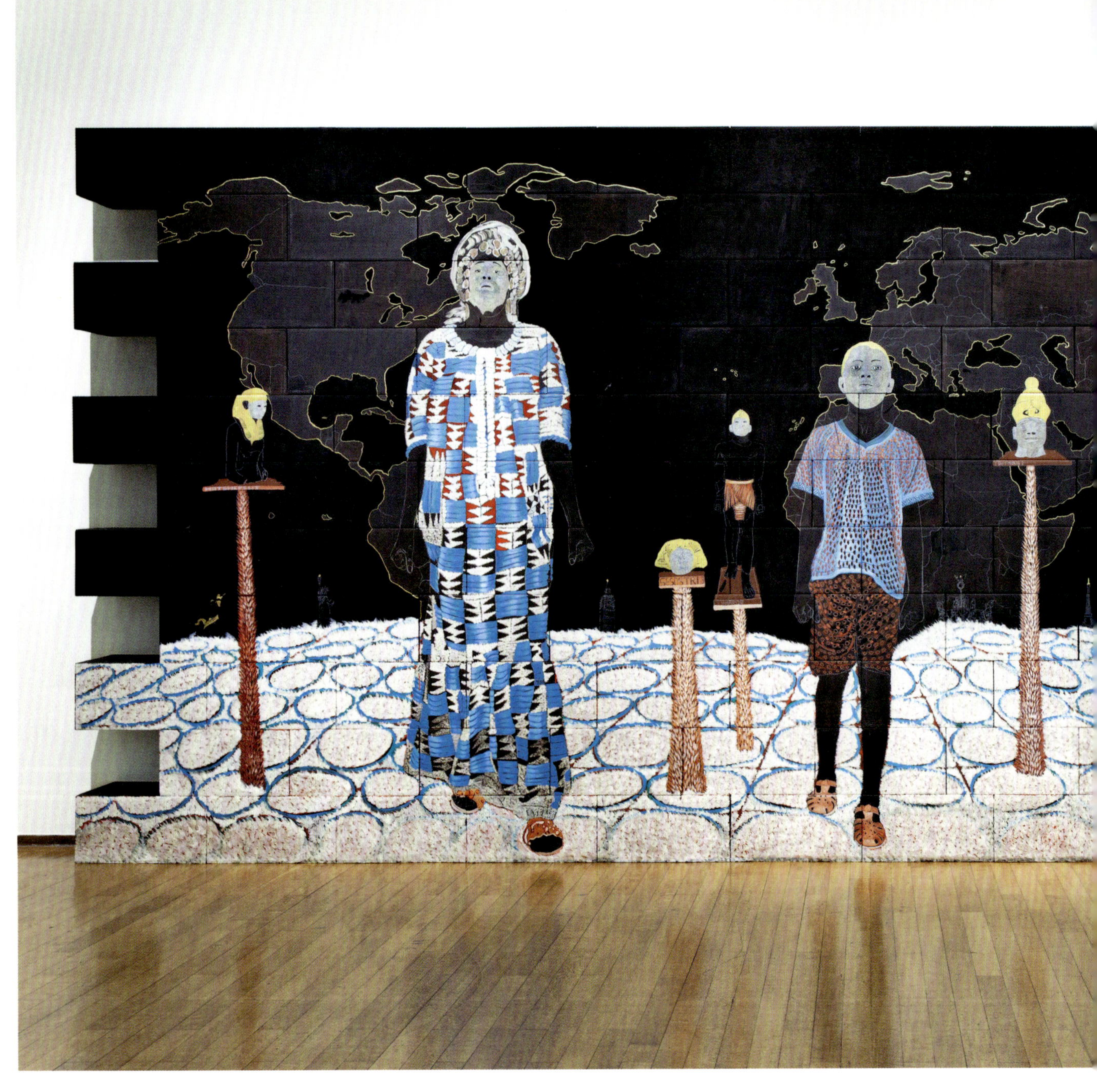

Omar Ba
*Clin d'œil à Cheikh Anta Diop − Un continent
à la recherche de son histoire*, 2017
Oil, pencil, acrylic, ink, gouache on
corrugated cardboard
330 × 718 × 40 cm

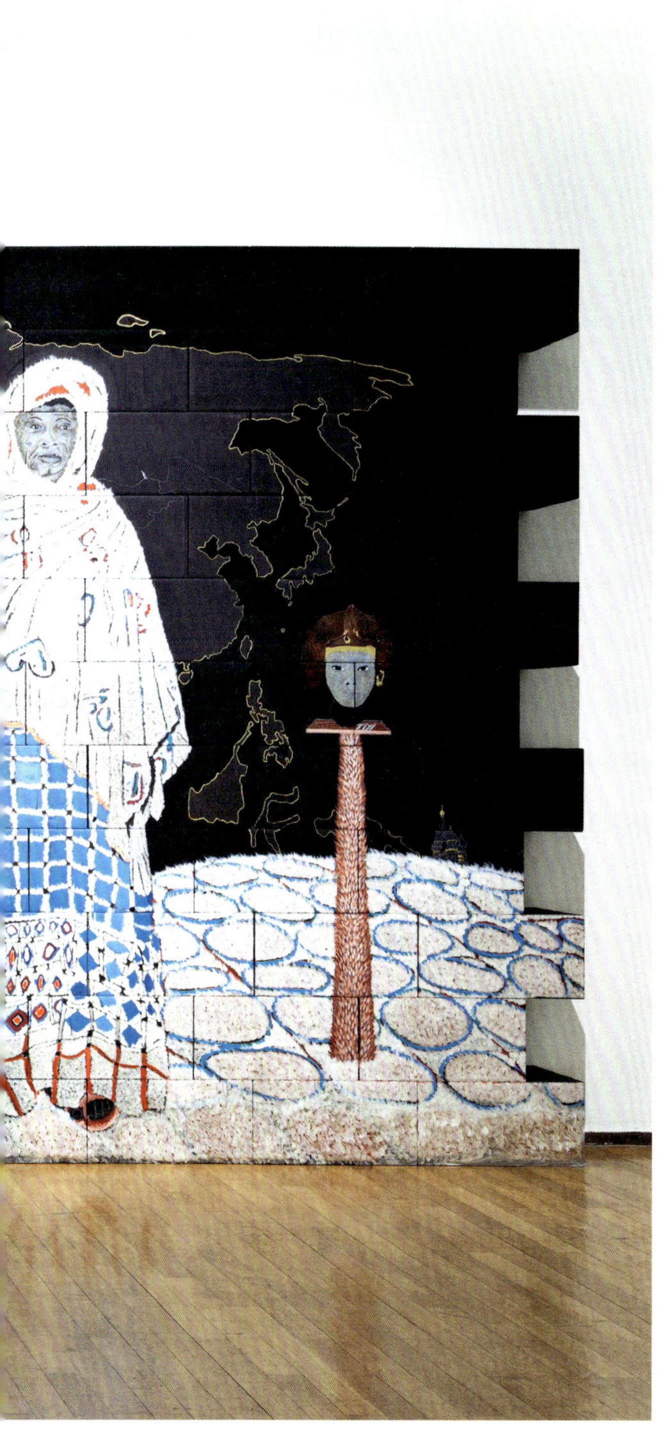

**OMAR BA
CLIN D'ŒIL À CHEIKH ANTA DIOP –
UN CONTINENT À LA RECHERCHE DE SON HISTOIRE
2017**

This work by Omar Ba is an impressive painted memorial to the era of African decolonization and to Cheikh Anta Diop as one of the leading intellectuals of that movement. Against the backdrop of a world map and Western buildings from the era of imperial modernity, such as the Eiffel Tower and the Big Ben, we see three figures in West African dress. In between them, artworks from ancient Egypt are depicted on narrow pedestals. Omar Ba is alluding here to the academic research carried out by the Senegalese anthropologist and historian Diop, who posited a historical connection between the cultures of sub-Saharan Africa and those of Egypt, which Western discourse has always described as white or Hamitic. Starting in the nineteen-fifties with publications such as *Nations nègres et culture* (The African Origin of Civilization), Diop characterized Egyptian civilization as Black and attempted to demonstrate its influence on Greek antiquity. Diop's anti-colonial historical scholarship, also referred to as "Afrocentric," had a major impact on liberation movements on the continent and in the African diaspora, bolstering efforts to develop postcolonial concepts of identity and history.

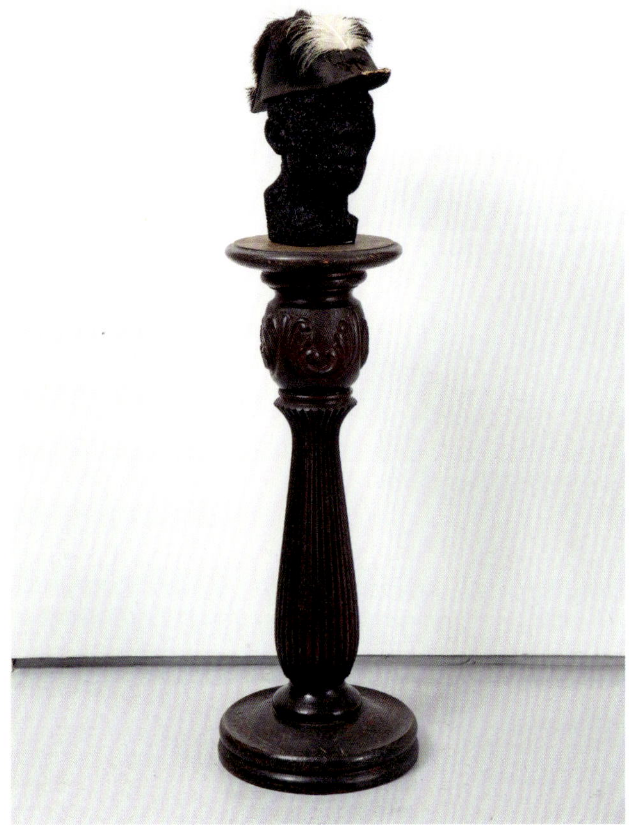

1

RADCLIFFE BAILEY

Black history and cultural lore are the central themes of
Radcliffe Bailey's art. Exploring subjects ranging from
traditional African art and the history of slavery, to
the anti-colonial revolutions and liberation movements
in the USA, and onward to African American music, the
artist has since the nineties dealt with many different
facets of this history of violence and resistance in his
paintings, sculptures, and installations. Bailey conceives
of memory as a medicine for treating the disease of
racism. His sculpture *Untitled* (2010) commemorates the
Haitian revolutionaries Toussaint Louverture and Jean-
Jacques Dessalines, who around 1800 overthrew French
colonialism and founded the first free Black Nation in
the Americas. Bailey's use of glitter in his work alludes to
the spiritual and healing practices of Haitian voodoo.
Mahalia (2021) is a pictorial tribute to the gospel singer
and civil rights activist Mahalia Jackson. The structure
of the image was inspired by the famous quilts of Gee's
Bend in Alabama. Characteristic of Bailey's process
is the fusion here of musical and textile techniques of
Black resilience, for which he also draws on his
childhood memories of living in his grandparents' home.

1   **Radcliffe Bailey**
     Untitled, **2010**
     Glitter, felt, feather, wood
     125×35.5×28 cm
2   **Radcliffe Bailey**
     Mahalia, **2021**
     **Mixed media including flock and acrylic
     paint components mounted on board,
     with window tint elements adhered to
     glazing**
     193×139×15.2 cm

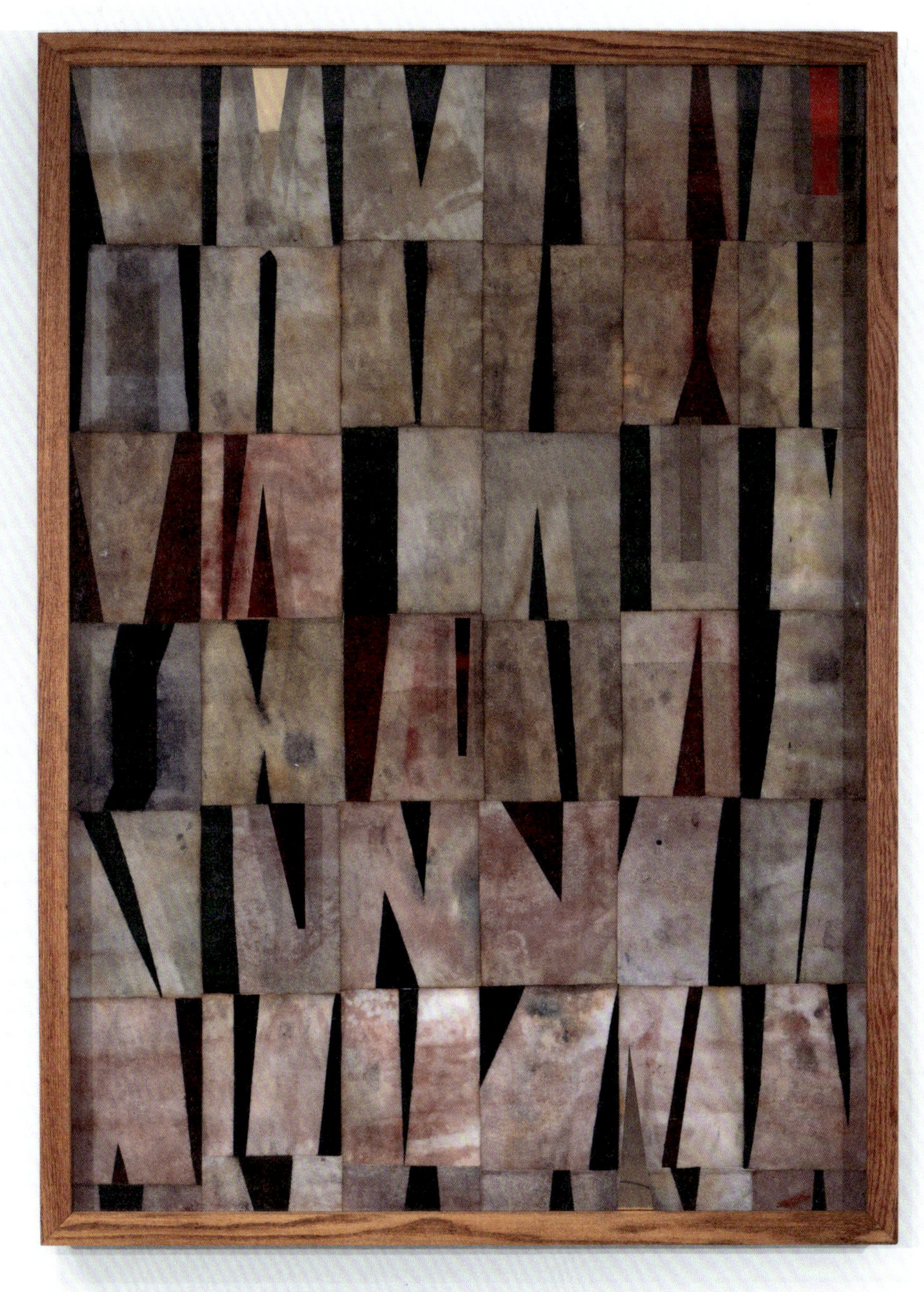

2

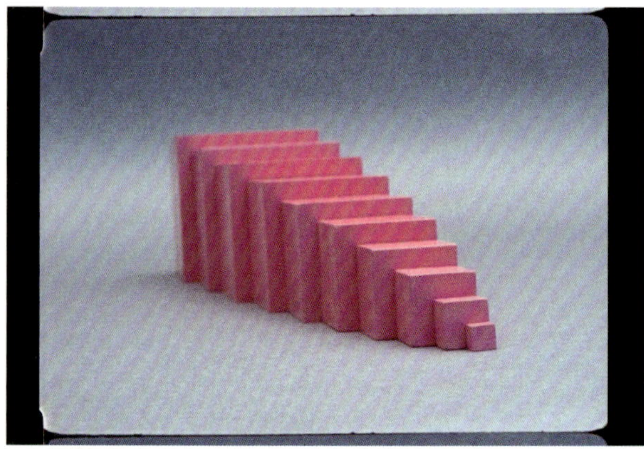

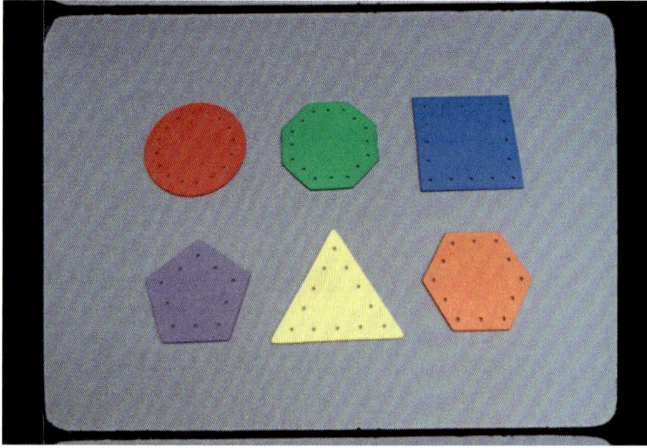

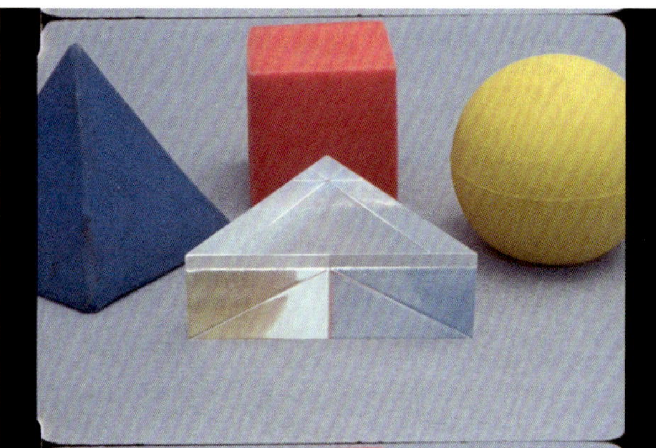

1

YTO BARRADA

In the tumultuous summer of 1966, Yto Barrada's mother, a twenty-three-year-old Moroccan student, was one of fifty "Young African Leaders" invited by the US State Department on a tour of the USA. Through play, poetry, and humor, the film *Tree Identification for Beginners* explores this staged encounter between North America and Africa and the burgeoning spirit of disobedience that would shape an entire generation—as expressed by the Pan-African, Tricontinental, and Anti-Vietnam War movements. The film combines 16 mm stop-motion animation using Montessori toys with voiceovers by Barrada's mother and other Crossroads Africa participants, as well as by historical figures such as Black Panther Stokely Carmichael. *Untitled (Nougat Cross Section Flavor Sampler)* (2016), Barrada's sculptural work made of Moroccan candy, relates to sculptures from the nineteen-sixties by Lebanese artist Saloua Raouda Choucair, now considered a central figure in Arab modernism.

1   Yto Barrada
Tree Identification for Beginners, 2017
16 mm film, transferred to digital, color, sound, 36 min
2   Yto Barrada
Untitled (Nougat Cross Section Flavor Sampler, fig. 1), 2016
Moroccan sweets, varnish
5-part, each ca. 28 × 15 × 4 cm

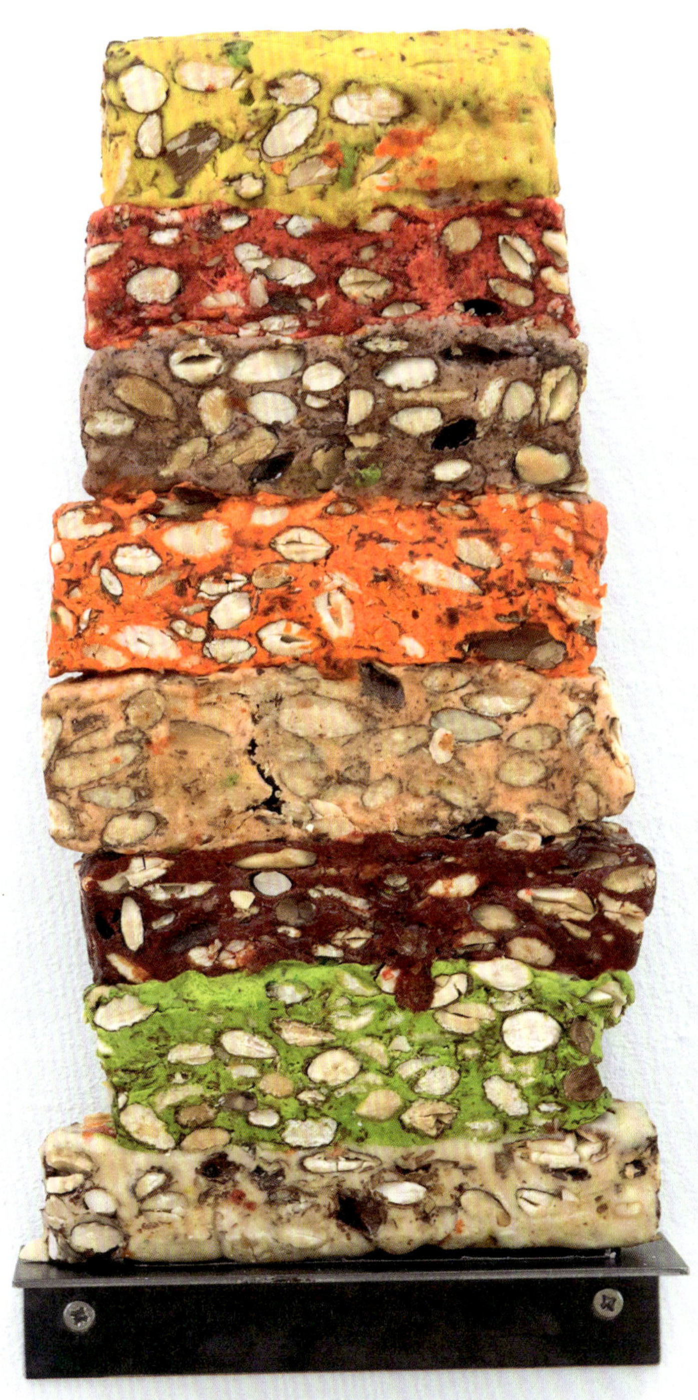

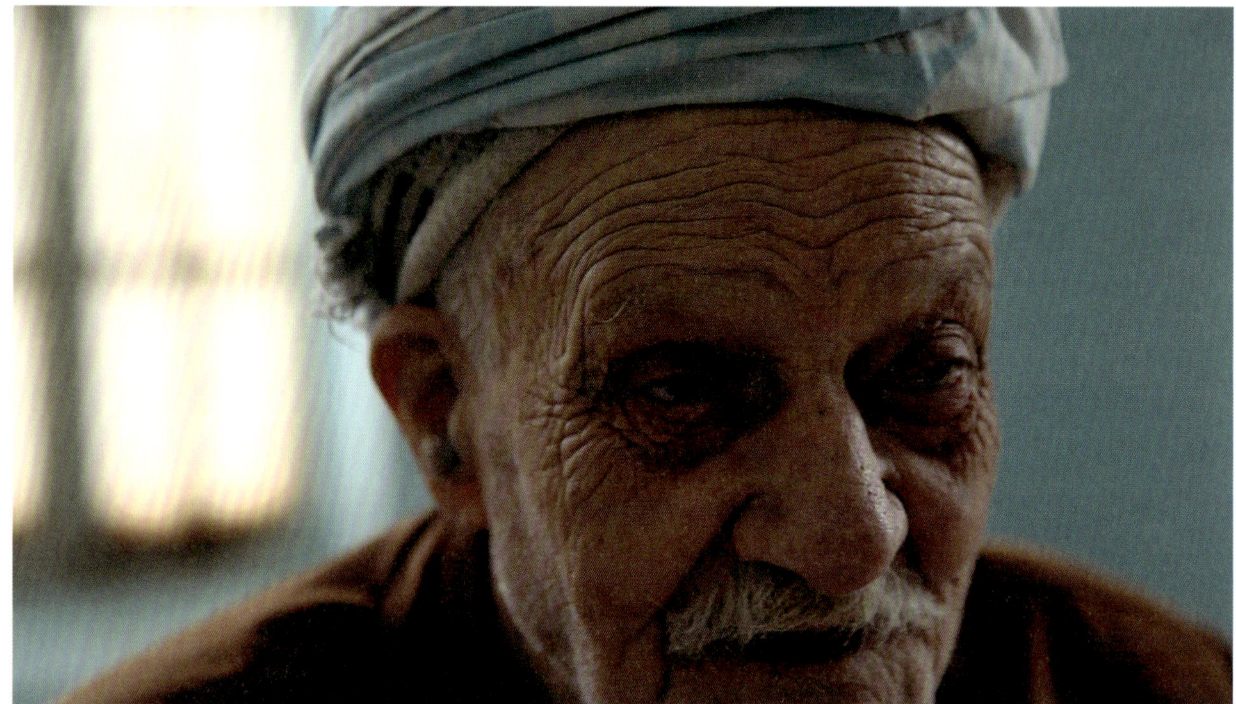

1

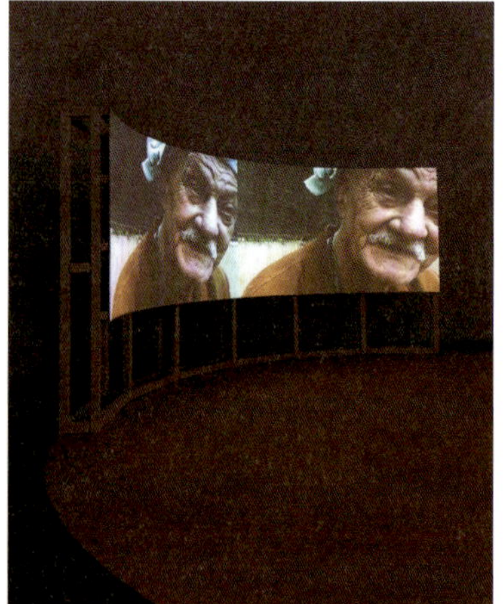

2

MOHAMED BOUROUISSA
THE WHISPERING OF GHOSTS
2018

In his photographs and films of the last two decades, Mohamed Bourouissa draws on his own personal experiences to examine the issues of migration and the exclusion of minorities, especially young men in the French suburbs, portraying their precarious living conditions and forms of cultural expression. For *The Whispering of Ghosts*, Bourouissa visited a mental institution in his hometown of Blida, Algeria, where Frantz Fanon worked as a psychiatrist in the fifties before joining the Algerian resistance movement against French colonial rule. In the film, the artist talks with Bourlem Mohamed, a former patient at the hospital, about his experiences as a freedom fighter in the anti-colonial war and also about the garden of the psychiatric institution, which he planted in 1969 and tended for many years. For Fanon, who as a doctor agitated against the segregation of French and Algerian patients at the clinic, gardening alongside others in therapy was a way to overcome the colonial dividing lines. "Bourlem Mohamed's work," writes Argentine curator Carlos Basualdo, "exists as a testimony of Fanon's clinical reforms, the embodied echo of an emancipatory gesture."

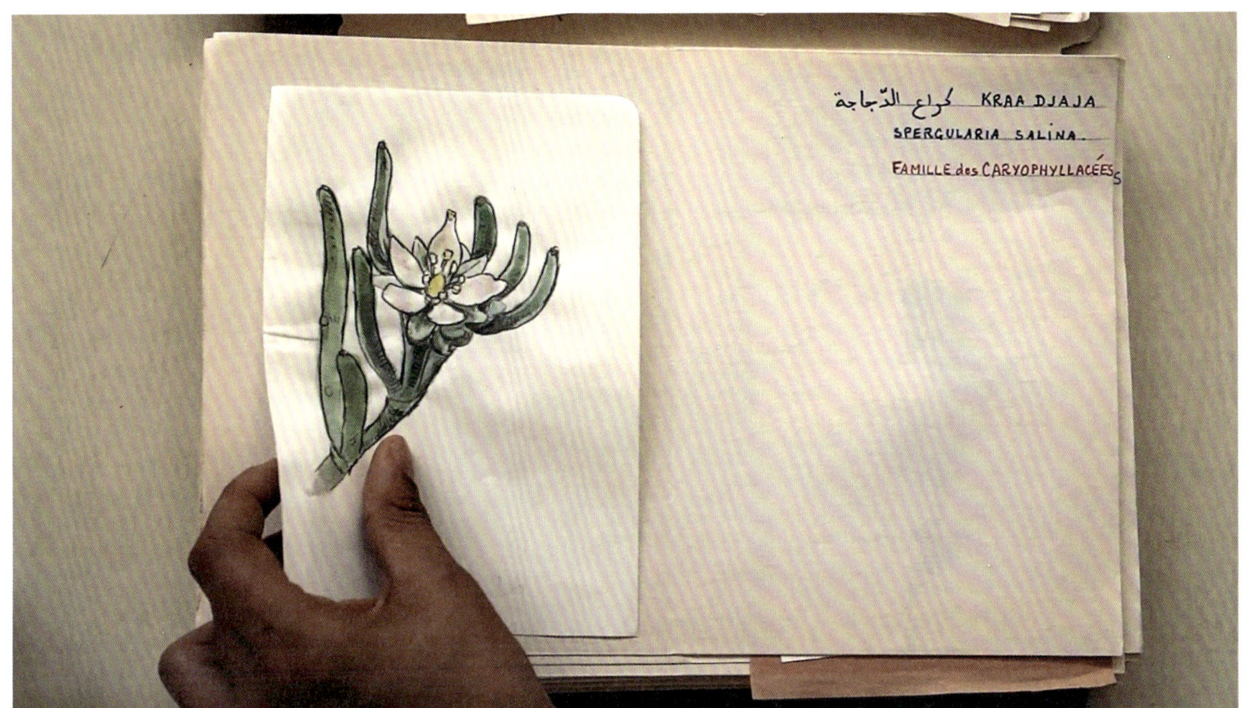

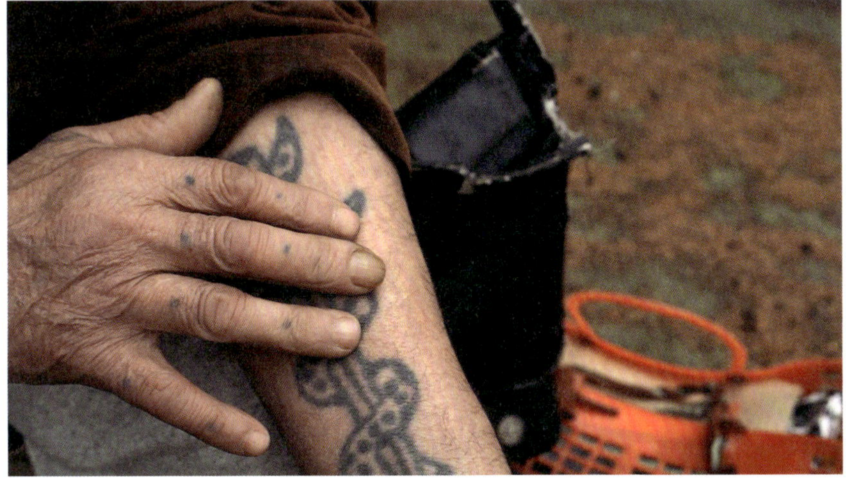

3

1   Mohamed Bourouissa
     The Whispering of Ghosts, 2018
     Video, color, sound, 13:15 min
2   Mohamed Bourouissa
     The Whispering of Ghosts, 2018
     Installation with video
     Installation view, Z33 House for
     Contemporary Art Design and Archi-
     tecture, Hasselt, 2021
3   Mohamed Bourouissa
     The Whispering of Ghosts, 2018
     Video, color, sound, 13:15 min

DIEDRICK BRACKENS

Diedrick Brackens sees himself as a weaver. In contrast
to the vast historical legacy of painting and sculpture,
Brackens conceives of weaving as a liberating practice
for a queer Black artist. His extremely tactile works
deal with issues of racism, queer identity, illness, and
death using their very own language of forms and symbols. Derived from West African weaving techniques,
the by turns abstract or figurative pieces reference
African American cultural traditions and the symbolic
worlds and rituals of the American South, as well as the
material of cotton, which is inextricably linked to slavery. Brackens is interested in relationships between
shapes, rhythms, and the tonal qualities of patterns, and
also in how a young artist today relates to ancestors
in the realms of both art and activism. He communes
with such ancestors in his textiles, from Aaron Douglas
of the Harlem Renaissance, to the rural modernism of
the quilt-makers of Gee's Bend, Alabama, to Felix
Gonzalez-Torres.

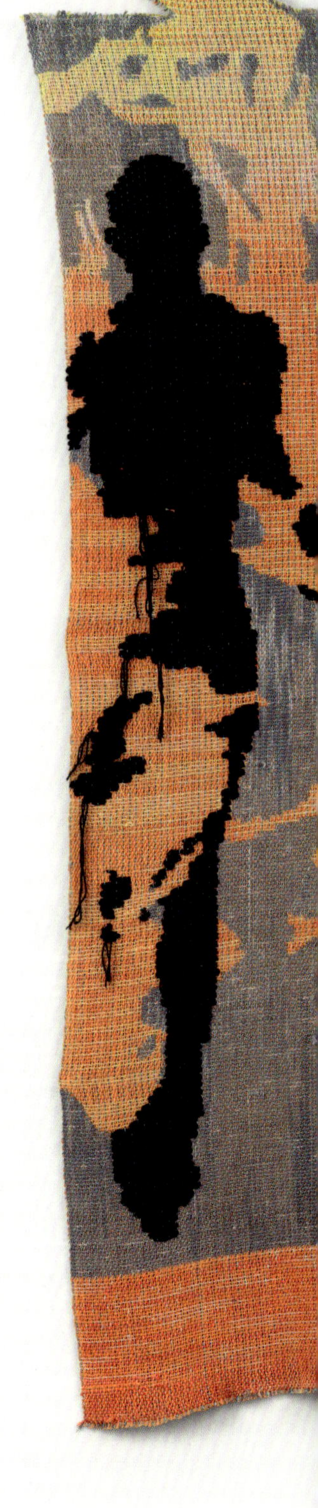

1

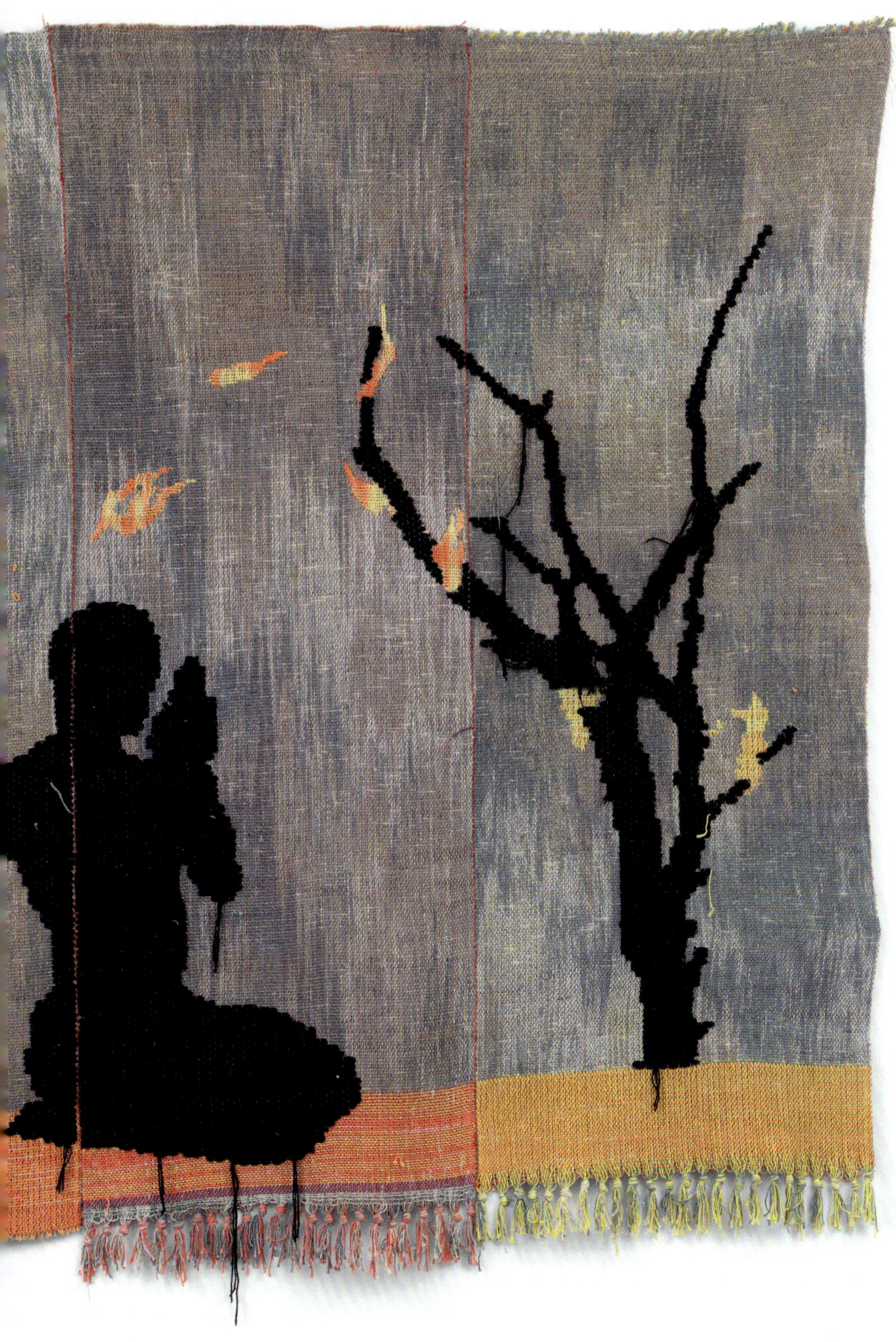

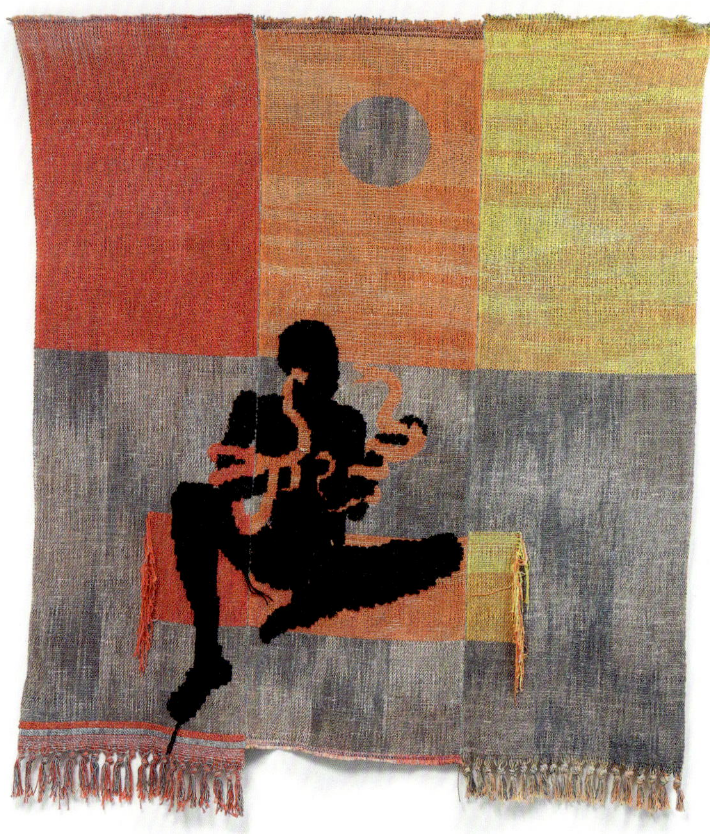

2

1   Diedrick Brackens
    infernal garden, 2022
    Woven cotton and acrylic yarn
    264.2 × 251.5 cm
2   Diedrick Brackens
    ingredients for lovers, 2022
    Woven cotton and acrylic yarn
    216 × 193 cm
3   Diedrick Brackens
    taste honey for nerves, 2021
    Woven cotton and acrylic yarn, charms
    228.6 × 205.7 cm

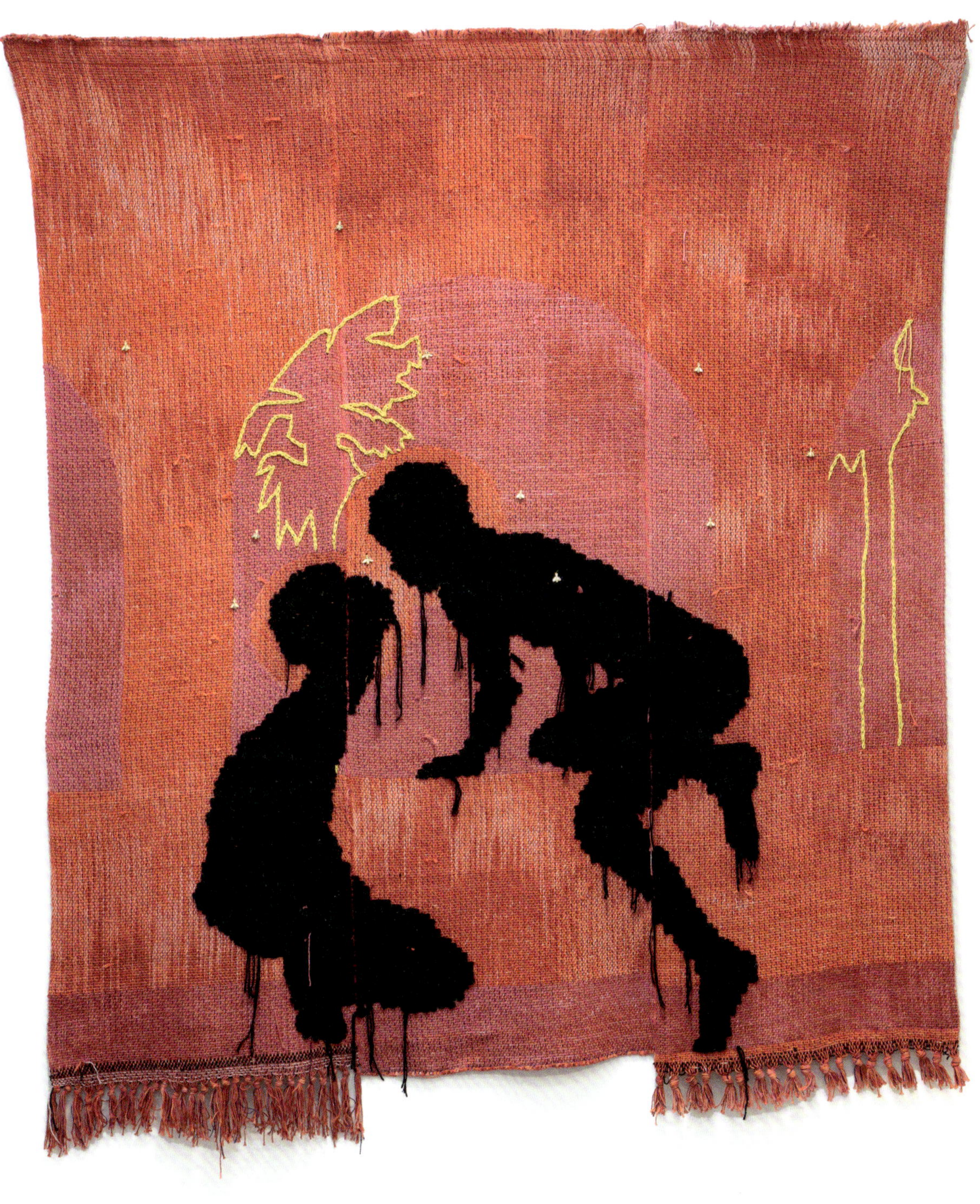

3

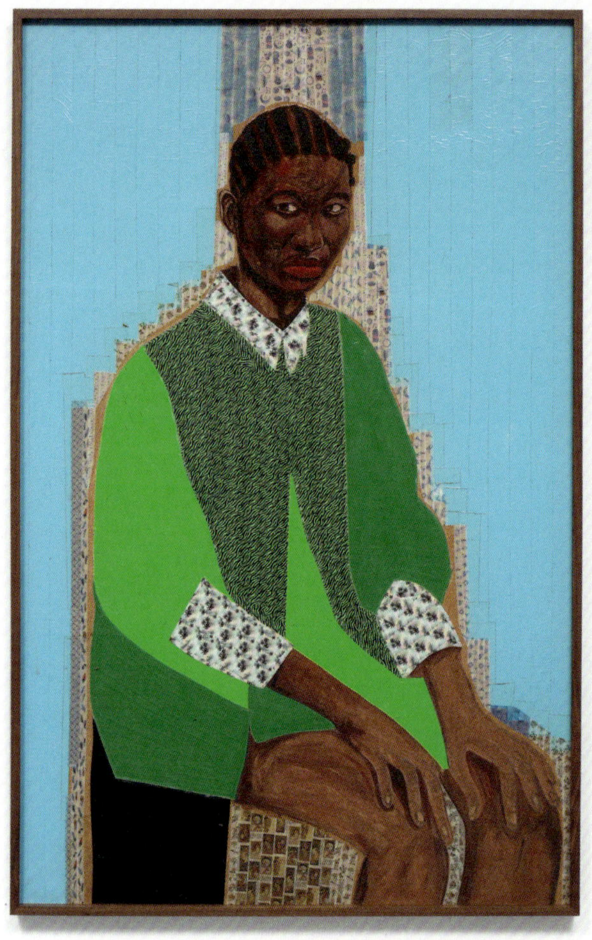

1

SERGE ATTUKWEI CLOTTEY

Serge Attukwei Clottey is known for his object paintings made from pieces of yellow plastic canisters, which reflect the legacy of colonialism in the horizon of ecological problems and the everyday life of people in Ghana. In addition to these "afrogallonist" works, Clottey's more recent paintings reference the first generation of photographers of African decolonization, particularly the studio photography of Seydou Keïta in Mali. Using a particular duct tape, however, the artist also recalls a case of racist state violence in Austria, where Clottey had an artist residency ten years ago. In 1999 the Nigerian asylum seeker Marcus Omofuma was killed by police during a detention flight after his mouth was taped to silence his protest. Clottey uses this material of oppression to paint images of liberation and African self-determination, as expressed in Keïta's photographs of the nineteen-fifties.

1   Serge Attukwei Clottey
     The Orphan, 2020–21
     **Oil paint and duct tape on cork board
     193 × 124.5 cm**
2   Serge Attukwei Clottey
     Yellow Sweater, 2020–21
     **Oil paint and duct tape on cork board
     160 × 124.5 cm**

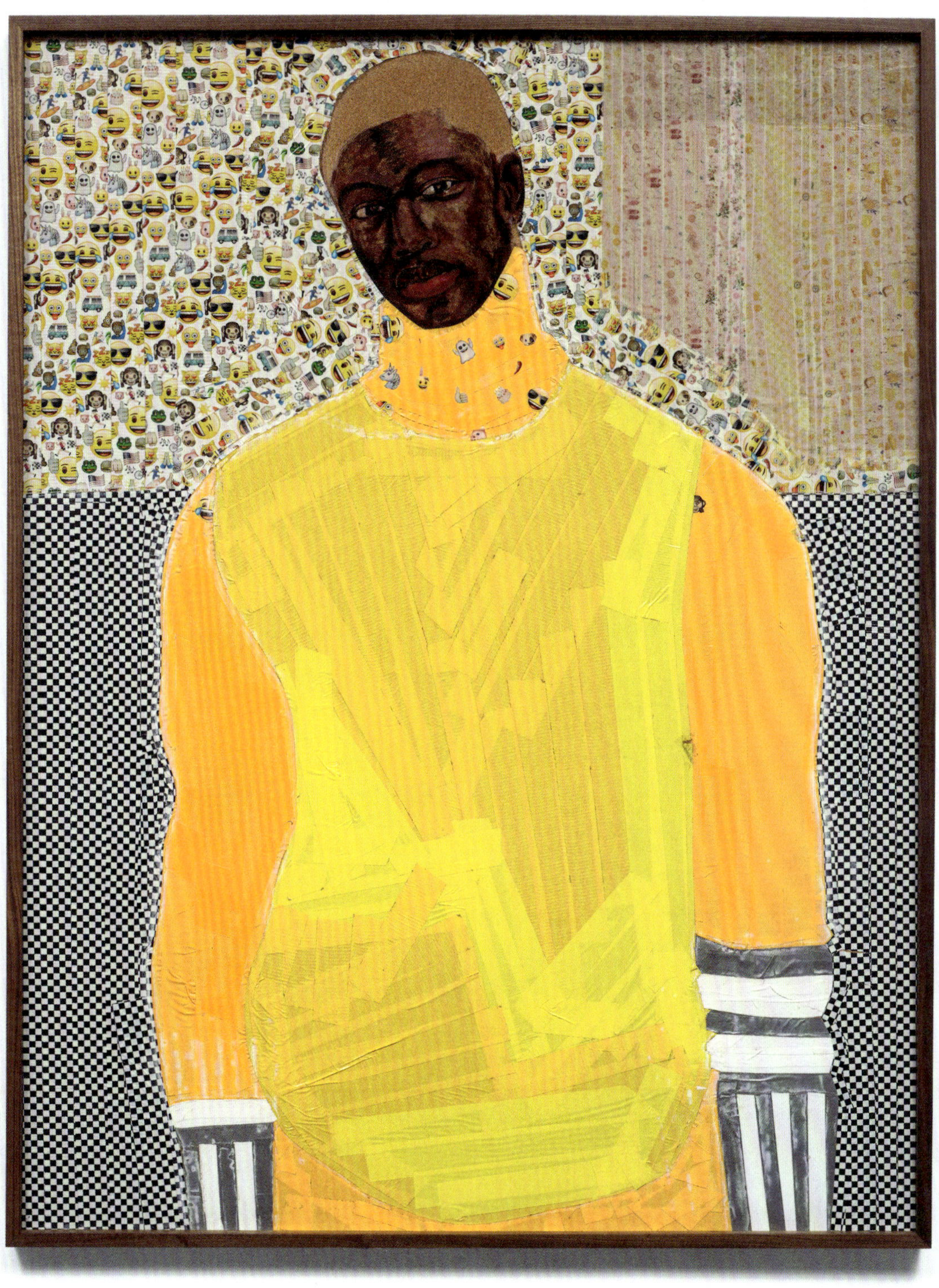

2

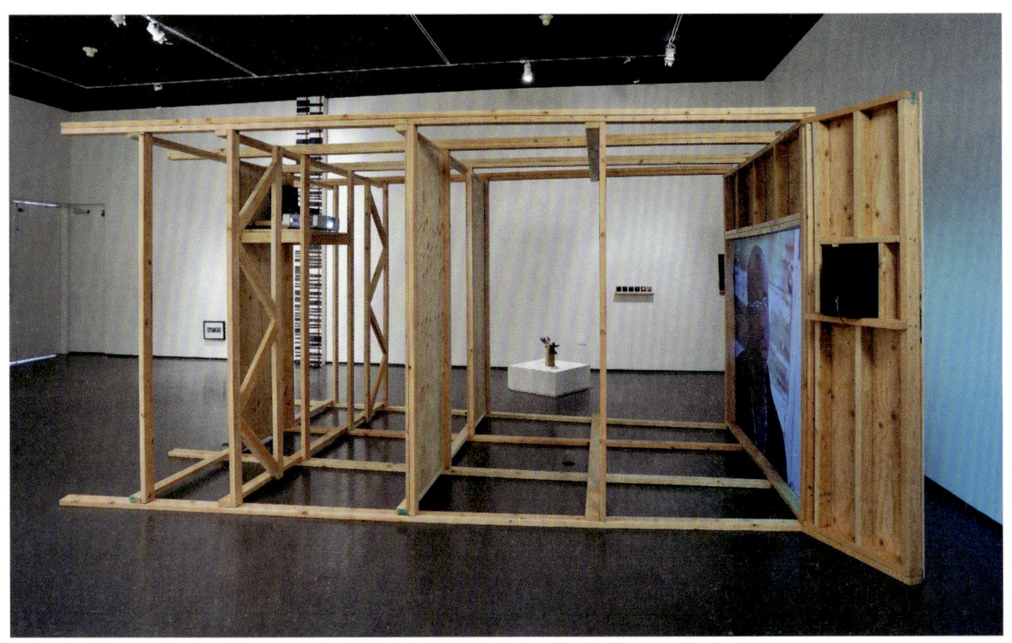

WILLIAM CORDOVA
THIS ONE'S 4U (PA' NOSOTROS)
2008–15

this one's 4U (pa' nosotros), a wooden scaffolding turned sideways to symbolize altered perception and function, incorporates a video projector and a large white screen that relate to concepts of Third Cinema, the genre coined by Argentine filmmakers Fernando Solanas and Octavio Getino in 1969. Third Cinema is the urgency to reject Hollywood film values in order to create, discuss, and invent examples that reflect a true representation of the quotidian life. The work provokes parallel narratives by simultaneously projecting two films: visually projecting, *Tupac Shakur: Thug Angel, the Life of an Outlaw* (2002) by Peter Spirer and, audio projecting, *Tupac Amaru* (1984) by Federico Garcia Hurtado. Garcia's *Tupac Amaru* is a cinematic narrative of the Andean leader's indigenous and African slave-led uprising in Peru against Spanish rule in 1780. *Tupac* by Peter Spirer documents the life and times of the often-misunderstood activist and Rap artist Tupac Amaru Shakur, who was named after the Andean Túpac Amaru. Both the eighteenth- and twentieth-century Tupacs are associated with civil disobedience and helped raise social political consciousness in the Americas, the Caribbean, and beyond. How we interpret bodies, ethnicity, languages, landscapes, race, the past, and presence is an increasing part of our changing reality. (william cordova)

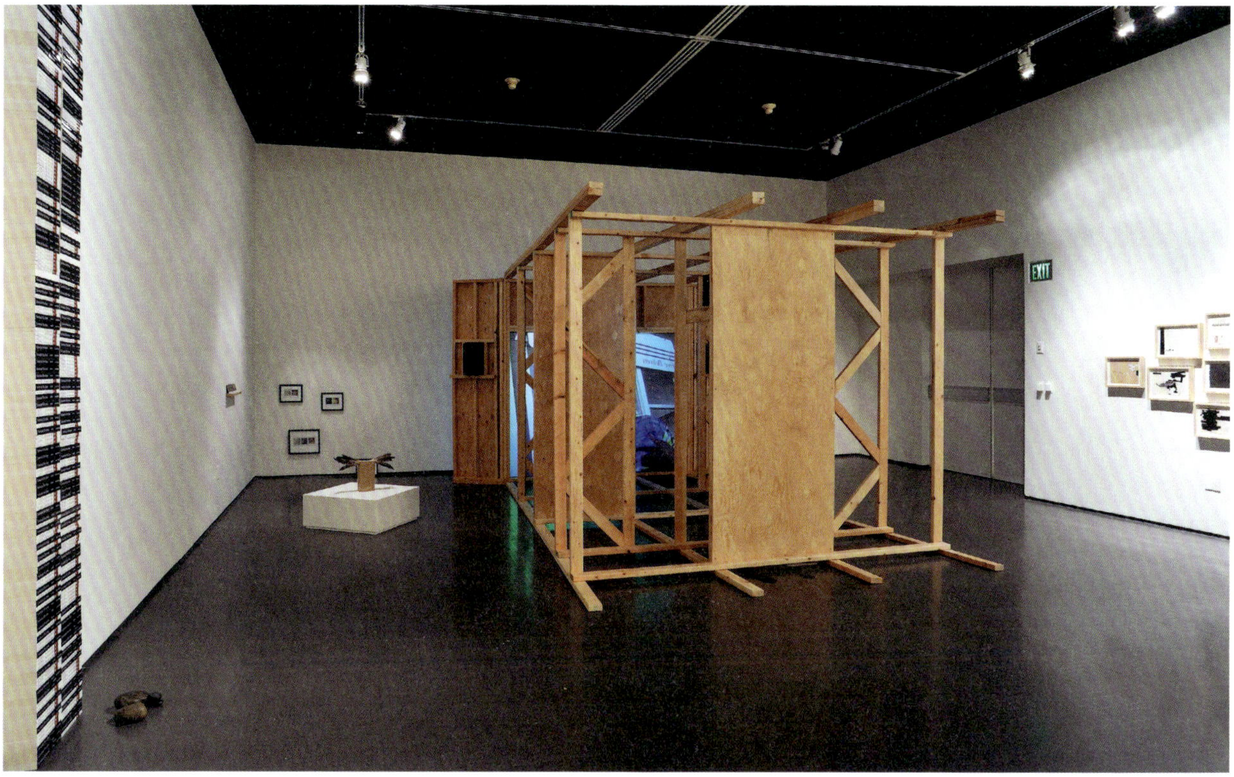

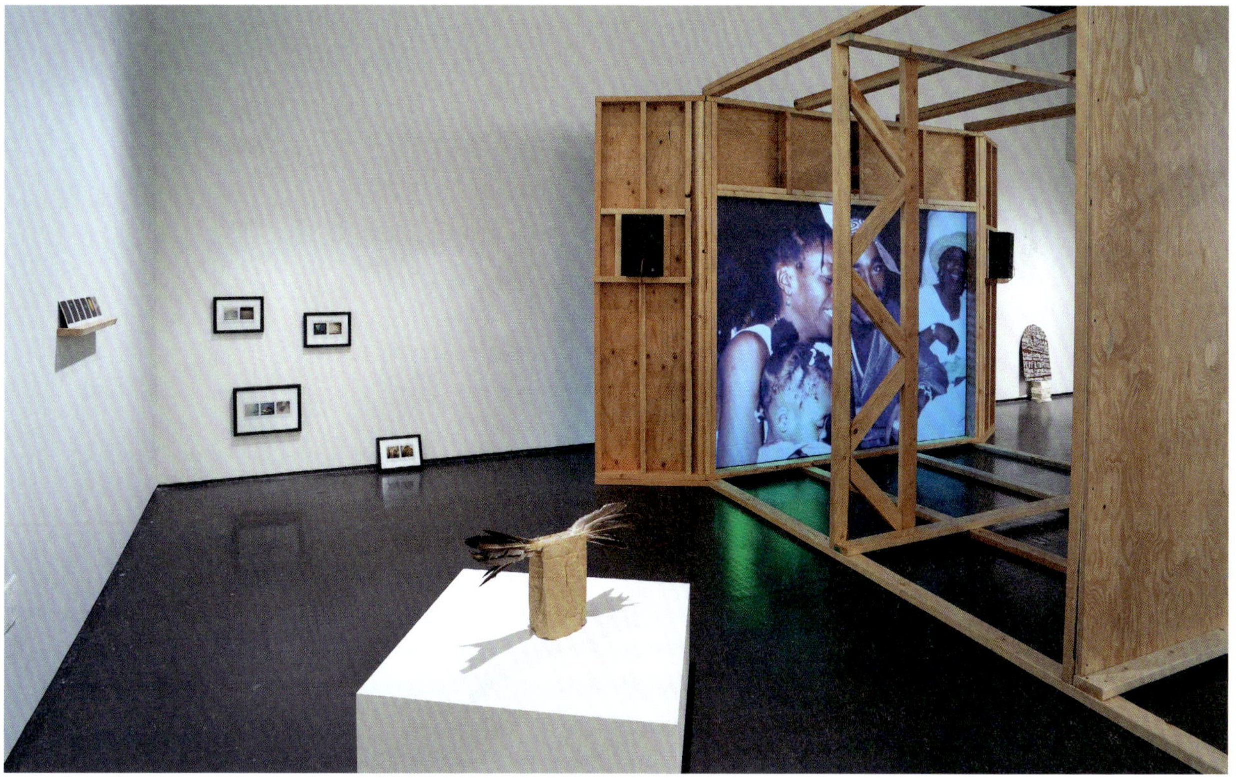

william cordova
this one's 4U (pa' nosotros), 2008–15
Installation views, Yerba Buena Center for
the Arts, San Francisco, 2012

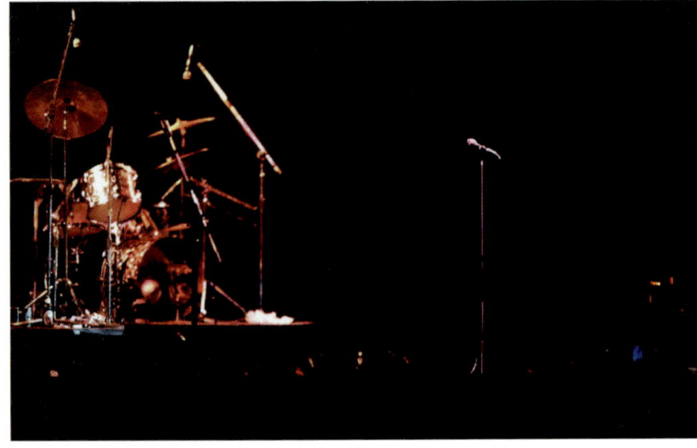

1

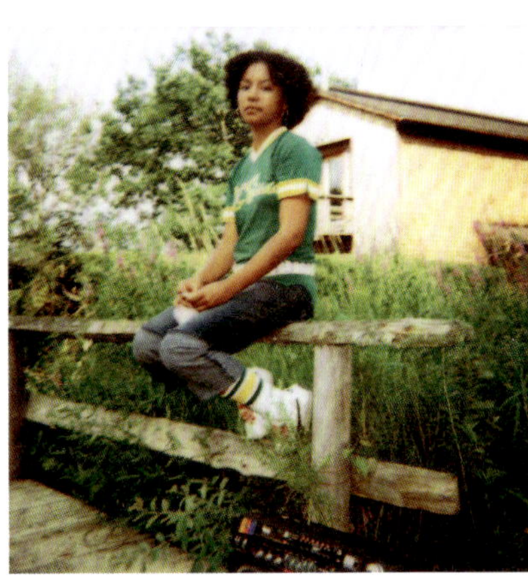

2

WILLIAM CORDOVA
FILMS

The stage from the last Sex Pistols concert in 1978 and
sentences from a speech given by Malcolm X in 1964;
the steps of the Manhattan courthouse and Jimi Hendrix's
Band of Gypsys touting the song "Voodoo Child" in
1969 as the "Black Panthers' national anthem": In his
short films from the last twenty years, some of them only
a few seconds long, william cordova combines audio
and video fragments from music events and instances of
political activism to create dialectical scenes of civil
disobedience and subcultural rebellion. He draws here
on techniques and aesthetic concepts from revolutionary schools of film, in particular Soviet cinema of the
nineteen-twenties and Latin American Third Cinema
from the sixties and seventies. In his miniatures, originally
shot on Super 8—often making use of bootlegs—
cordova experiments with diverse conceptions of time
and forms of storytelling as he interrogates the complex
cross-fertilization between movements for political
and artistic liberation.

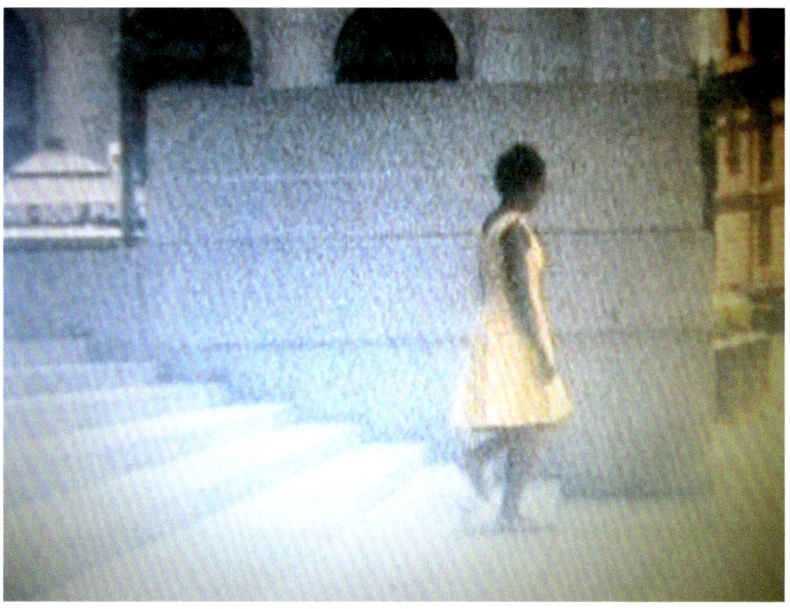

3

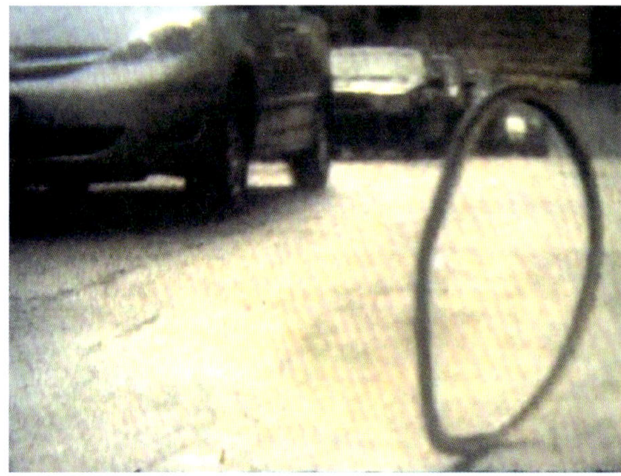

4

1   william cordova
    2 cents, 2005
    Digital video, transferiert from ¾-inch
    video, color, sound, 4 min
2   william cordova
    Badussy (or machu picchu after dark),
    2003
    Digital video, transferred from Super
    8 mm film, sound, 2:30 min
3   william cordova
    *Sacsayhuaman (Stand Up Next 2 A
    Mountain)*, 2006–08
    Digital video, transferred from Super
    8 mm film, sound, 1:10 min
4   william cordova
    *18˚6' 11.87" N, 94˚2' 24.69" W (de cero
    a la infinidad)*, 2009
    Digital video, transferred from Super
    8 mm film, sound, color, 0:30 min

ATUL DODIYA

Atul Dodiya's pictures quote elements from the paintings of the poet Rabindranath Tagore, which are super-
imposed over motifs from the political life of Mahatma
Gandhi. Early twenty-first-century Indian society
has been marked by the rise of the Hindu nationalist
BJP party and its policy of identifying Indian culture with
the Hindu religion. Against a backdrop of intolerance,
oppression, and violence, especially against Muslims,
Dodiya's art persistently harks back to the concepts of a
secular society and nonviolence from the era of India's
independence movement. The works presented in
Avant-Garde and Liberation come from a series in which
the artist invokes the media presence of Mahatma
Gandhi: "There are images of Gandhi everywhere. Every
second street is named after him, his face is on stamps,
on currency, in government offices, but his spirit is no-
where. As I reflected on him I began to realize that Gandhi
had much in common with a new art technique called
conceptual art. The series changed my life, and my
concerns shifted to the social arena. Today, I feel Gandhi
is more relevant than ever before." Of apparent equal
topicality for the artist is the cosmopolitan spirit of
Tagore, who understood India's identity as consisting
in the unification of all cultural differences. Atop scenes
from Gandhi's campaigns, Dodiya paints motifs lifted
from Tagore's abstract calligraphic pictures from the
nineteen-twenties and -thirties, which form a poetic
counterpart to Gandhi's performative politics of liberation.

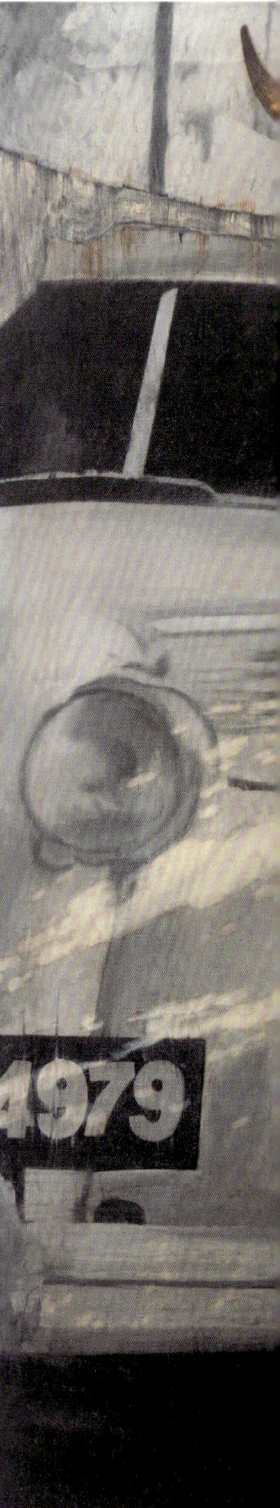

1

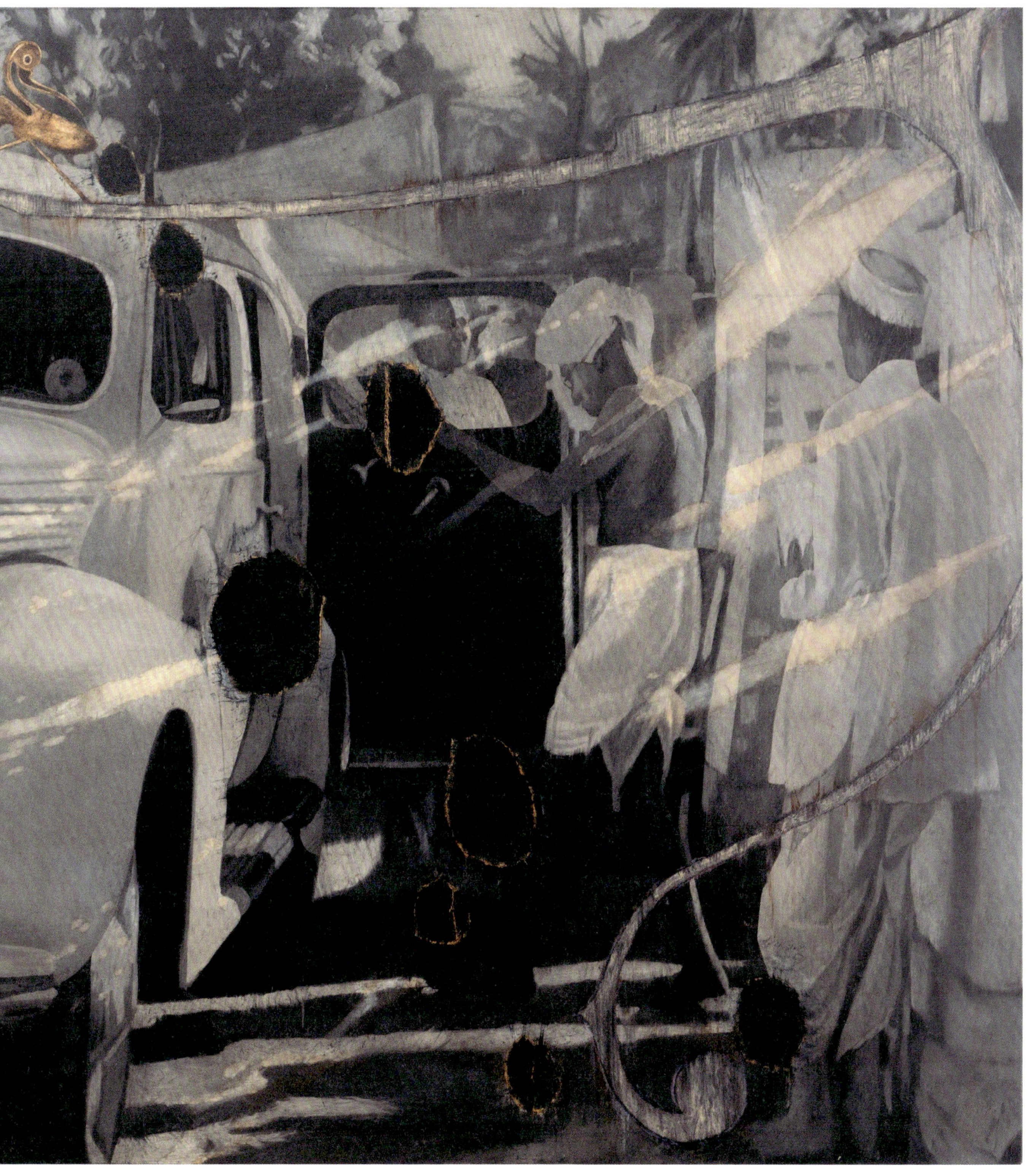

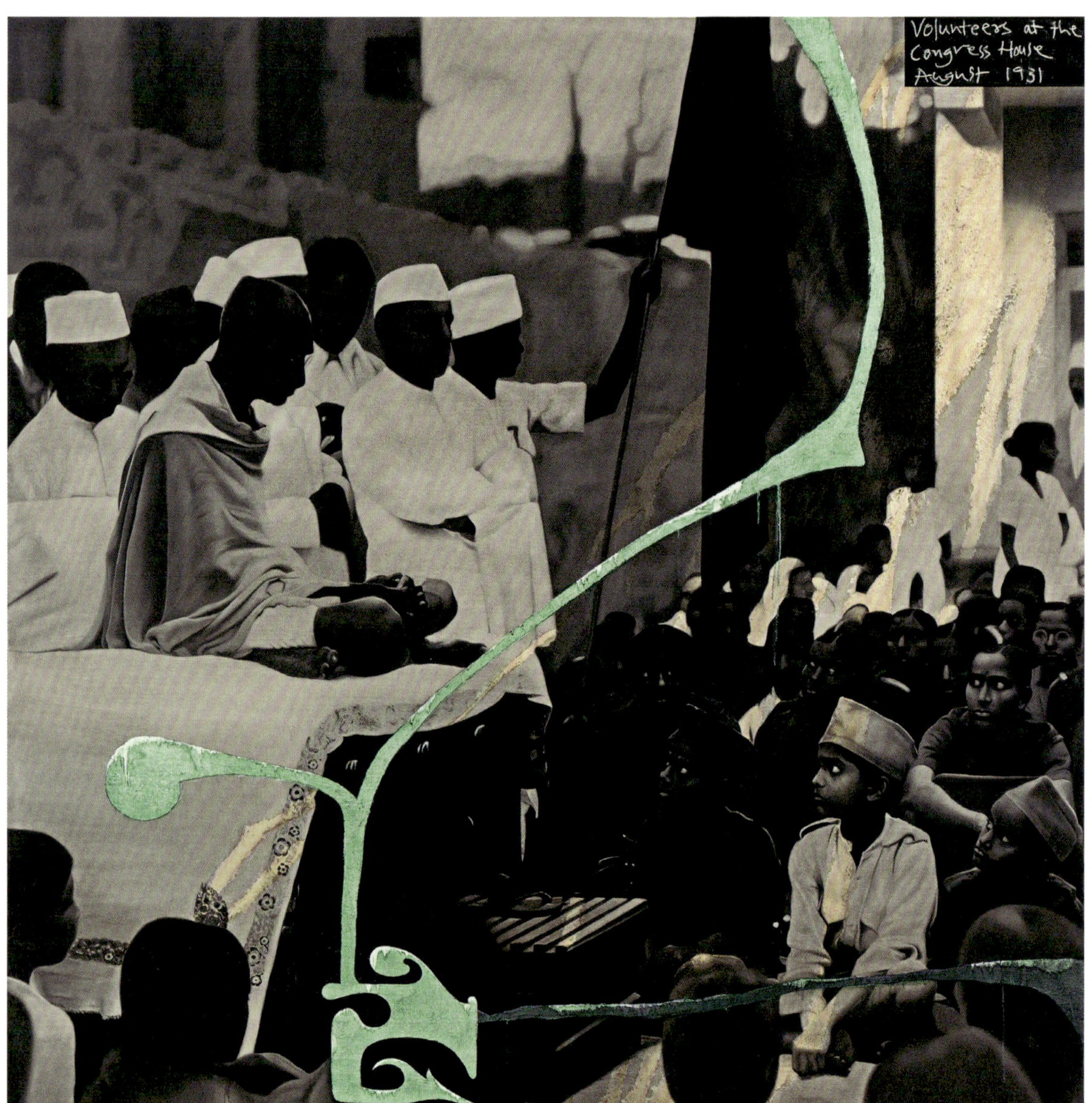

2

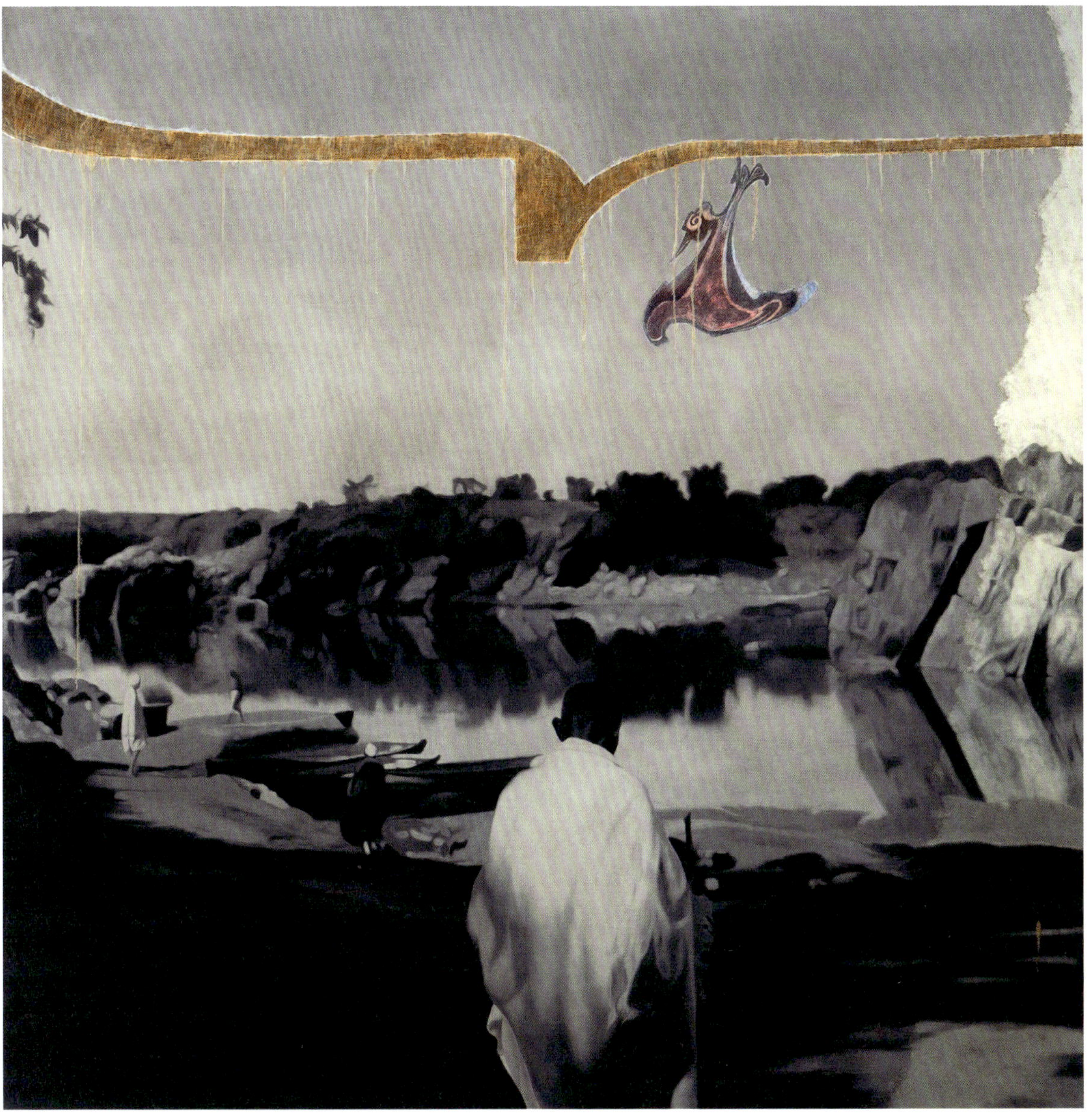

3

1   Atul Dodiya
     *Mahatma Gandhi entering G D
     Birla's Packard*, 2016–18
     Oil on canvas
     183×212.6 cm
2   Atul Dodiya
     *Volunteers at the Congress
     House—August 1931*, 2014
     Oil, acrylic with marble dust and
     oil-stick on canvas
     183×183 cm
3   Atul Dodiya
     *Visit to the marble rocks at
     Jabalpur, 1941*, 2016
     Oil on canvas
     183×183 cm

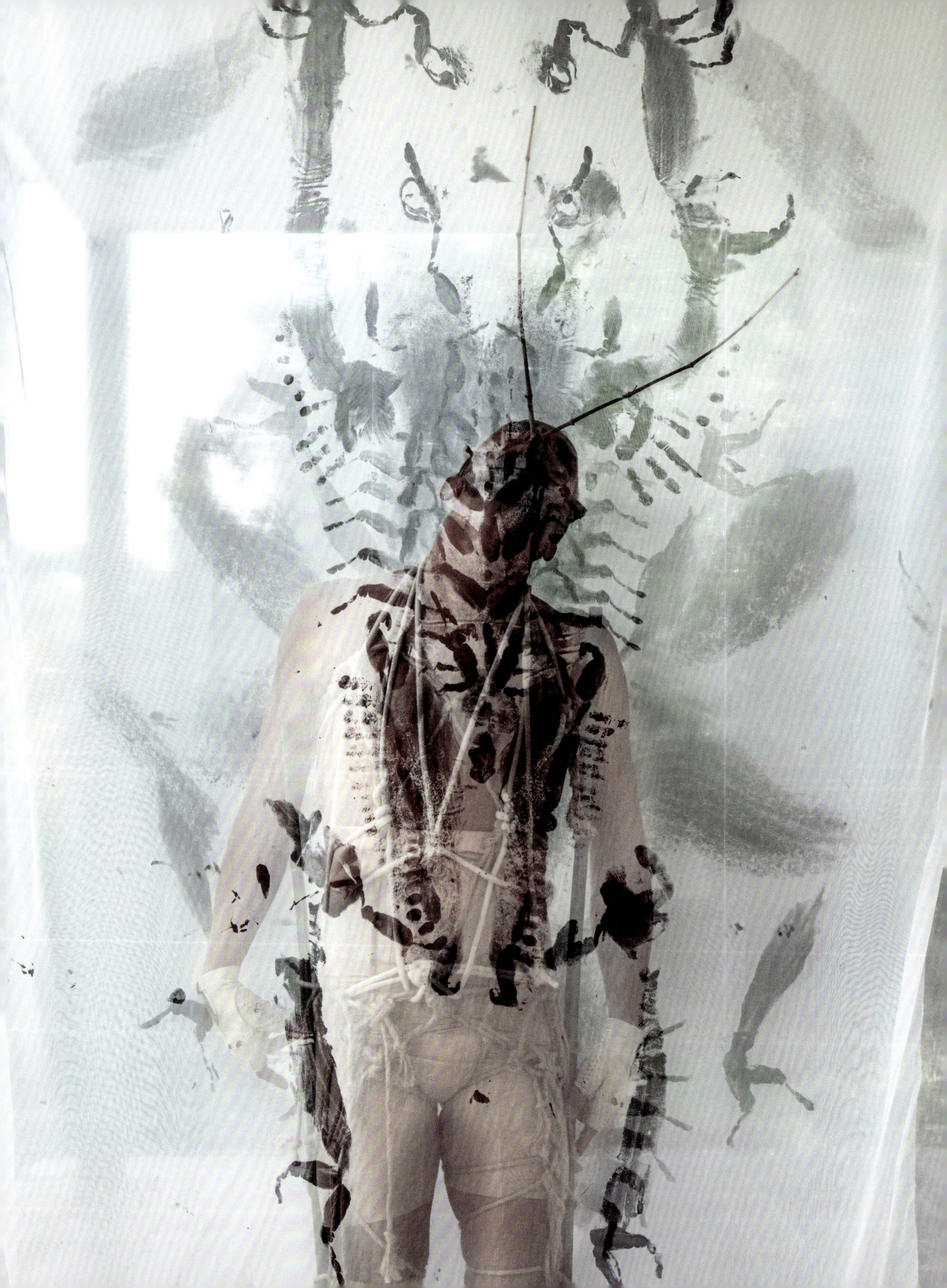

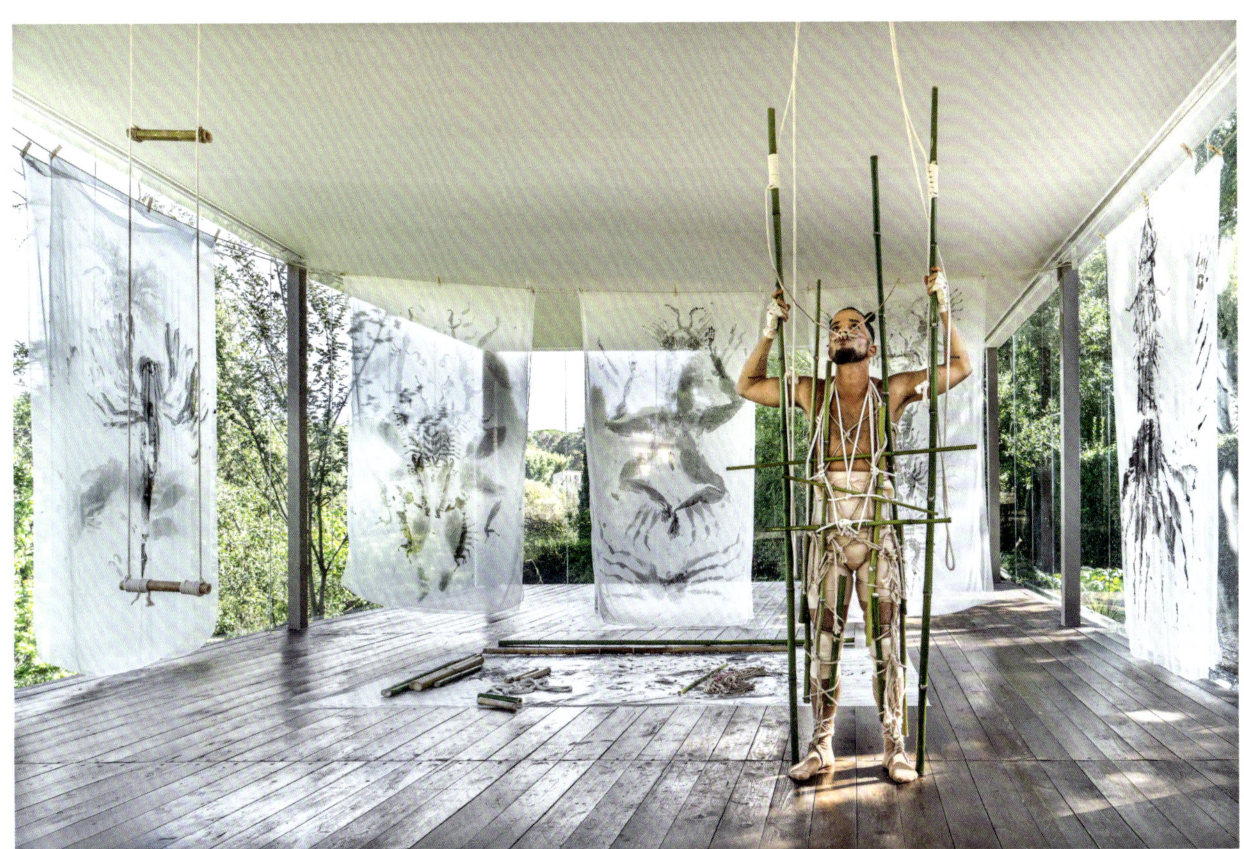

Robert Gabris
Insectopia, 2020
Performance and installation view with "autoprints," Villa Romana, Florence, 2020

ROBERT GABRIS

In *Insectopia*, Robert Gabris responds to the impositions and attributions that an artist whose work evokes the experience of a queer Rom*nja person must face in many art institutions in a society marked by racist and sexist notions. The body prints allude to scientific and police practices of collecting and classifying plants and animals—and ultimately also humans, who have been made into exhibits and study objects as a way to exert control and power over those who deviate from the bourgeois and heterosexual norm. The artist expresses his "skepticism about anthropology, ethnography, and the institutional power of museums" in works on paper, large fabric panels, and a video of a performance in Florence. Using the technique of the body print, Gabris recalls the *Body Prints* made by the African American artist David Hammons as part of the Black Arts Movement of the nineteen-sixties. Gabris's own transformation into an insect in the drawings and performances of *Insectopia* can be understood as an expression of resistance to the social and institutional power of classification and as an assertion of self-determination: "I don't emigrate, I don't assimilate, I don't integrate. If you want to identify my fingerprints, you have to go through my *Insectopia*."

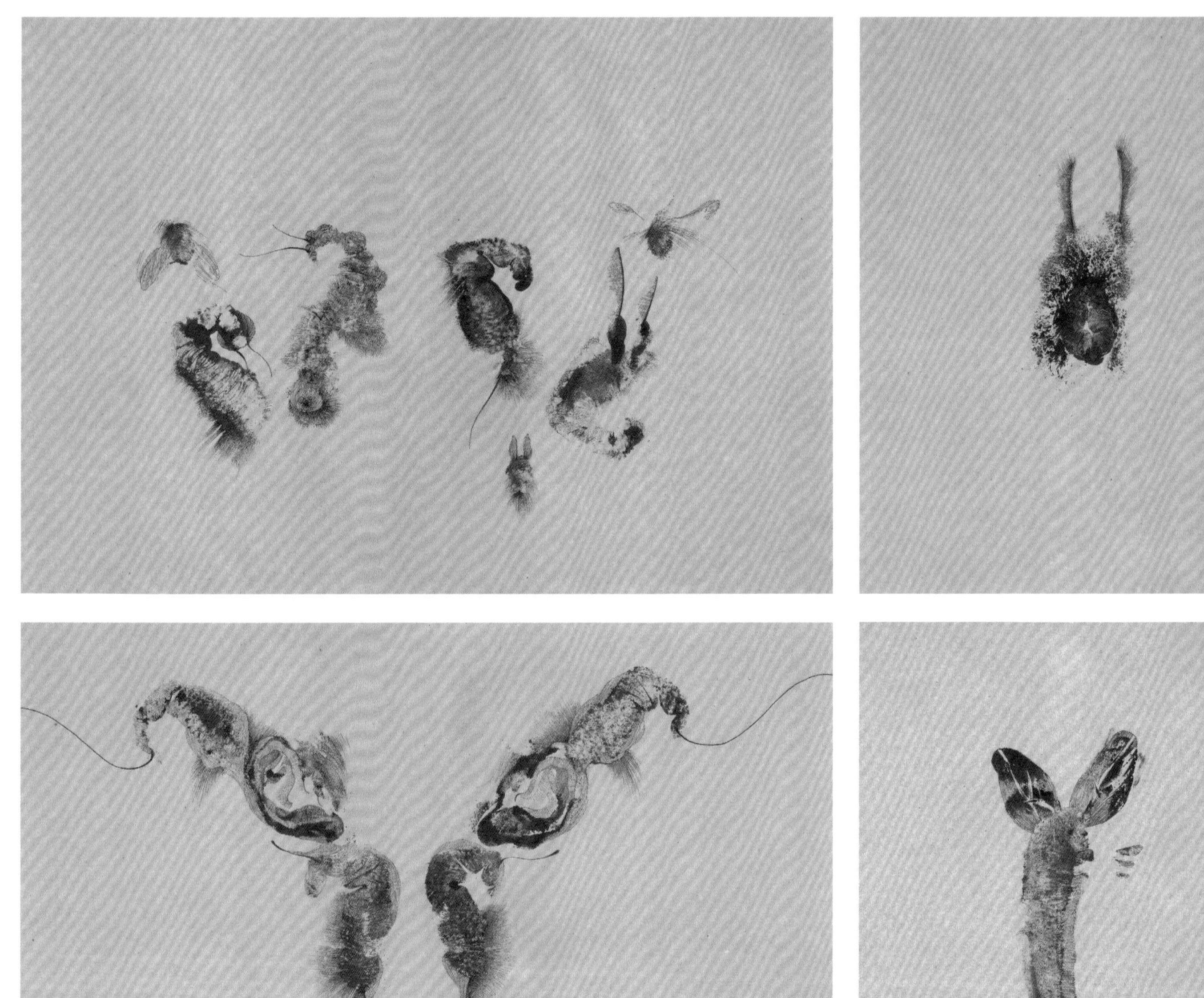

Robert Gabris
Insectology in My Body, 2020
"Autoprints," black ink and fineliner 0.25 mm
29 × 41 cm each

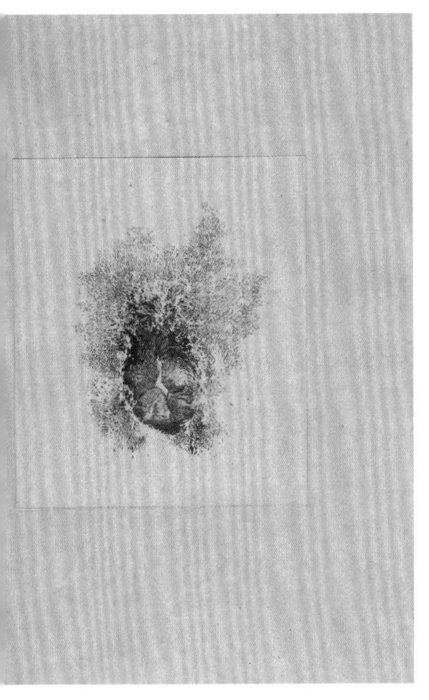

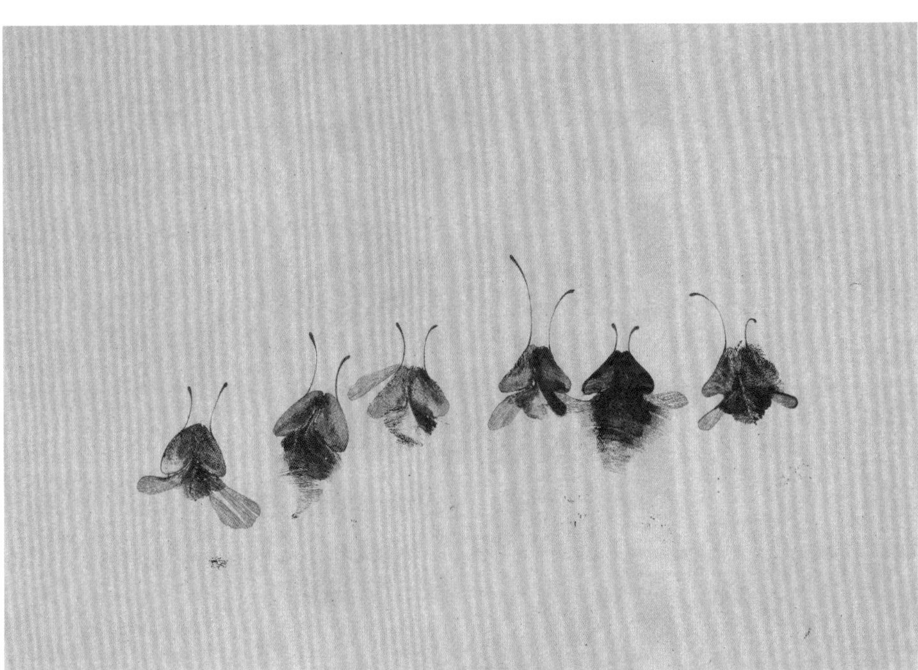

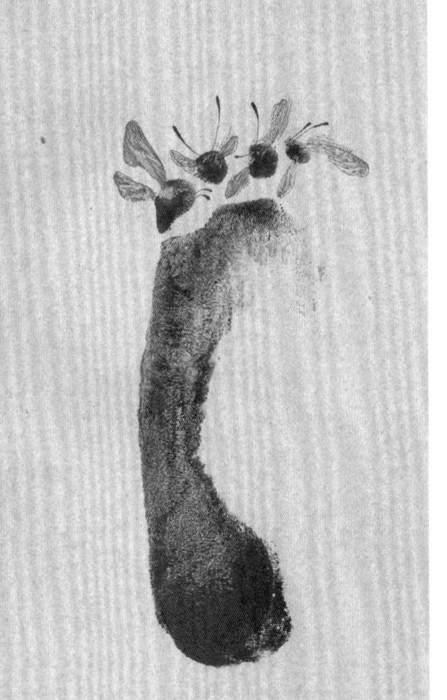

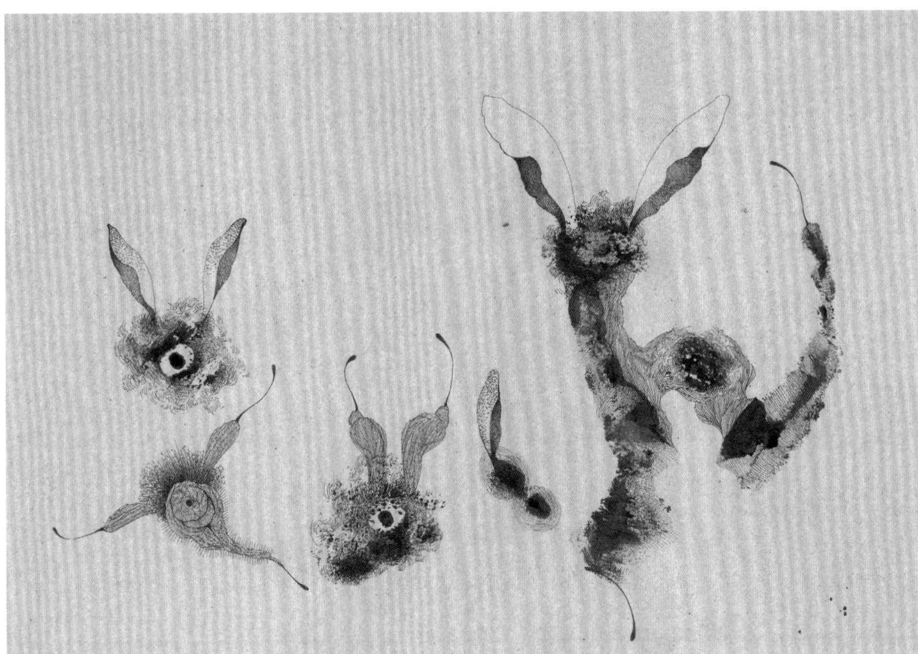

JOJO GRONOSTAY
AVANT-GARDE CITY
2023

The political awakening of African countries during the independence era brought with it new forms of expression in literature, film, art, and photography, as well as a specific building culture. As in the other arts of decolonization, the architecture of the nineteen-sixties and -seventies features forms and concepts that stood for liberation and pointed to the future of African societies after the end of colonialism. In *Avant-Garde City* (2023), Jojo Gronostay looks at examples of avant-garde architecture in cities such as Accra, Abidjan, and Dakar. Modernist and brutalist buildings dating from the independence era appear—as if casually taken from the movement and backed with a sound piece by Sami Mandee—among examples of profane functional construction and built manifestations of globalized capitalism. Gronostay, who for many years has been examining neocolonial aspects of the circulation of people and goods between Europe and Africa, shows us the architectural avant-garde of decolonization in an urban context. The way the work is displayed in the exhibition space furthermore calls to mind the freestanding video walls that ply us in popular shopping streets with moving advertising images.

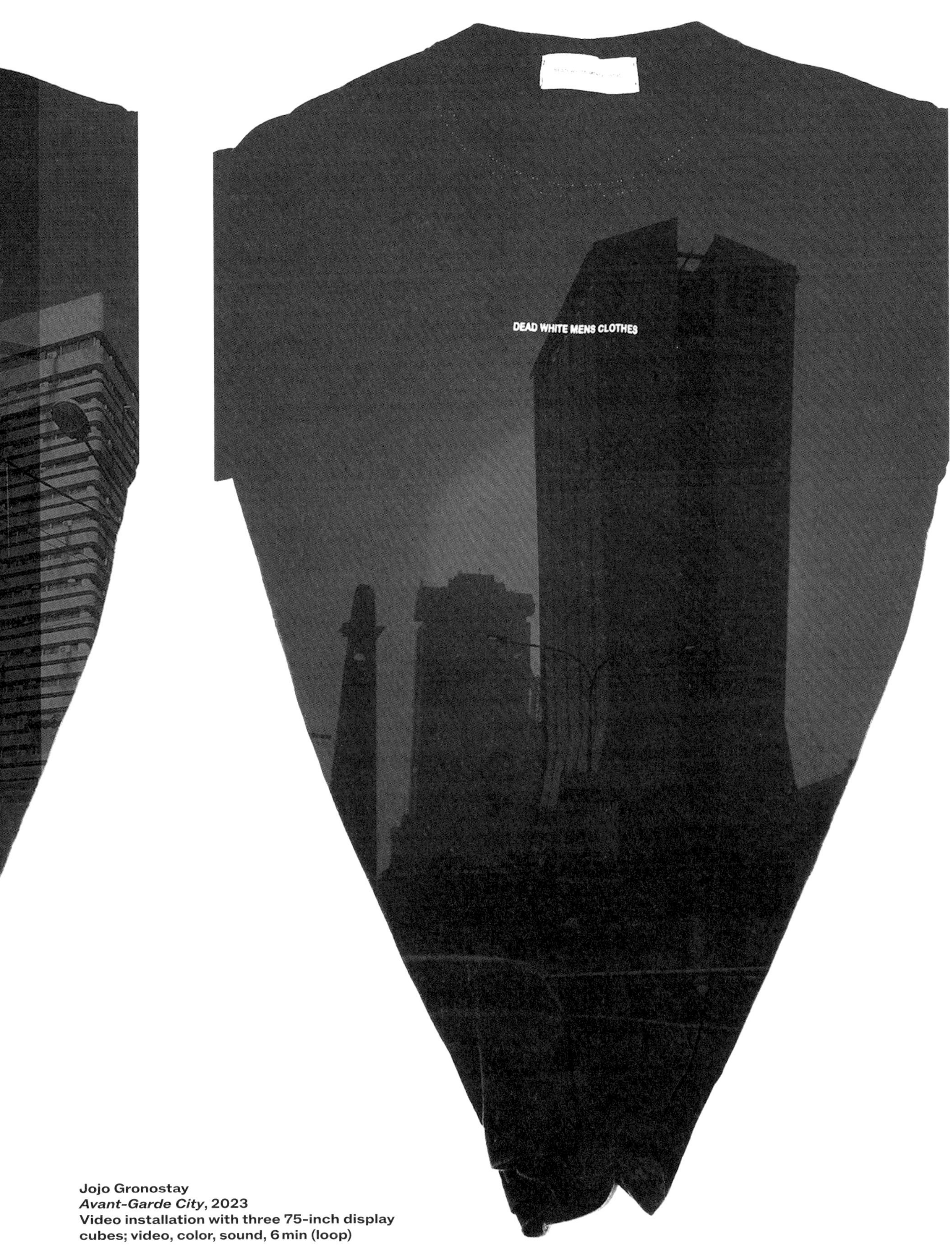

Jojo Gronostay
Avant-Garde City, 2023
Video installation with three 75-inch display
cubes; video, color, sound, 6 min (loop)

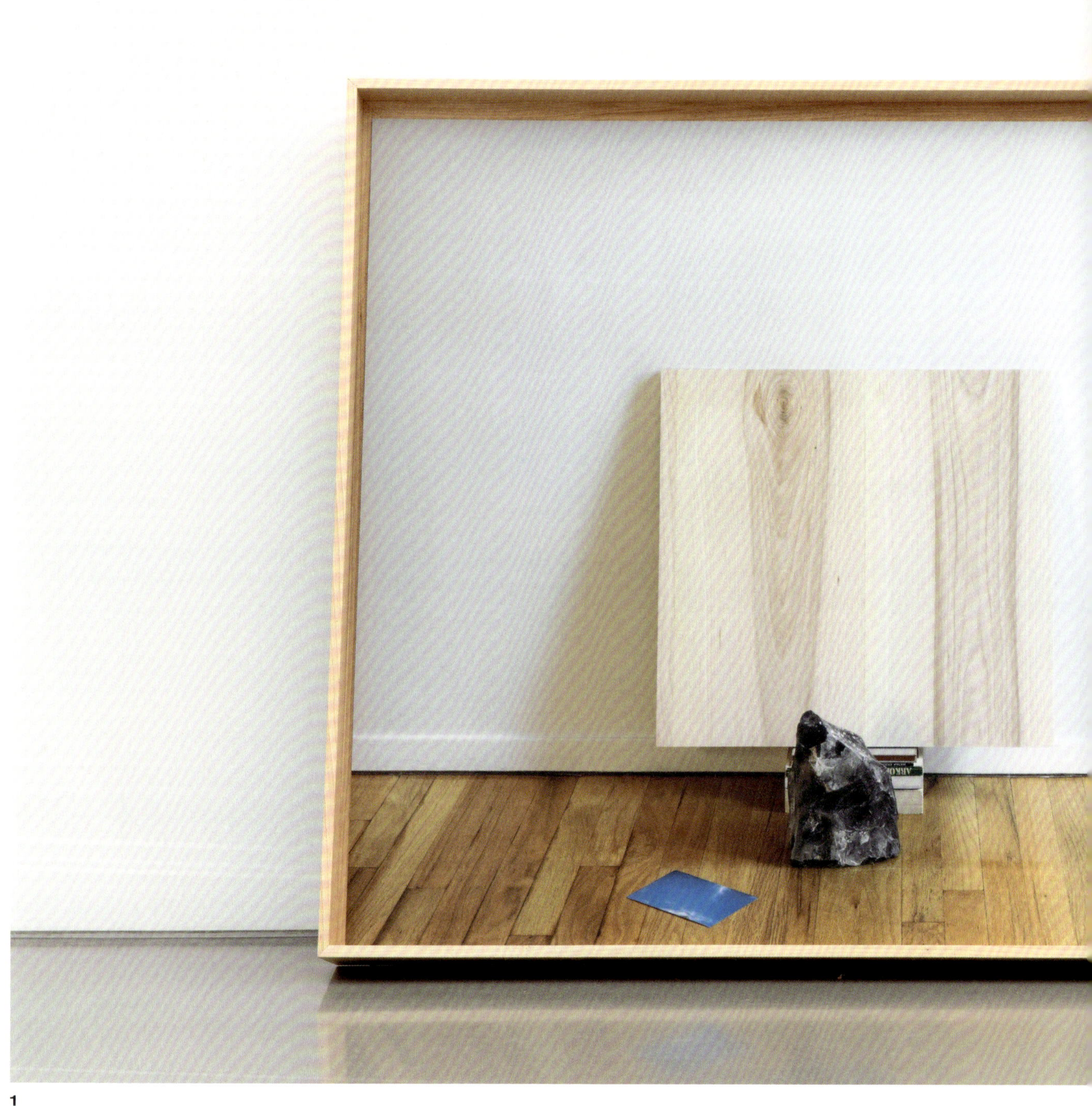

1

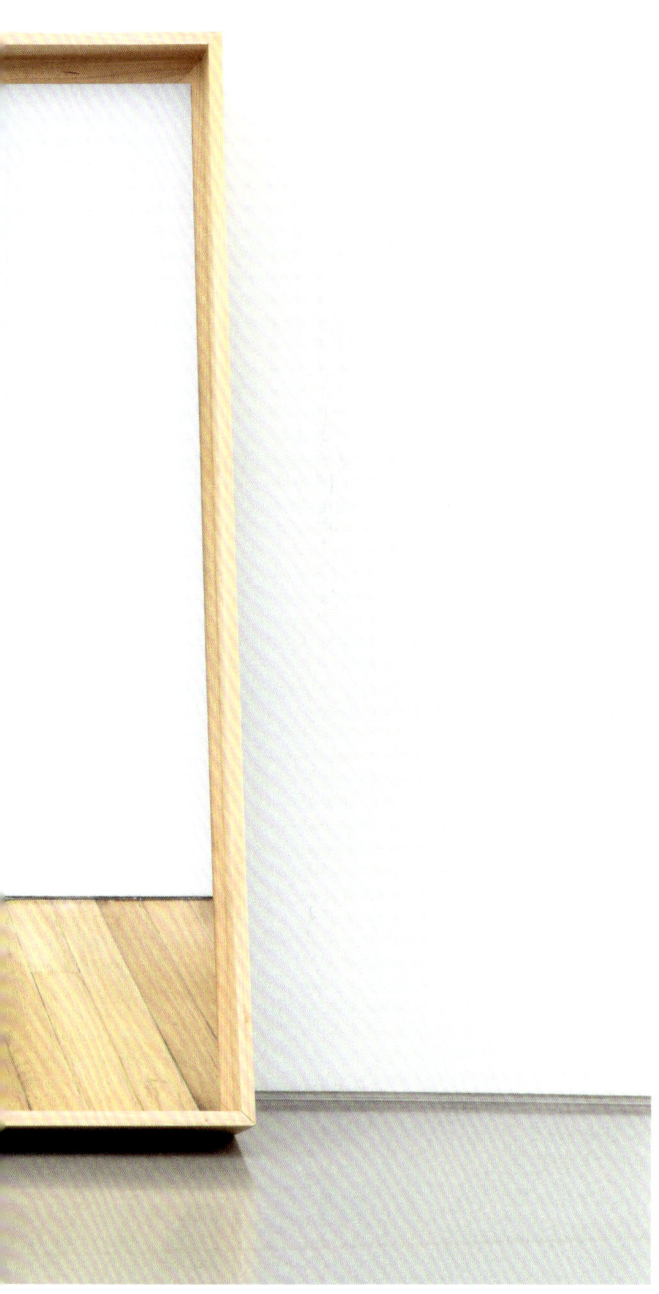

LESLIE HEWITT

Leslie Hewitt's photographic and sculptural works raise complex questions regarding temporality, memory, and history. Displayed in heavy wooden frames leaning against the wall, the photographs show still-life arrangements, likewise placed against a wall, made up of photos, books, plywood panels, and stones or shells. Similar to seventeenth-century Dutch still lifes, in which objects are what they are but at the same time function as symbols—of life's transience, among other things—while also making reference to the global Dutch trading empire, Hewitt's works trigger a gradual process of decoding, even though it often seems that the objects are trying to turn away from the viewer's gaze. This resistance to a consumerist mode of perception is underscored by Hewitt's citations of publications by the pan-African publishing house Présence Africaine, founded in Paris in 1947, and of stories written by the Afro-Surrealist author Henry Dumas, a member of the Black Arts Movement of the nineteen-sixties. In the postcolonial still life, the internationalism of Black art and liberation politics takes the place of colonial trade in its seventeenth-century counterpart.

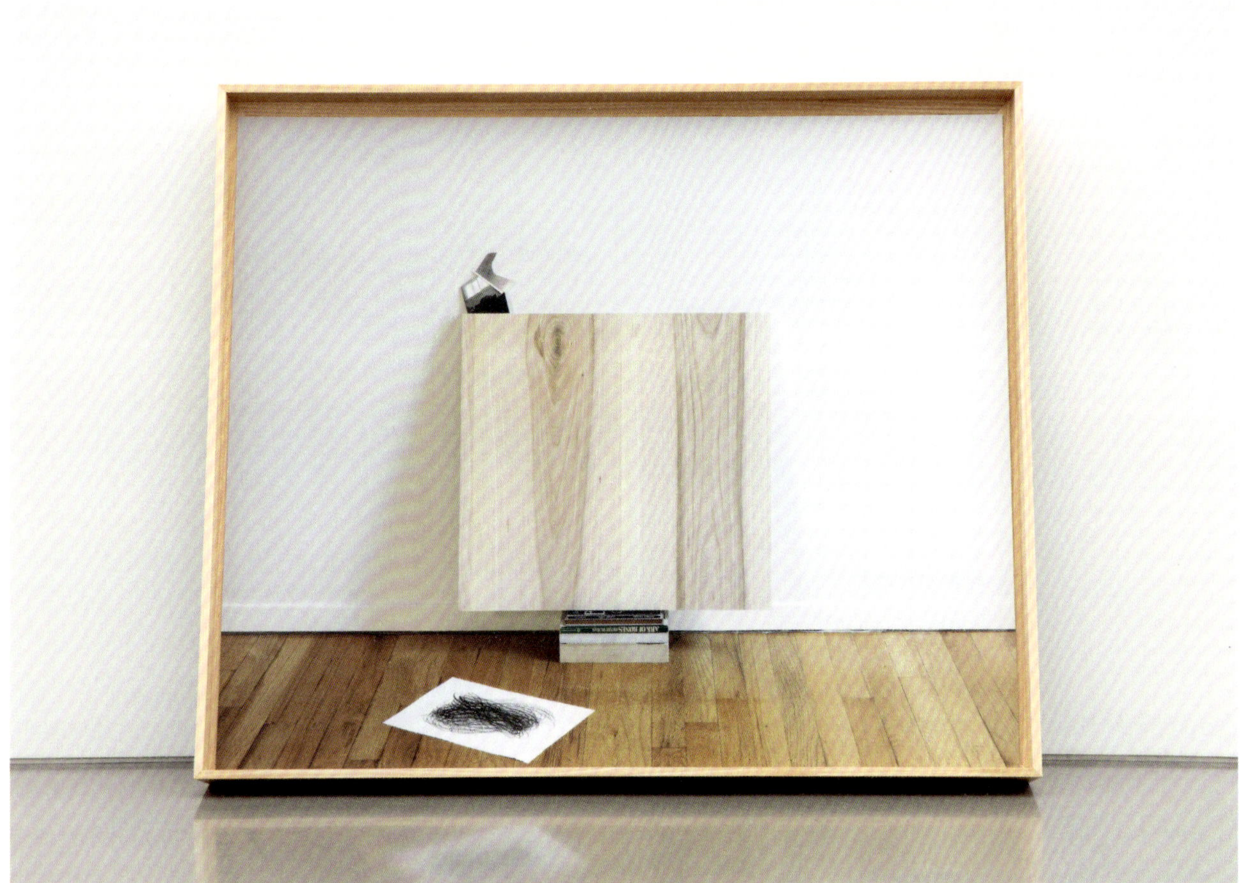

2

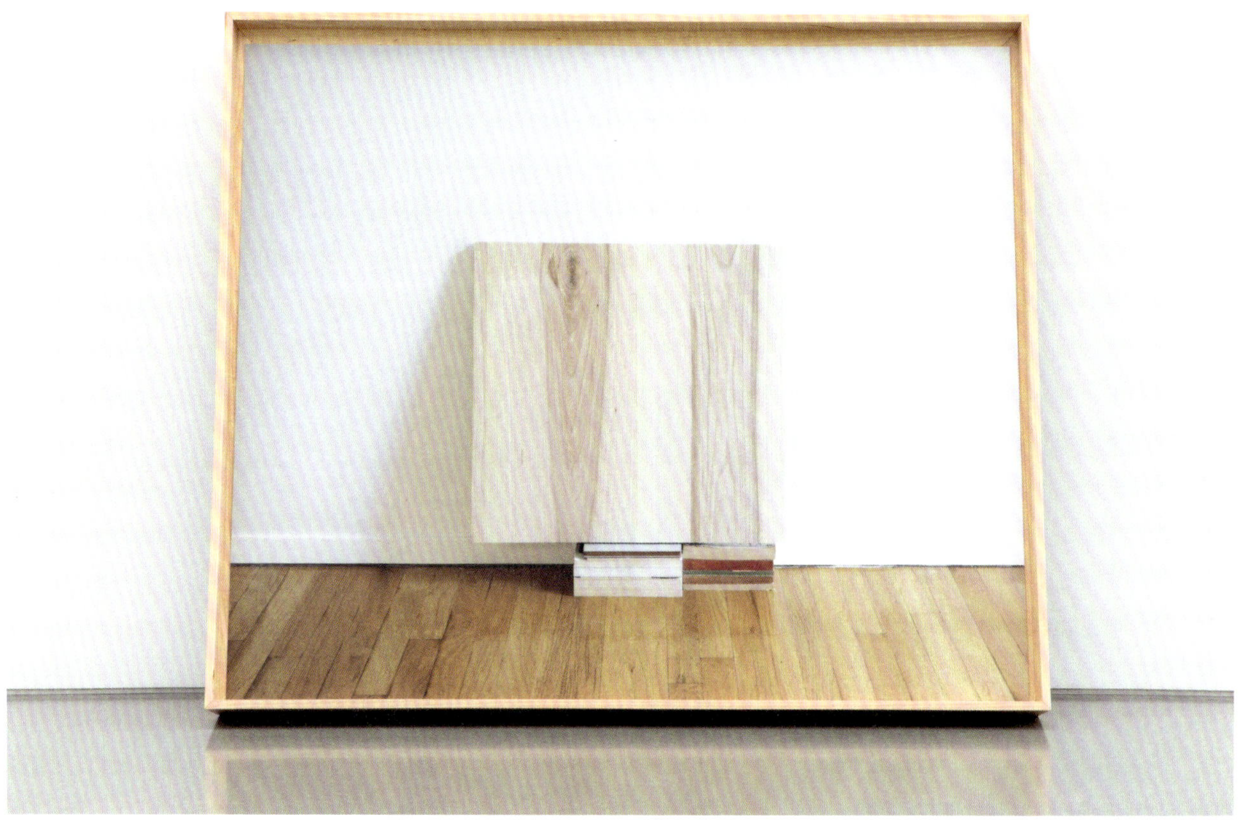

3

1   Leslie Hewitt
     Untitled (Double Entendre), 2019
     Digital C-print, framed
     133 × 158 × 18 cm
2   Leslie Hewitt
     *Untitled (Dreambook or Axis of the
     Ellipse)*, 2019
     Digital C-print, framed
     133 × 158 × 18 cm
3   Leslie Hewitt
     Untitled (The Notion of Labor), 2019
     Digital C-print, framed
     133 × 158 × 18 cm

IMAN ISSA
PROXIES, WITH A LIFE OF THEIR OWN
2020–22

The four displays by Iman Issa exhibited in *Avant-Garde and Liberation* are part of an ongoing series of self-portraits as others or, as their title suggests, proxies that take on a life of their own. Bordering on abstract, these works neatly encapsulate the problem dealt with in this exhibition: How can we describe or represent the way in which contemporary artists are engaging with key figures in decolonial modernism? What does it mean to identify with a historical personality and their art, or with their position in relation to society? Issa's (self-)portraits start with a schematic head shape that is modified to fit the particular individual she is portraying herself as. The objects on view refer to Doria Shafik, a leading figure in the mid-twentieth-century Egyptian women's movement; the poet Georges Henein, a founding member of the Cairo Surrealist group Art et Liberté in the nineteen-thirties; the Egyptian poet and educational reformer Taha Hussein; and the philosopher of art and religion Ananda Coomaraswamy, who was involved in the Swadeshi Movement for Indian independence and sought to reconcile Western and Eastern thought. Issa's *Self-Portraits* are accompanied by short texts that tell us a little about the artist's relationship to these personalities but do not explain it. Most of us know what it feels like to identify with someone else, even if we cannot put it into words. As the artist says: "I relate exactly but at the same time I don't fully understand."

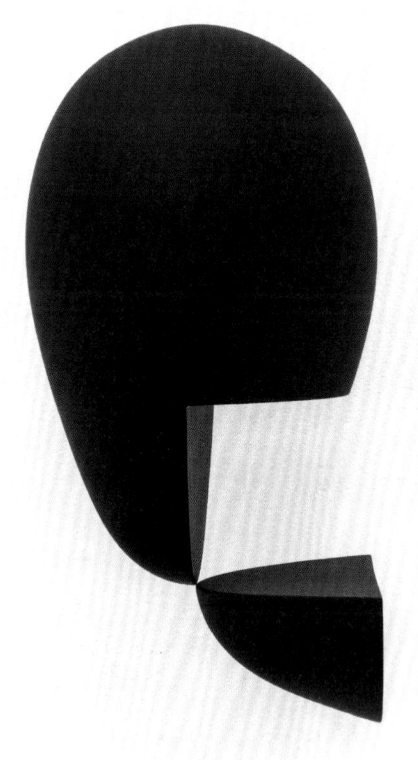

1

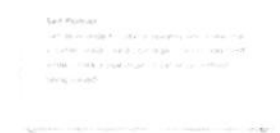

2

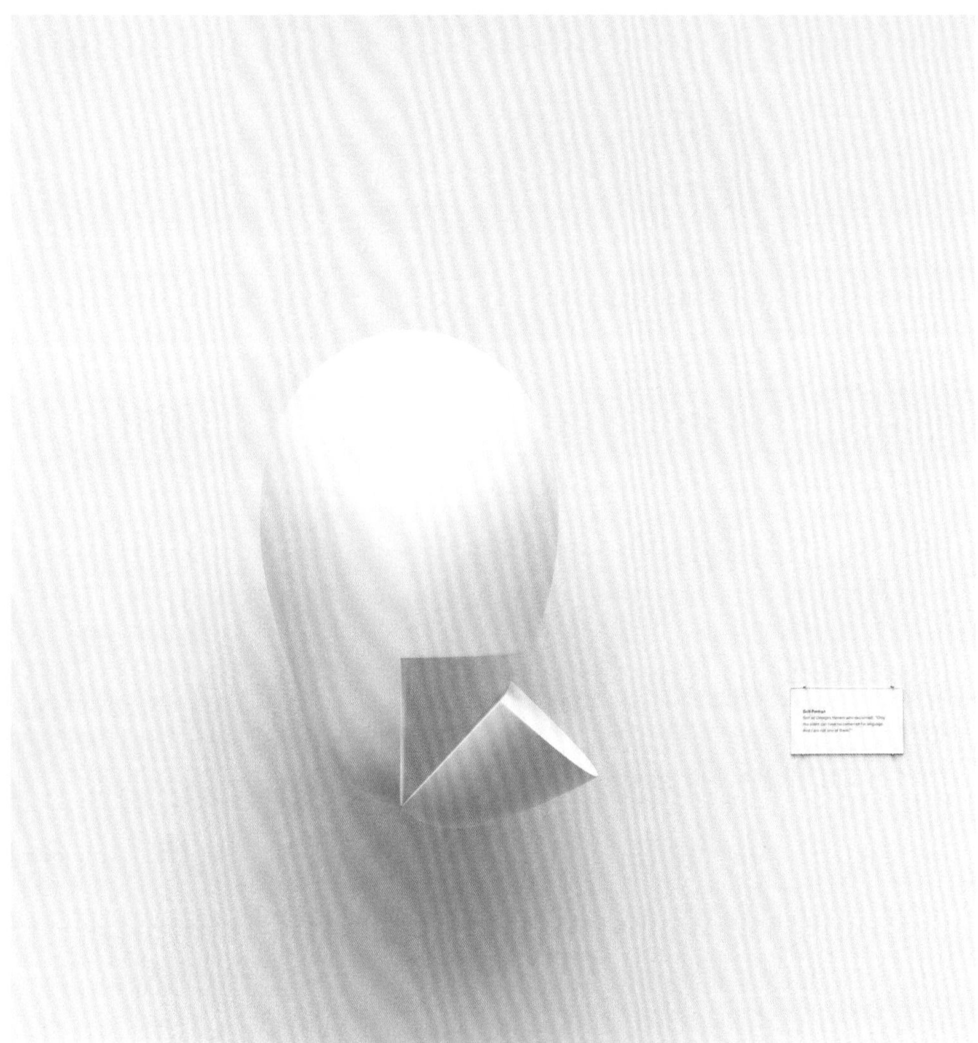

3

Self-Portrait
Self as Georges Henein who exclaimed:
"Only the silent can have no contempt for
language. And I am not one of them?"

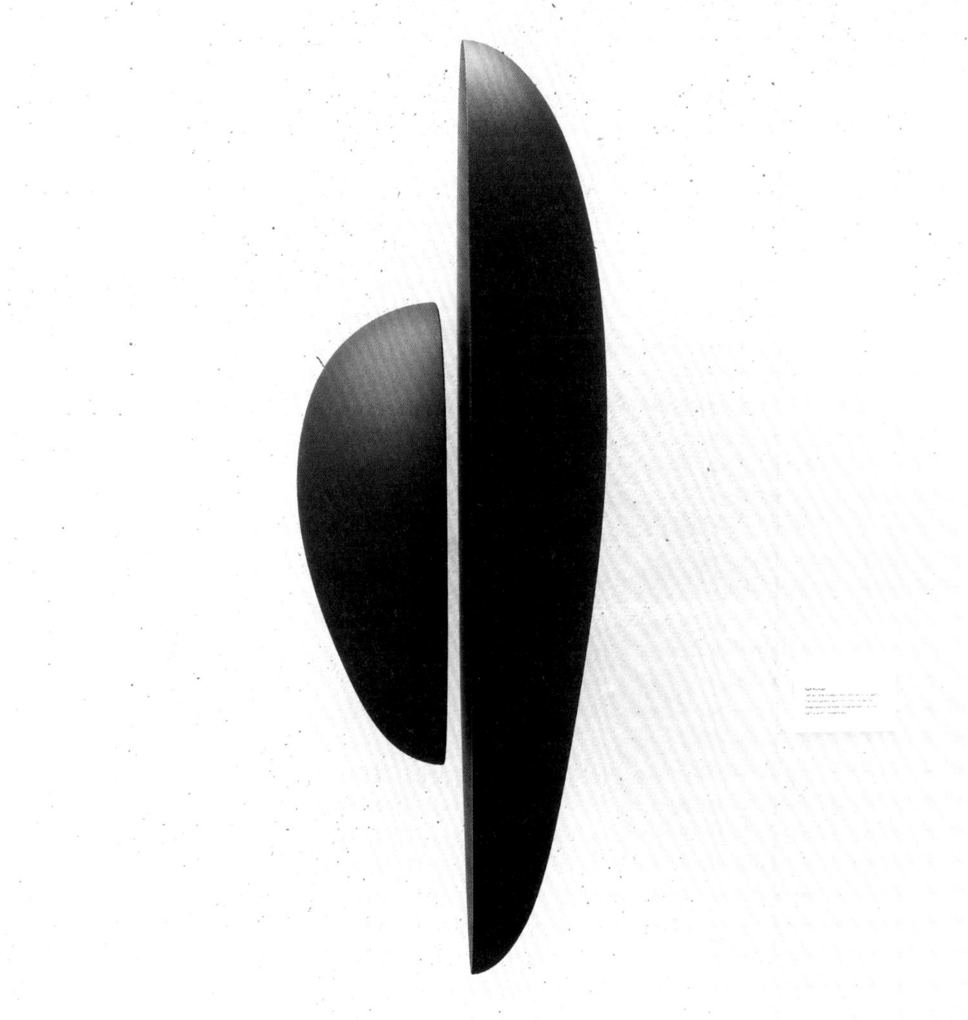

4

Self-Portrait
Self as Taha Hussein who referred to himself
in the third person, and who often divided his
observations between those sensed from his
right and left, respectively.

1   Iman Issa
    *Self-Portrait (Self as Ananda K.
    Coomaraswamy)*, 2022
    3D print, paint, metal poles
    53 × 34 × 43 cm
    Text panel under glass, 7 × 12 cm
2   Iman Issa
    Self-Portrait (Self as Doria Shafik), 2020
    3D print, paint, metal poles
    60 × 33.5 × 43.5 cm
    Text panel under glass, 7 × 12 cm
3   Iman Issa
    Self-Portrait (Self as Georges Henein),
    2021
    3D print, acrylic, epoxy, paint, metal poles
    48 × 33 × 43 cm
    Text panel under glass, 7 × 12 cm
4   Iman Issa
    Self-Portrait (Self as Taha Hussein),
    2020
    3D print, acrylic, epoxy, paint, metal poles
    90 × 32.5 × 42.5 cm
    Text panel under glass, 7 × 12 cm

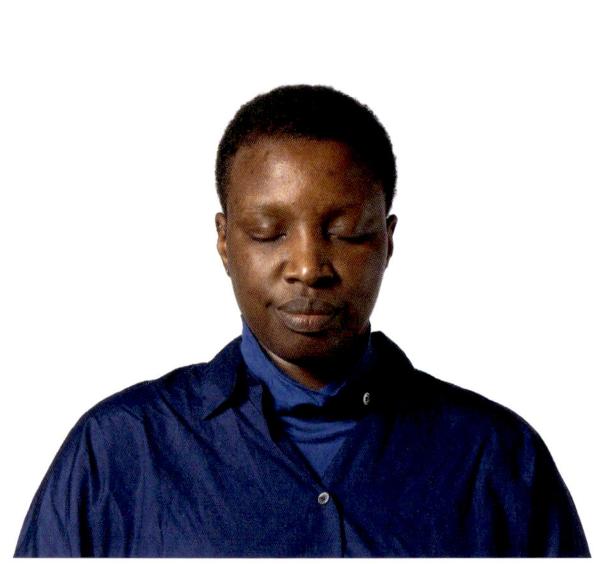 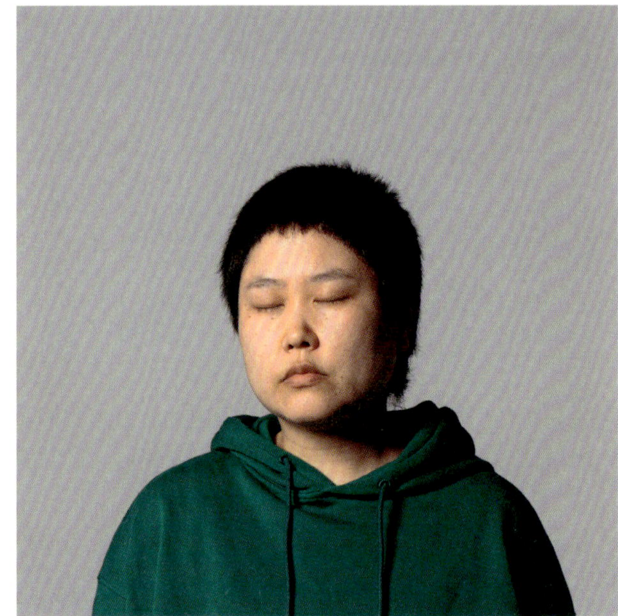

JANINE JEMBERE
CHANNELLING (VIENNA)
2023

For the photo series *Channelling (Vienna)* (2023), Janine Jembere photographed artists in Vienna with their eyes closed. As viewers, we look into the faces of the portrait subjects but not into their eyes, giving us the feeling that they see more than we do. As if they were in spiritual contact with deceased or distant persons, the sitters meld with artists, musicians, and poets from the liberation movements of the twentieth century, including the anti-colonial filmmaker Sarah Maldoror and the African American artist Faith Ringgold. Jembere made her analogue photographs after speaking with each portrait subject about the respective historical person who inspired them. *Channelling (Vienna)* thus serves to spotlight the continuity of resistance movements and the strength gained from community. "My intent is twofold," says the artist: "to create a record of 'who is here,' and to acknowledge those who are present with us—in a broader sense—our ancestors in spirit or those whose dreams we cherish and whose work we continue. I also hope for new connections to emerge through shared (or newly found) references and desires."

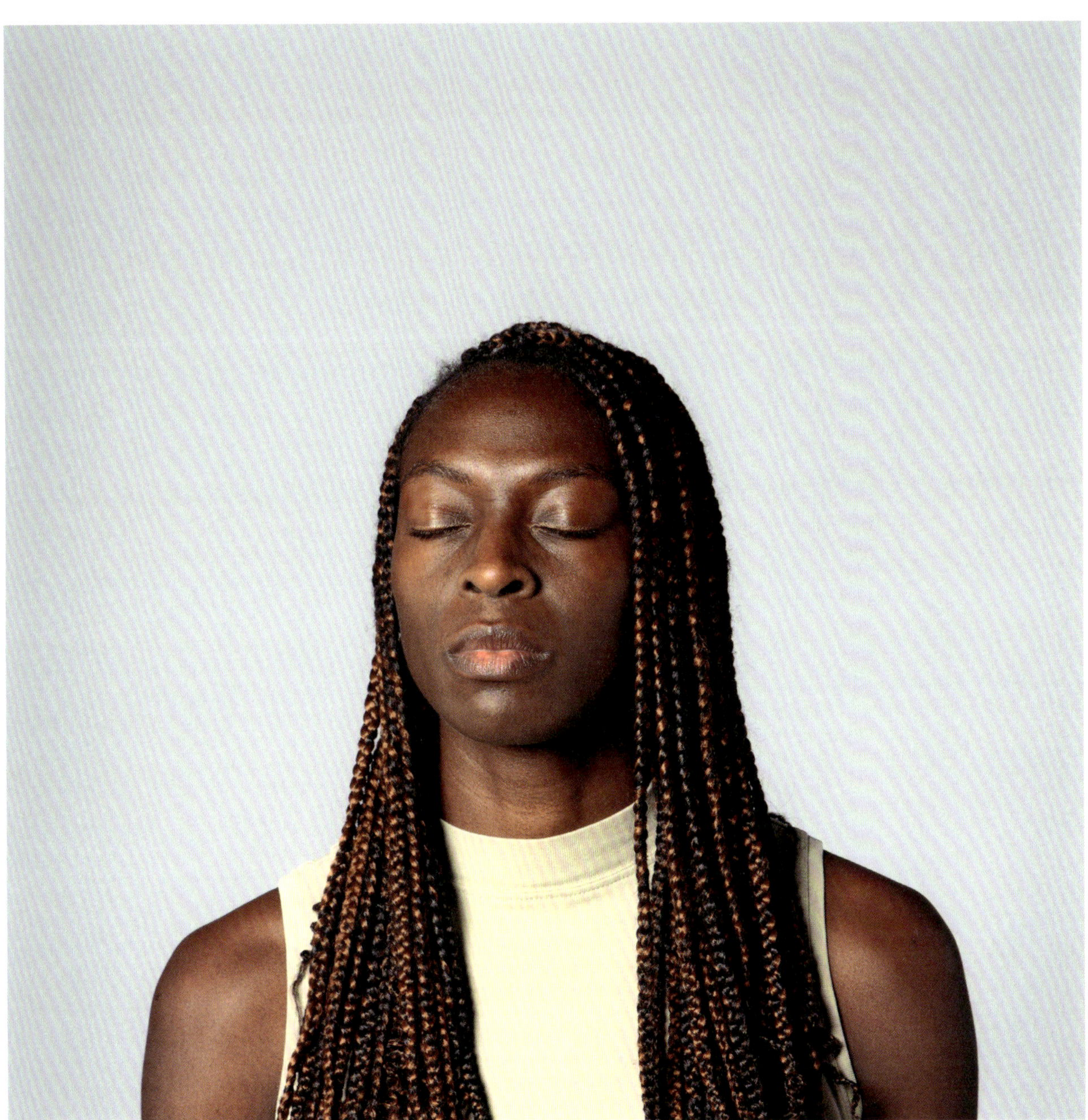

3

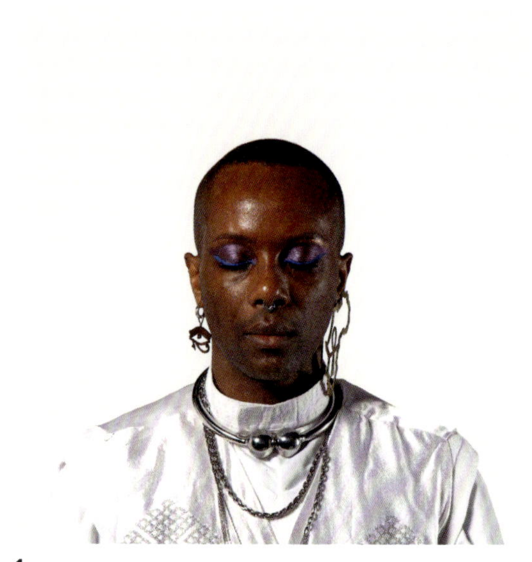

4

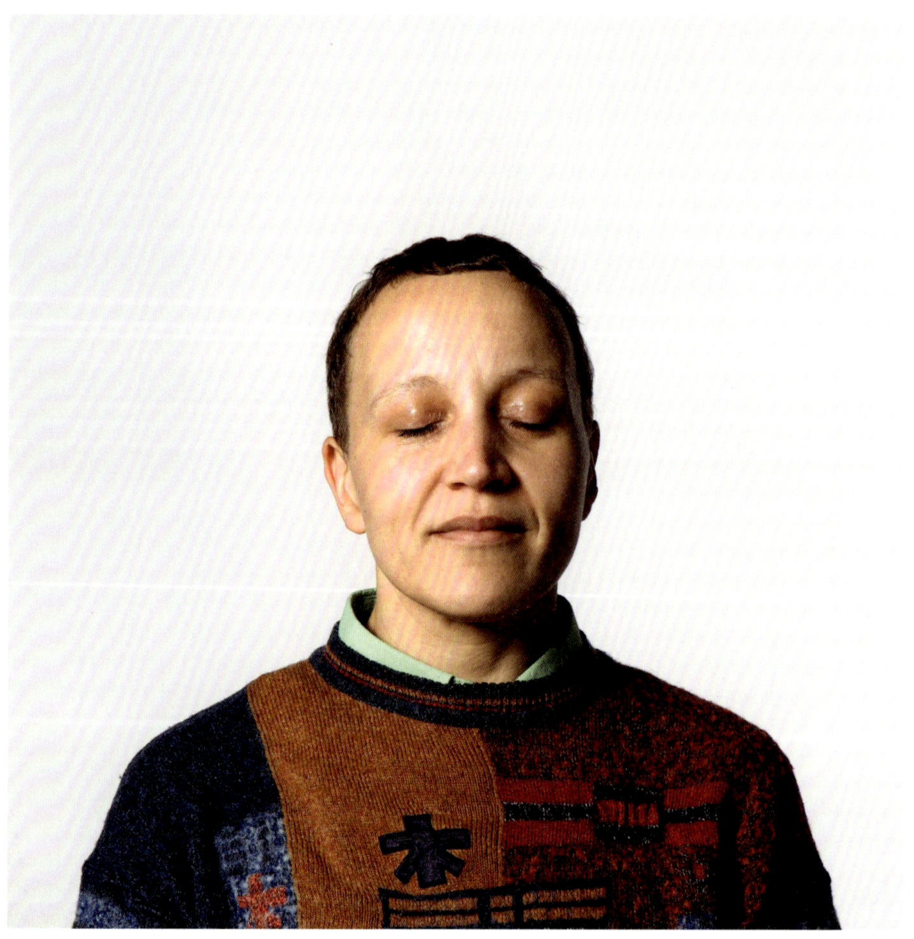

5

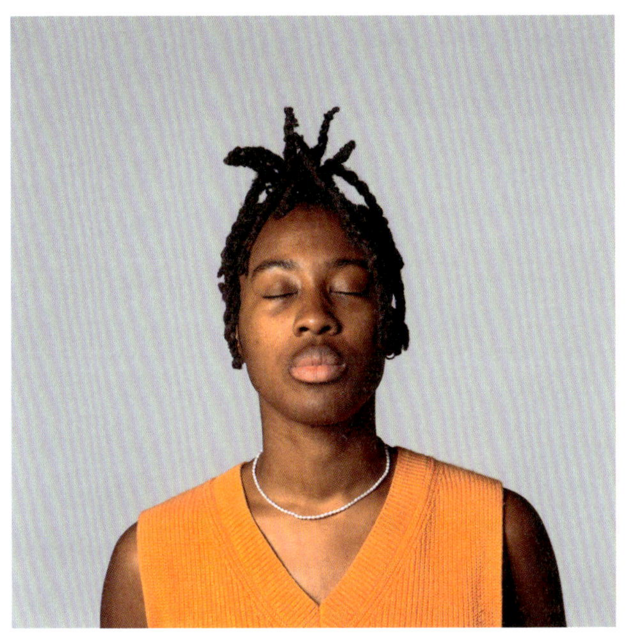

6

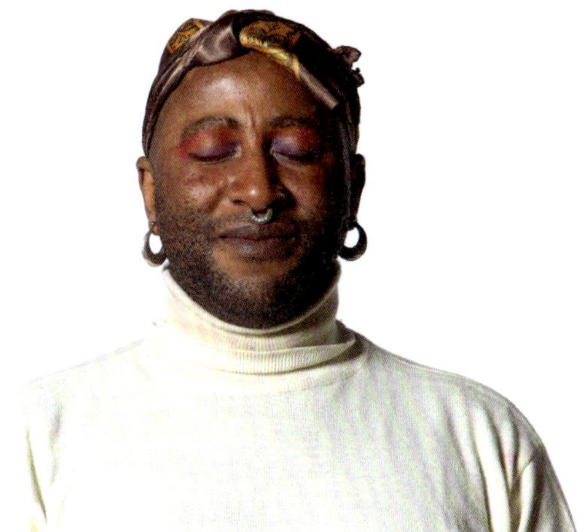

7

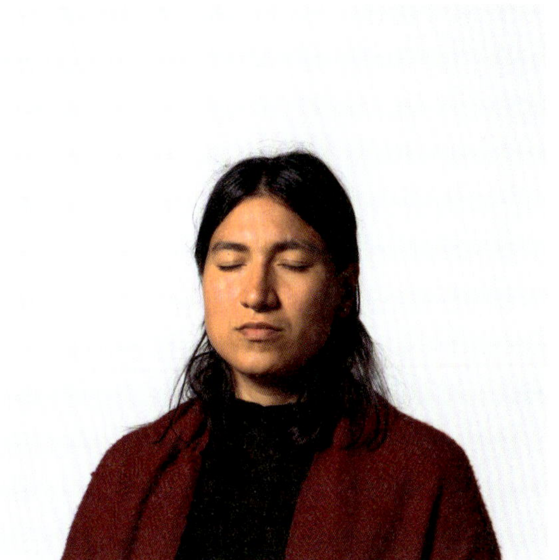

8

Janine Jembere
From the series *Channelling (Vienna)*, 2023
C-prints, 20 × 20 cm each

1   *Belinda Kazeem-Kamiński channelling
    Funmilayo Aníkúlápó-Kuti*
2   *Hyo Lee channelling José Esteban Muñoz*
3   *Abiona Esther Ojo channelling Faith
    Ringgold*
4   *Faris Cuchi Gezahegn channelling
    ሸዋዬ ደገፋ (Shewaye Degefa), Toni Morrison
    and Lama Rod Owens*
5   *Janine Jembere channelling Sarah
    Maldoror*
6   *Tonica Hunter channelling Beverly
    Glenn-Copeland*
7   *Mzamo Nondlwana channelling Winnie
    Nomzamo Madikizela-Mandela, Simon
    Nkoli and Alvin Ailey*
8   *Verena Melgarejo Weinandt channelling
    Waman Puma de Ayala*

99

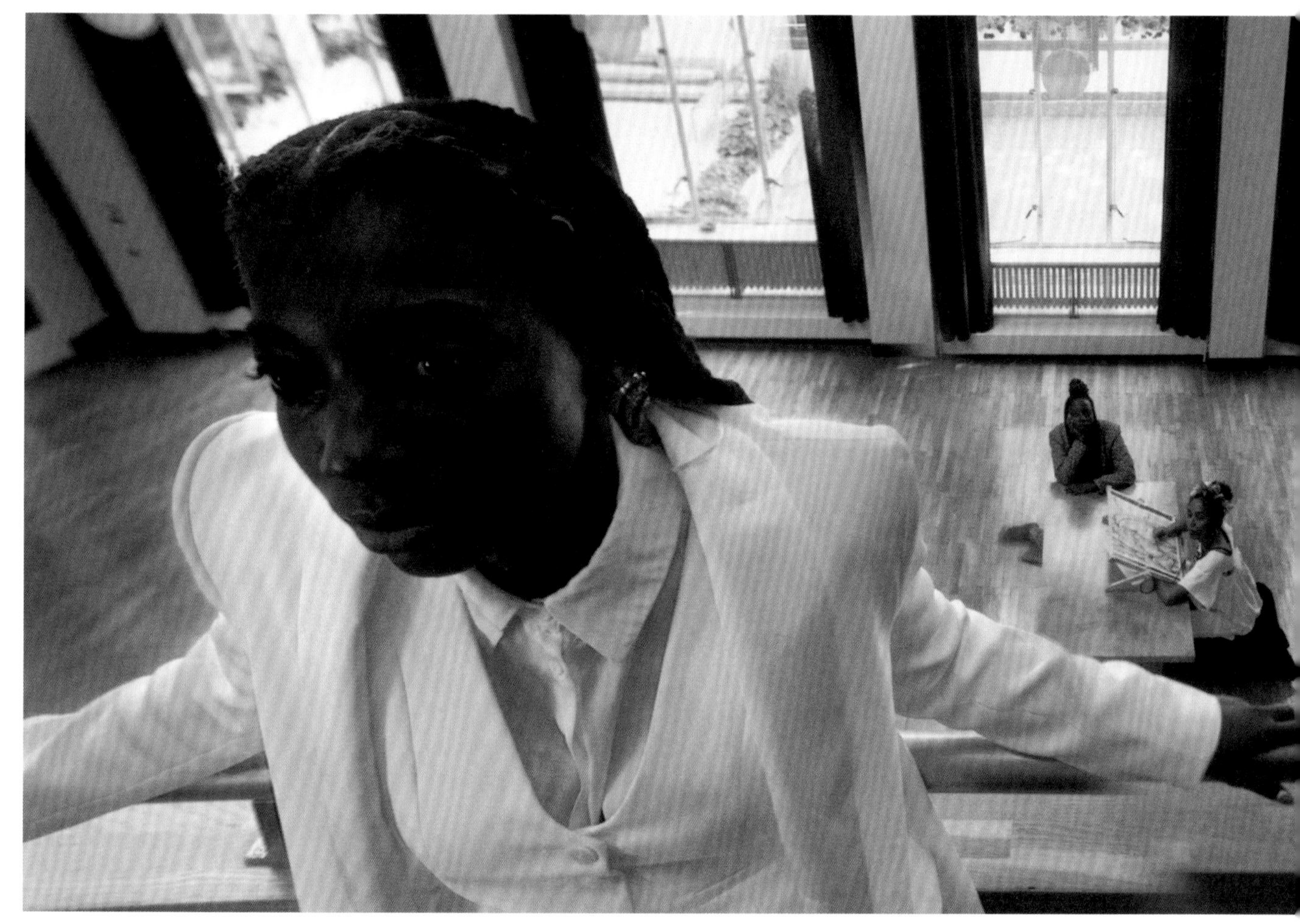

PATRICIA KAERSENHOUT
LE RETOUR DES FEMMES COLIBRIS
2022

Artistic engagement with contemporary forms of racism in the Netherlands (and Europe in general) has over the past twenty years led patricia kaersenhout to critically reexamine the history of slavery, colonialism, and anti-colonial resistance. In her new film, the artist places the women of the Négritude Movement at the center of a historically speculative reflection on emancipatory Black identity concepts and constricting gender relations. Taking the First International Congress of Black Writers and Artists in Paris in 1956 as her springboard, kaersenhout addresses the invisibility of Black women on the stages of the Pan-African Liberation Movement. Embodied by actresses, Suzanne Césaire and the sisters Jeanne and Paulette Nardal, who along with Léopold Sédar Senghor and Aimé Césaire were among the co-founders of Négritude in the thirties, meet up with the artists Josephine Baker and Frida Kahlo to discuss Surrealism, decolonization, art, and sexuality. A poetic-aesthetic tribute to the female Black avant-garde between Paris, Martinique, Mexico, and Mississippi.

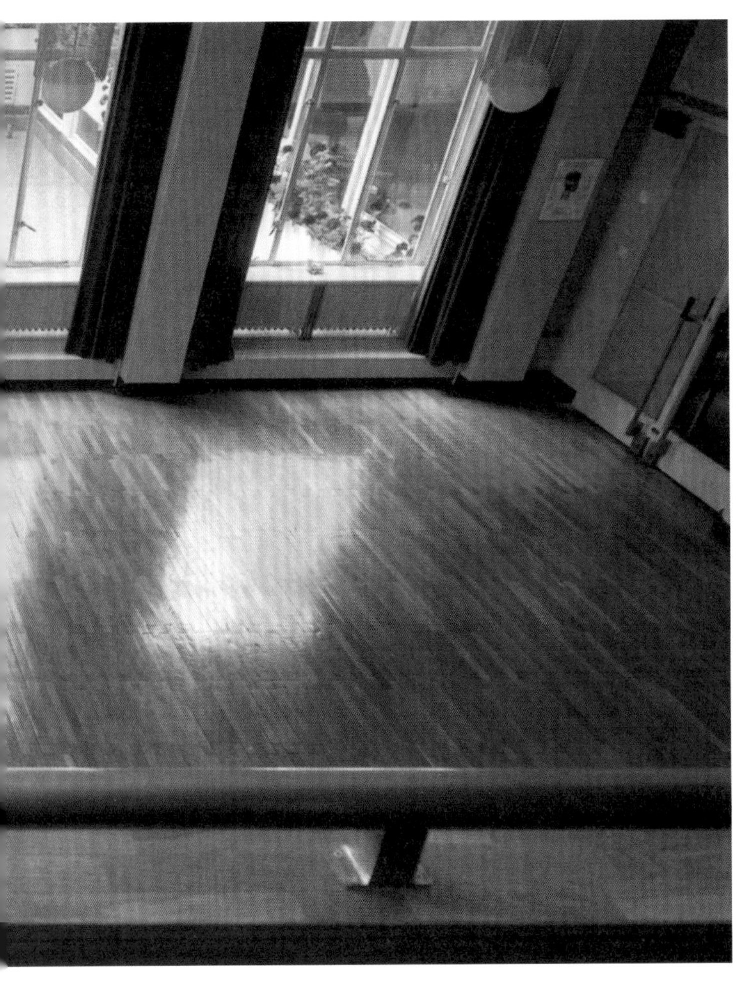

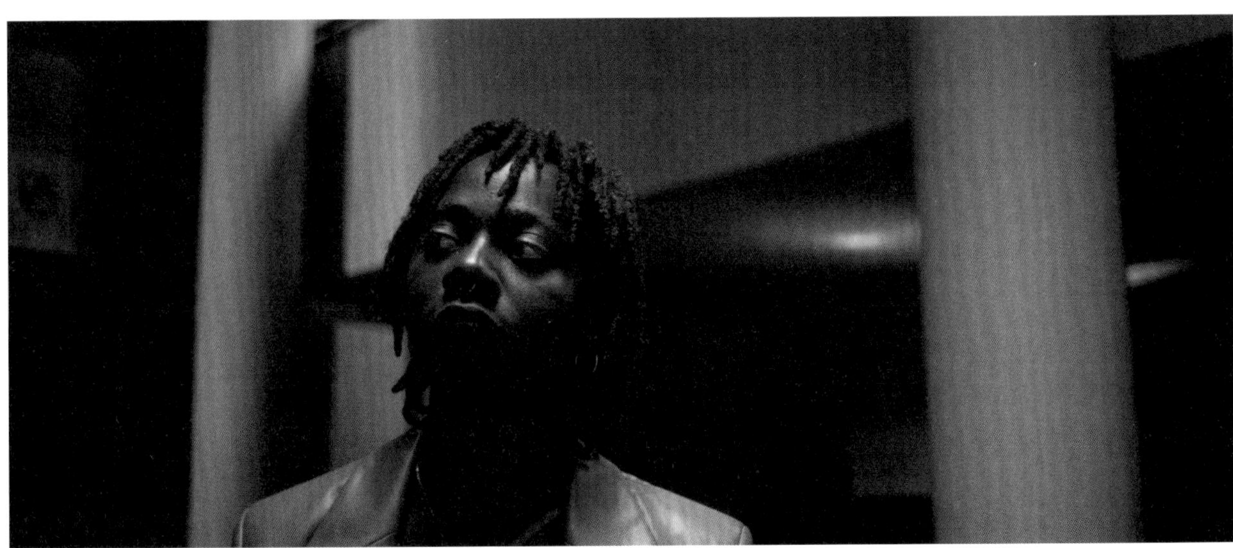

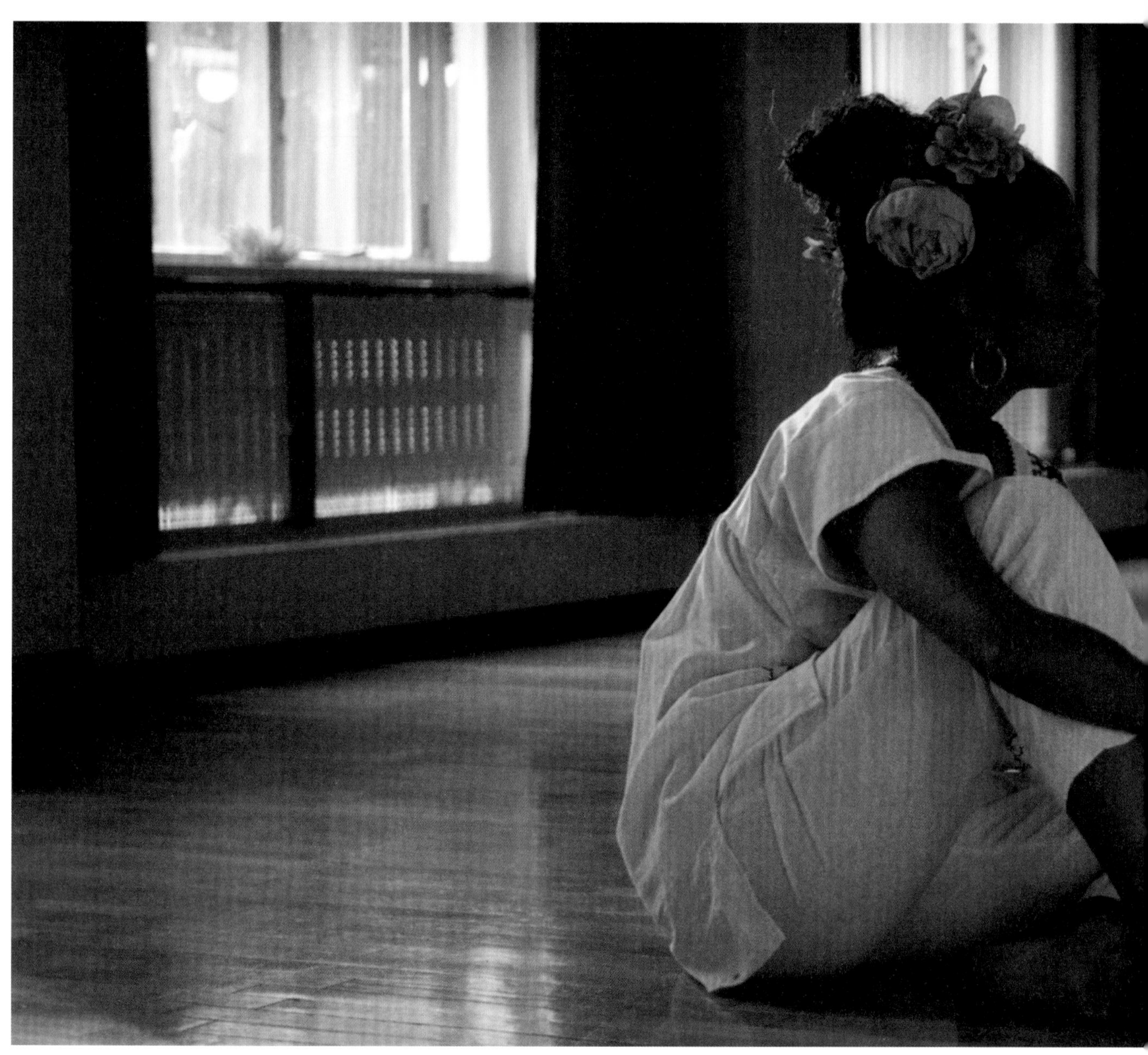

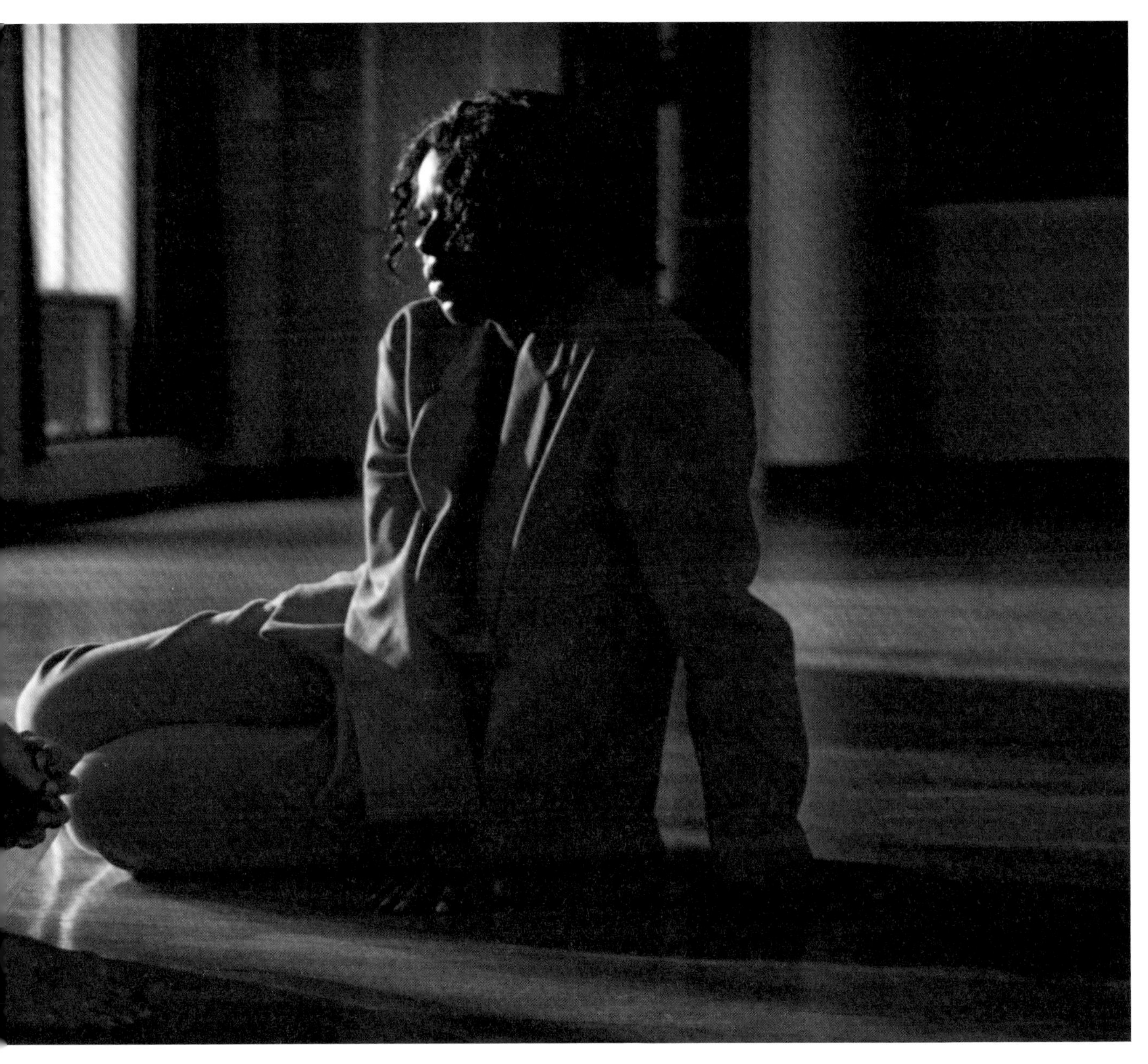

patricia kaersenhout
Le retour des femmes colibris, 2022
Film, black-and-white, sound, 18:23 min

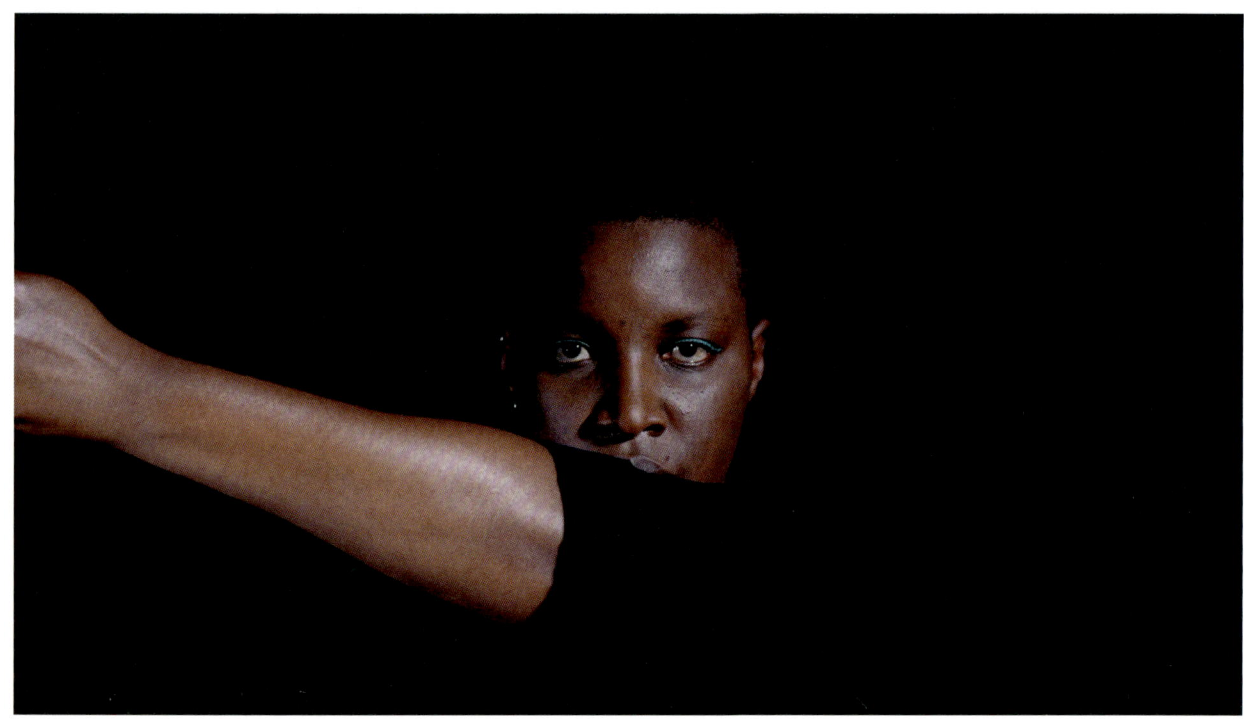

BELINDA KAZEEM-KAMIŃSKI
UNTITLED, K. T. C. I.
2022

In the video work *Untitled, K. T. C. I.* (2022), Belinda
Kazeem-Kamiński performs wearing a black jumpsuit, so
that only her forearms and face stand out against the
dark background. Using sign-like body language, the artist
writes a short sentence with outstretched arms that
spells out what the initials of the title stand for: "Kill the
Cop Inside" is a call to free the mind from the power of
oppressive violence. The phrase comes from the Brazilian
theater director Augusto Boal, who in the nineteen-
sixties developed a performative art of liberation he
called the "Theater of the Oppressed." Boal coined the
notion of the "cop in the head" as an image of internal-
ized oppression that prevents many people from participating in any form of political resistance. Against the
backdrop of current police violence against Black people,
the language of outstretched arms and clenched fists
that the artist uses to represent the call to self-liberation
invokes the Black Power gesture of the sixties. "The
stories of yesterday are the tools for today and the
answers for tomorrow," wrote Cindy Sissokho of Kazeem-
Kamiński's practice of taking up and carrying forward
historical movements to decolonize consciousness.

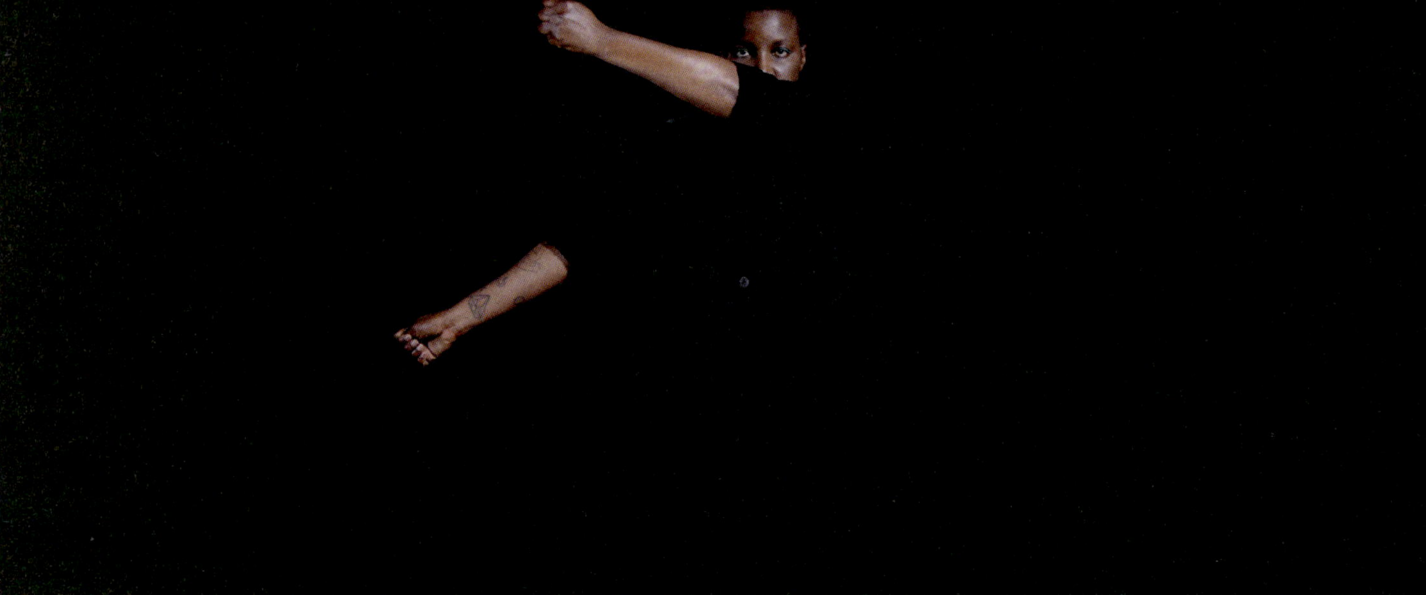

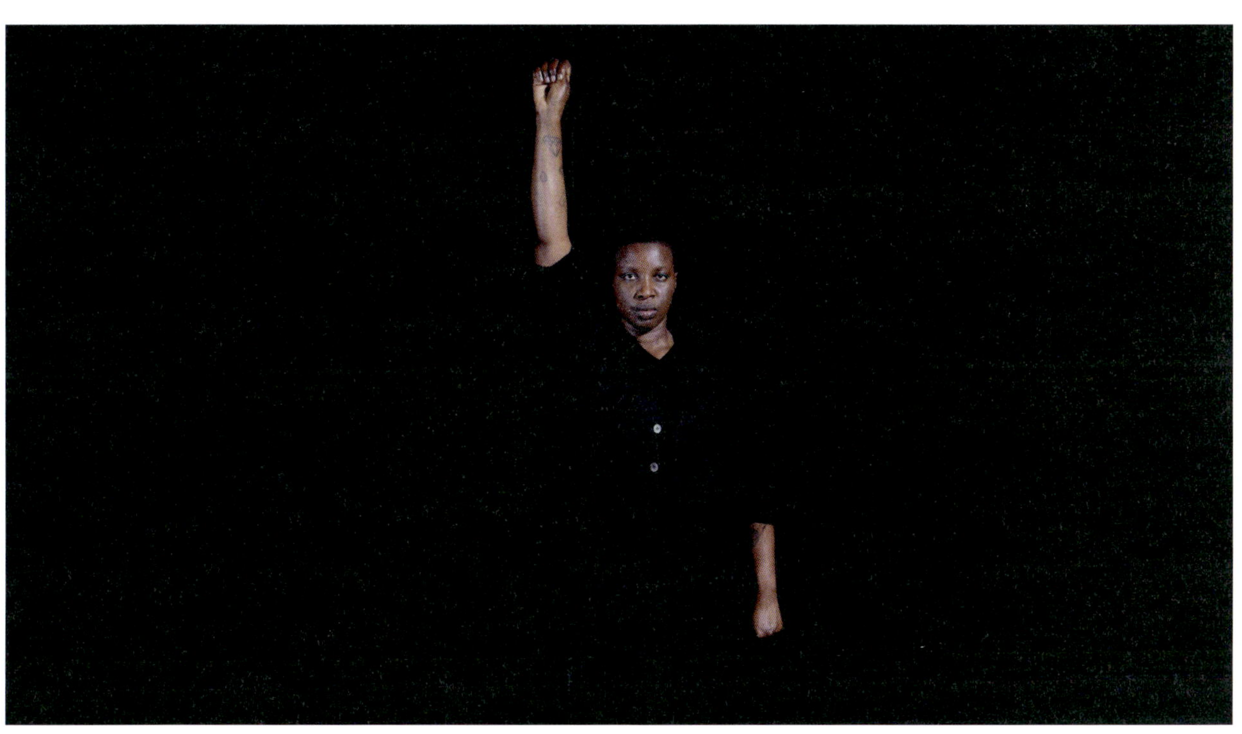

Belinda Kazeem–Kamiński
Untitled, K. T. C. I., 2022
Video, color, sound, 5 min (loop)

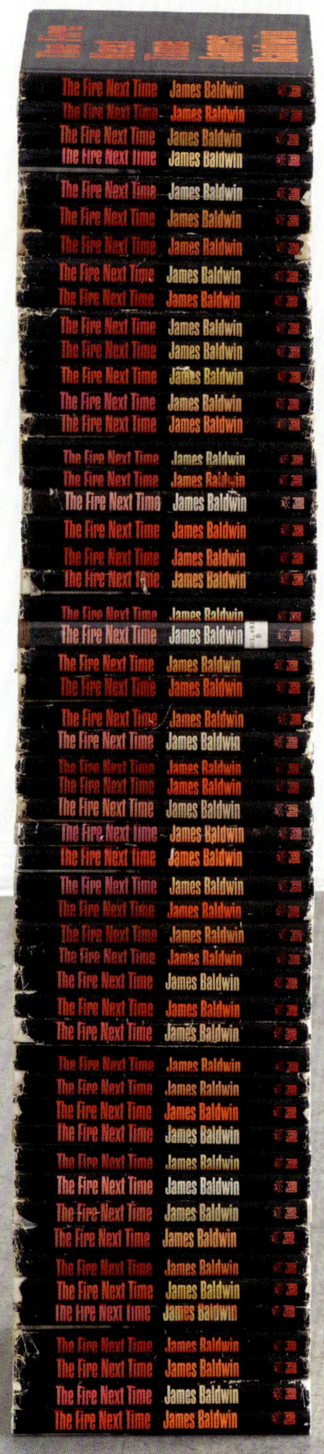

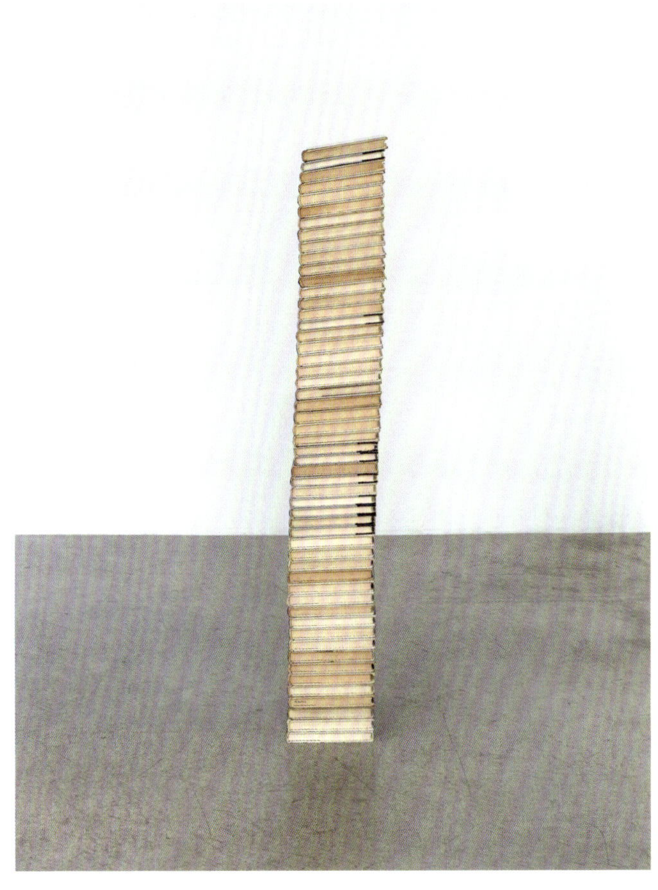

ZOE LEONARD
TIPPING POINT
2016

For *Tipping Point*, Zoe Leonard collected fifty-three copies of the first edition of James Baldwin's book *The Fire Next Time* (1963) and arranged them in a stack. The number of books corresponds to the years that elapsed between the publication of Baldwin's book on the destructive power of racism in the USA and the execution of Leonard's work. The artist, whose work has since the eighties subtly addressed instances of oppression and resistance, had long been preoccupied with Baldwin's famous warning to American society. Appalled by the numerous police killings of unarmed Black people in the twenty-tens, Leonard then felt compelled to turn Baldwin's book into a work that, like few others, articulates both simply and yet with deep complexity the timeliness of historical struggles. The form taken by the sculpture is reminiscent of Minimal Art objects that came to the fore simultaneously with Baldwin's *The Fire Next Time*, also calling to mind their seriality. In *Tipping Point*, however, the motif of repetition is to be understood politically: How many more times does this warning, voiced frequently since Baldwin, still have to be repeated? And when will the social tipping point be reached?

Zoe Leonard
Tipping Point, 2016
Stack of 53 books (James Baldwin: *The Fire Next Time*, first edition, New York: Dial Press, 1963)
100 × 15 × 20 cm

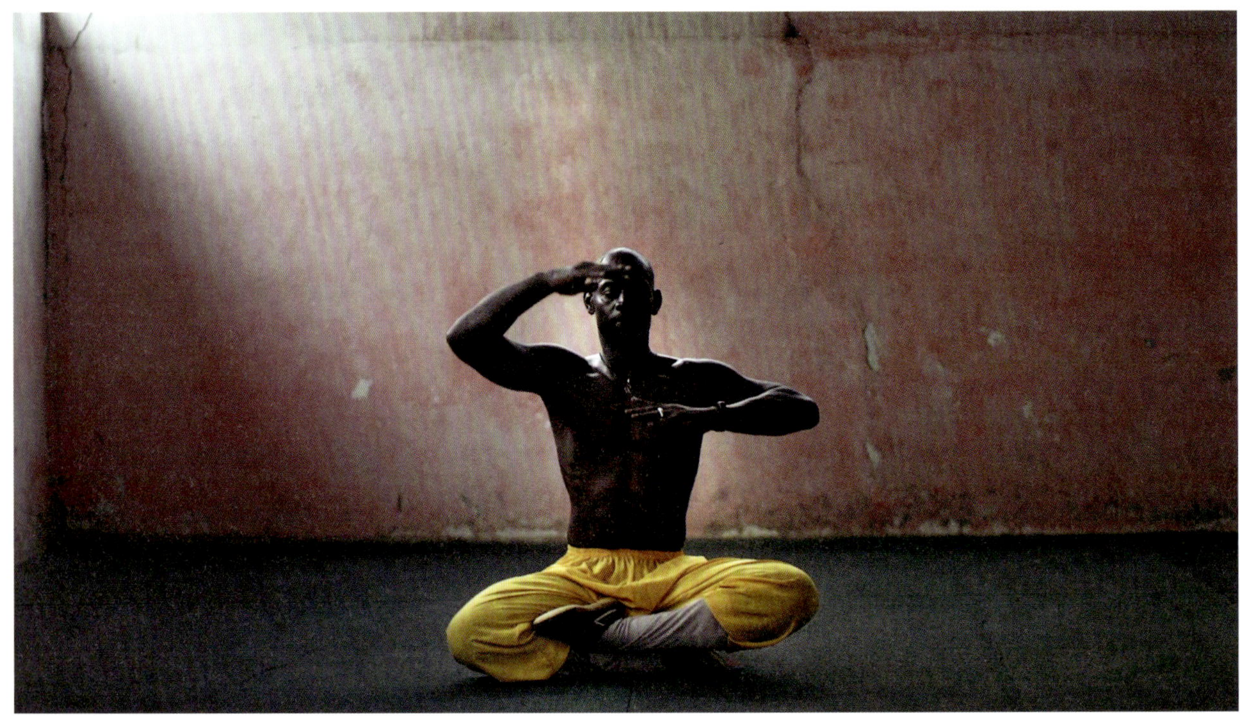

1

VINCENT MEESSEN
JUSTE UN MOUVEMENT
2021

In Jean-Luc Godard's feature film *La Chinoise* (1967), about a Maoist group that took part in the student movement in France, Omar Blondin Diop plays a militant African philosophy student and, by extension, himself. A short time later, Diop, who was inspired by the Situationists, conceived an African theater of life. He also wrote about Andy Warhol's film *Chelsea Girls* (1966) and co-founded a Marxist-Leninist group that agitated against neocolonial policies in Senegal under Léopold Sédar Senghor. Convicted of participating in a plan to free imprisoned comrades, Diop died in prison in Gorée in 1973 under unexplained circumstances. Vincent Meessen's film *Juste un mouvement* was shot in Dakar with amateur actors and Diop's relatives as well as former companions, including the artist Issa Samb. The film updates Godard's *La Chinoise* as a reflection on the liberation movements of decolonization and on the global uprisings of the late sixties, on African-European-Chinese relations today, on the persistence of Omar Diop's political ideals, and on the revolutionary potential of art and cinema.

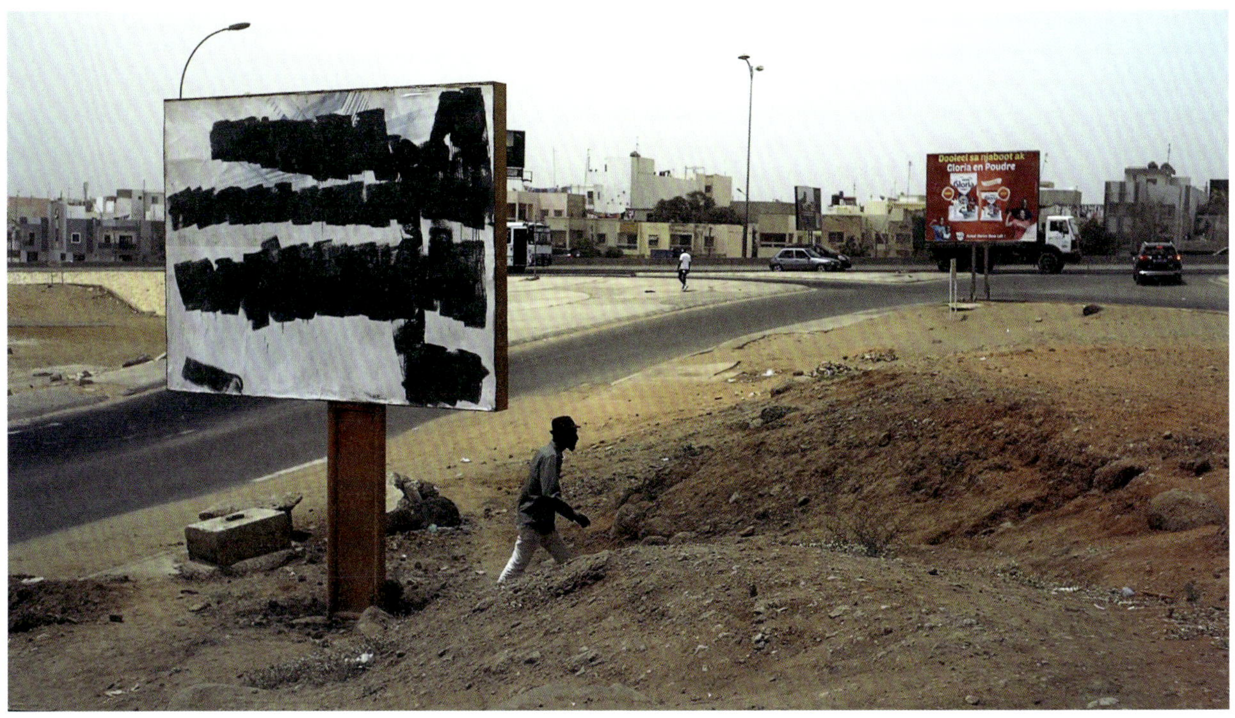

2

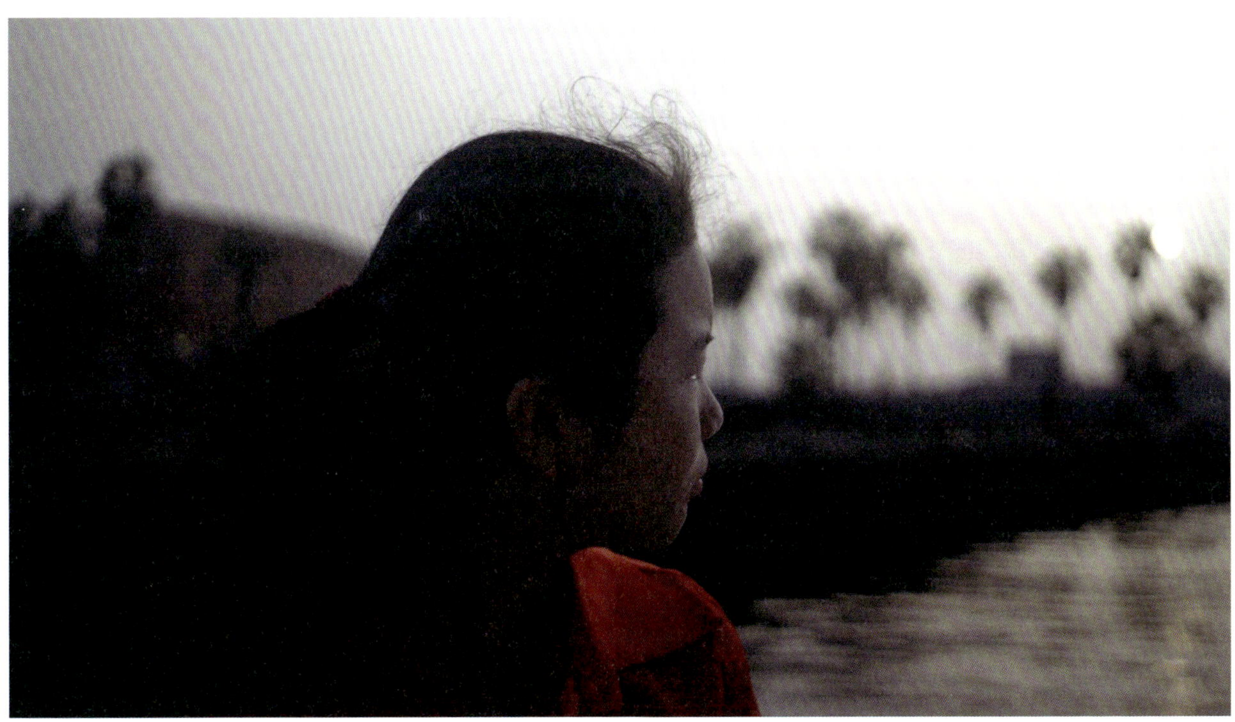

3

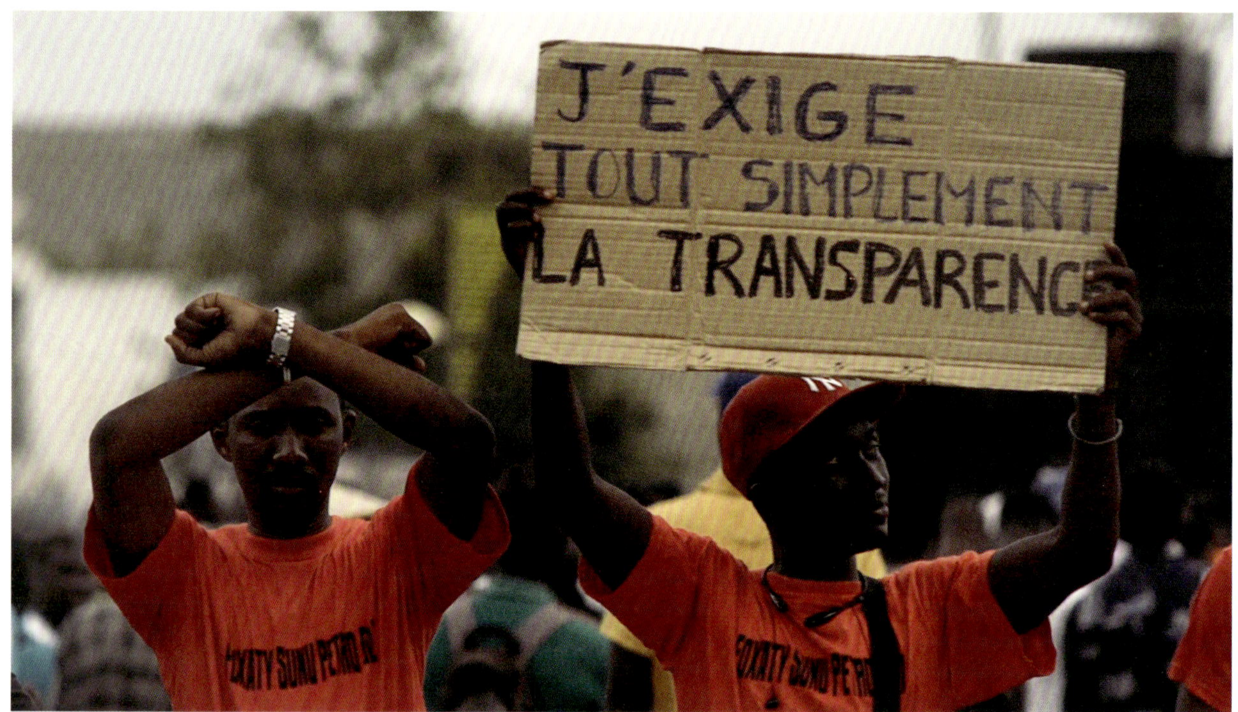

4

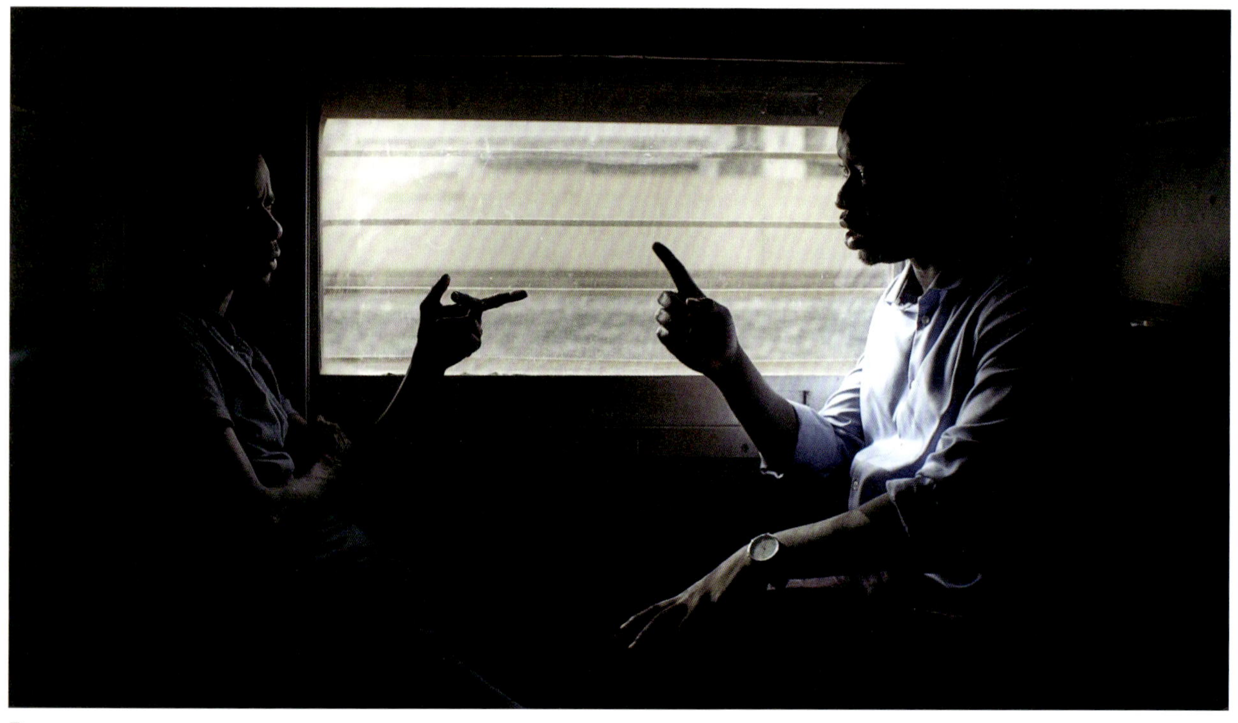

5

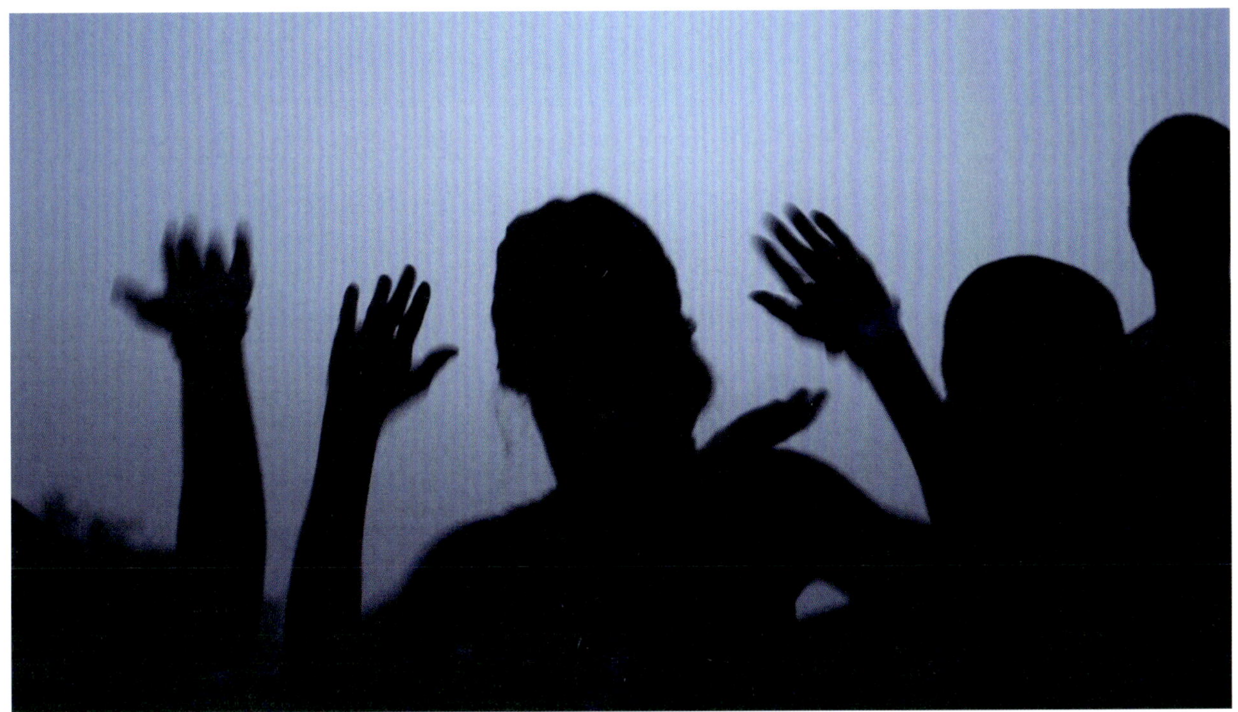

6

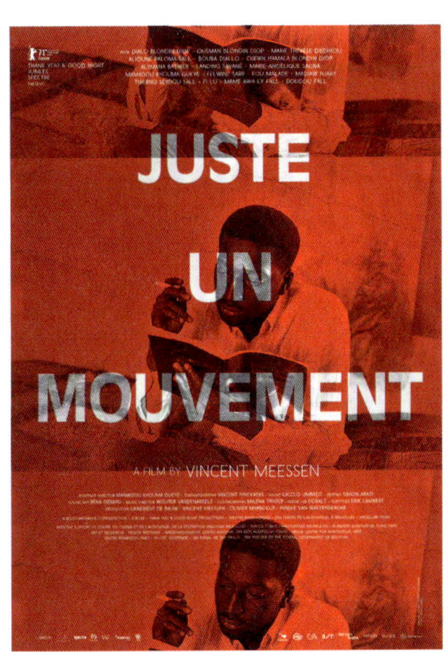

1–6 Vincent Meessen
Juste un mouvement, 2021
Video, color, sound, 110 min
7 Poster for *Juste un movement*, 2021
Graphic design: Speculoos

7

"Today, in a hundred years,
who are you sitting reading this poem of mine
filled with curiosity?
Today, in a hundred years?"

– Rabindranath Tagore, *The Year 1400*

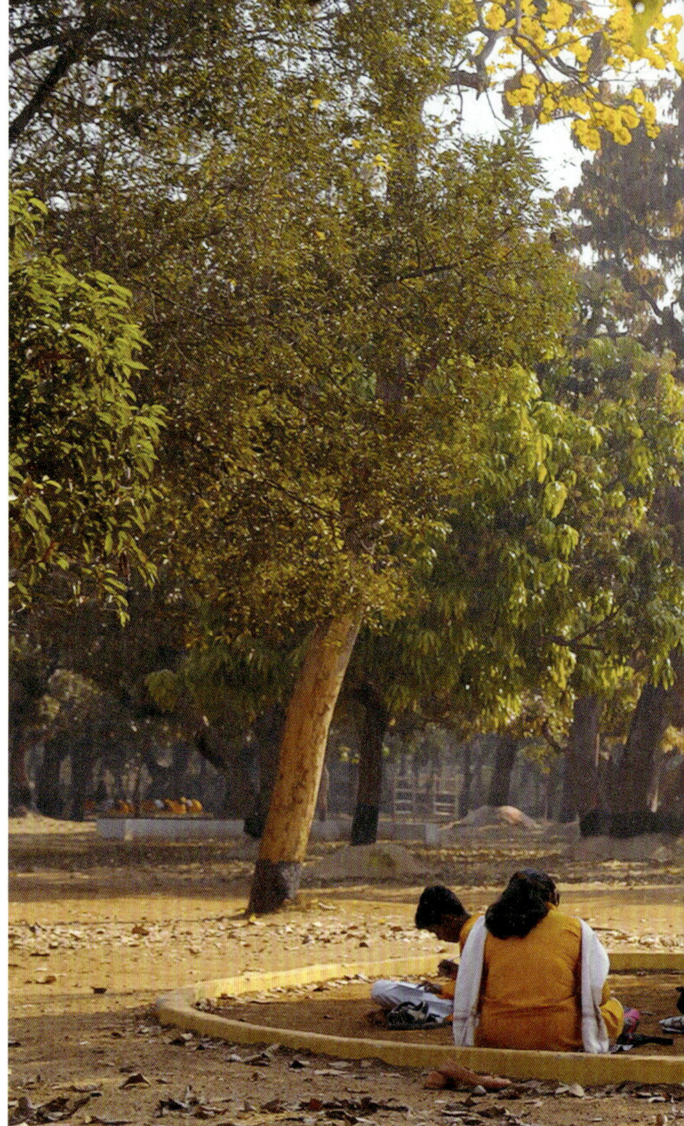

THE OTOLITH GROUP
O HORIZON
2018

The film begins with the recitation of a poem written in
Bengali in the late nineteenth century in which Rabindranath Tagore wonders about how the here and now will
figure in the future, and about how art will be viewed in a
hundred years. A century later, *O Horizon* responds by
looking back at the Indian poet's progressive educational
projects. The Otolith Group view their film as a study of
learning, showing us people practicing and learning
everything from dancing to Chinese to history to gardening. Tagore developed his holistic, socially and ecologically oriented schools and the cosmopolitan Visva-Bharati
world university in Santiniketan as an alternative to the
British educational system. Now that the university has
come under threat from the Modi government's Hindu
nationalist policies, *O Horizon* reminds us of the liberating potential of learning, as embodied by Ramkinkar
Baij's avant-garde sculptures on the campus of this institution of decolonization.

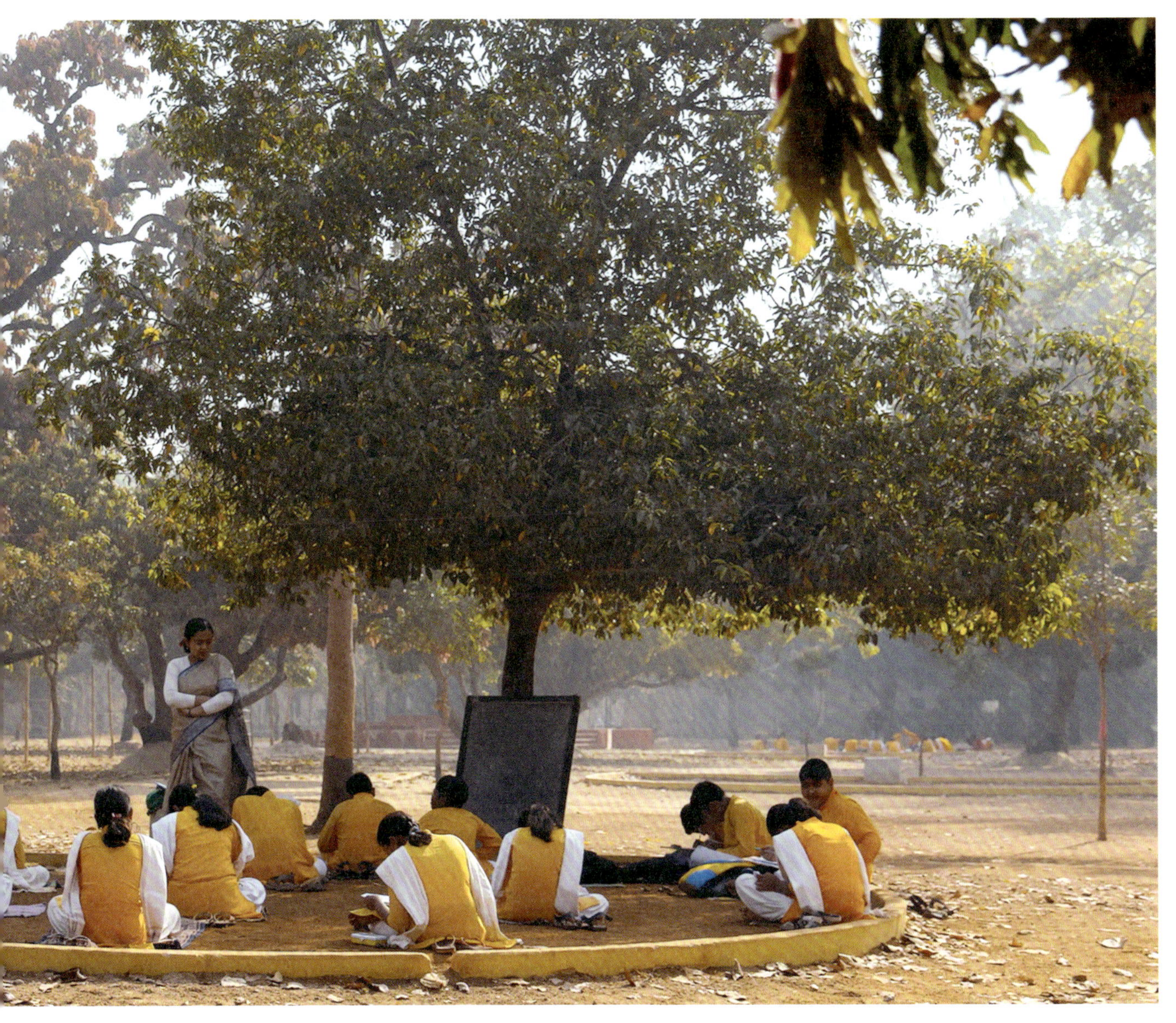

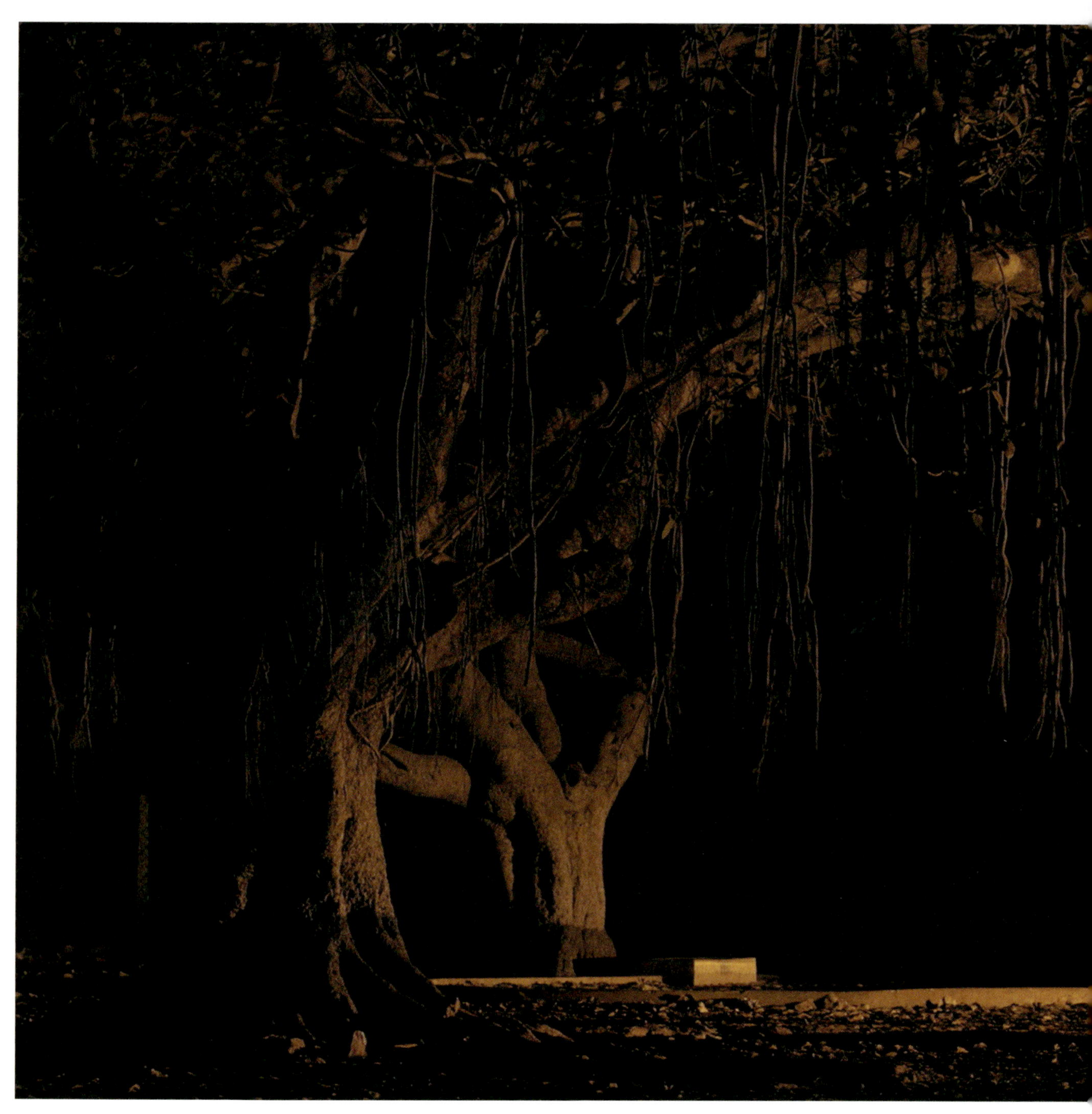

The Otolith Group
O Horizon, 2018
Video, color, sound, 81 min

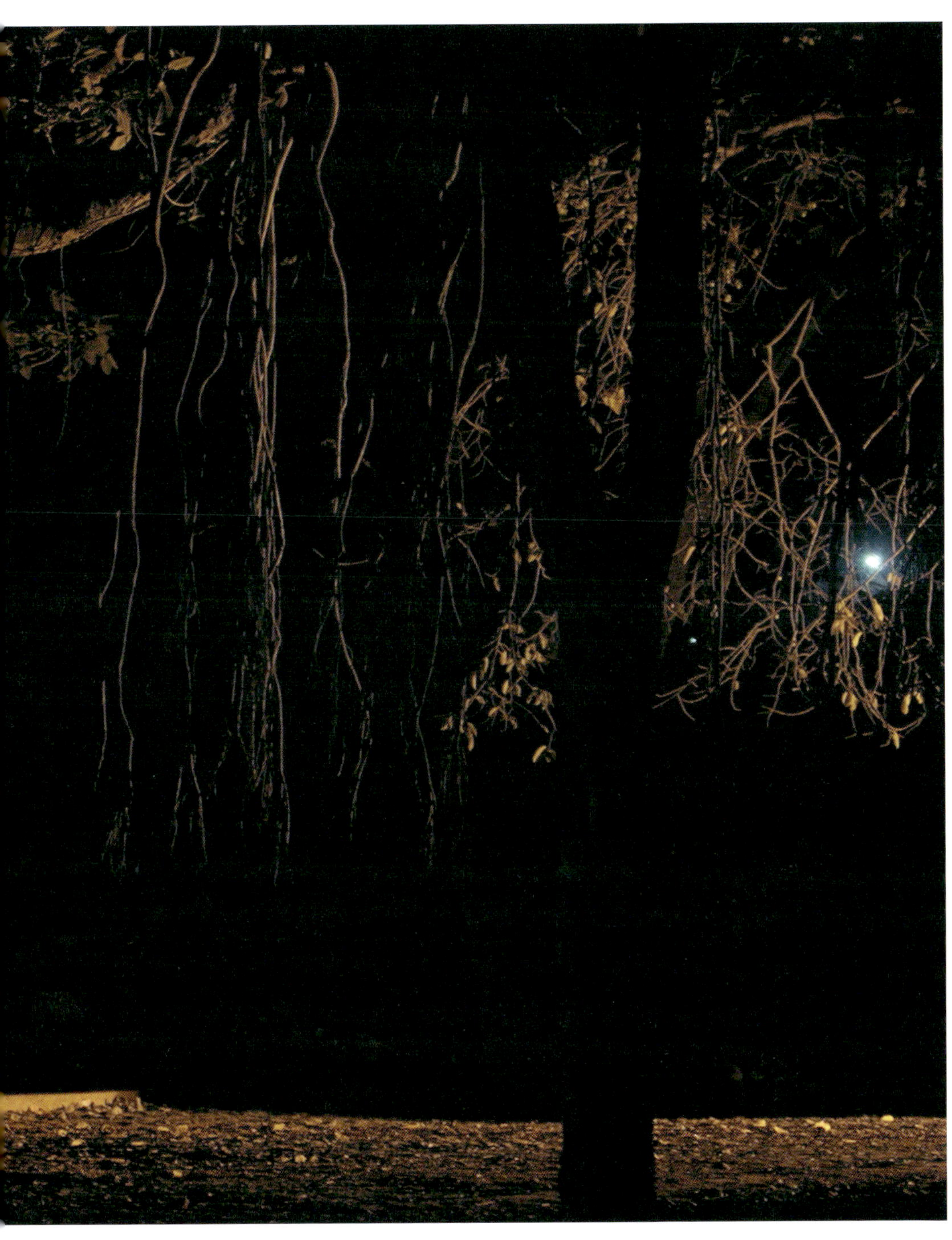

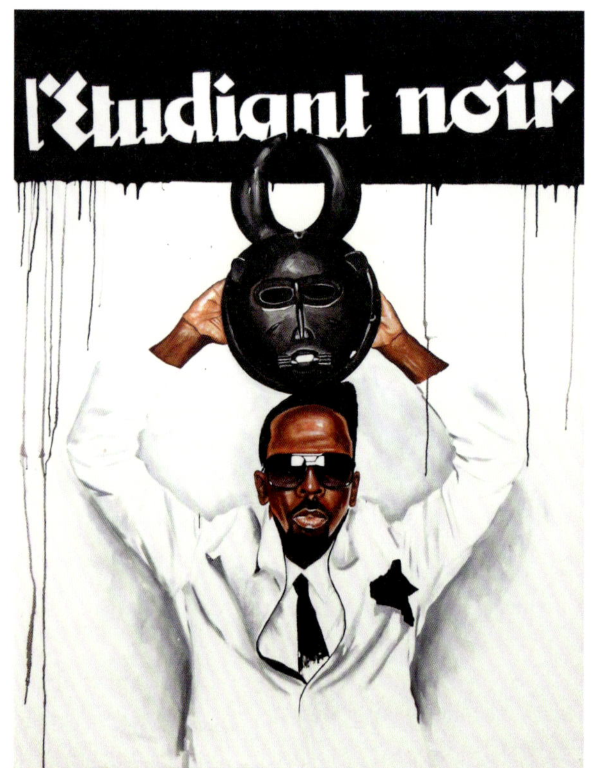

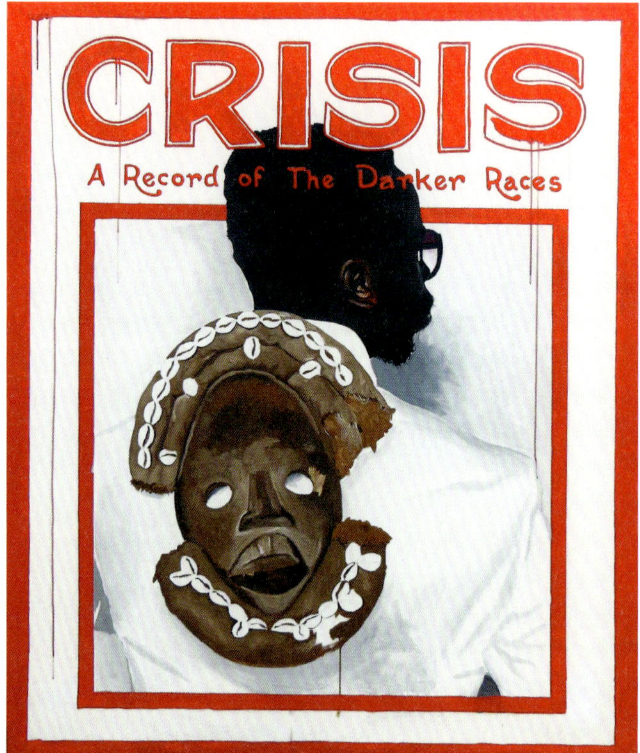

1   2

FAHAMU PECOU

Fahamu Pecou's works explore the image of Black mas-
culinity in the visual culture of US society, from the
allegedly threatening youth, to the cool rapper, to the
spectacle of Black death in the media. The artist sees
his paintings as an interrogation of the Black body, mind,
and spirit, represented respectively by concepts of
hip-hop culture, Négritude, and Ifá (Yoruba spiritual cos-
mology). With the titles *Fire!!*, *Revue du Monde Noir*,
The Crisis, and *L'Etudiant noir* the paintings on view in
the show quote the covers of important publications that
expressed the new Black self-confidence of the Harlem
Renaissance and the Négritude Movement of the nineteen-twenties to -forties. The artist projects himself
into the historical scenarios as an elegantly styled young
man accompanied by African sculptures. Titles such
as *Real NEGUS do Real Things* play on variations on the
names of hip-hop numbers—in this case one by Noto-
rious B.I.G., Negus being the title of the Ethiopian king—
while others, such as *Return to My Native…* refer to
classics of anti-colonial poetry, here Aimé Césaire's
Cahier d'un retour au pays natal, published in 1939.

1   Fahamu Pecou
    Real NEGUS do Real Things, 2012
    Acrylic on canvas
    178 × 137 cm
2   Fahamu Pecou
    Corps perdu, l'âme se retrouve, 2012
    Acrylic on canvas
    178 × 148 cm
3   Fahamu Pecou
    A.W.N. (Artist with Negritude), 2012
    Acrylic on canvas
    178 × 147 cm

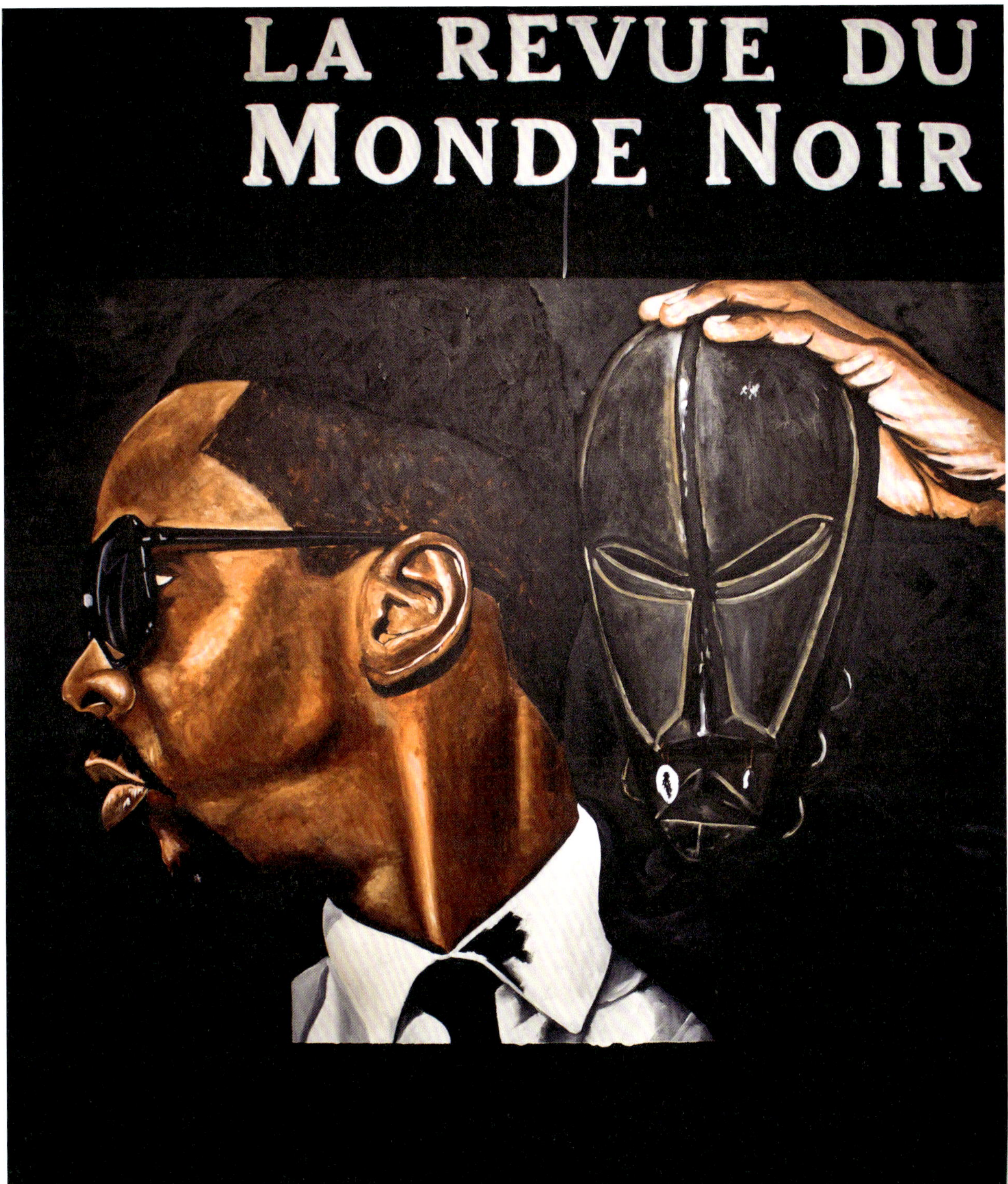

3

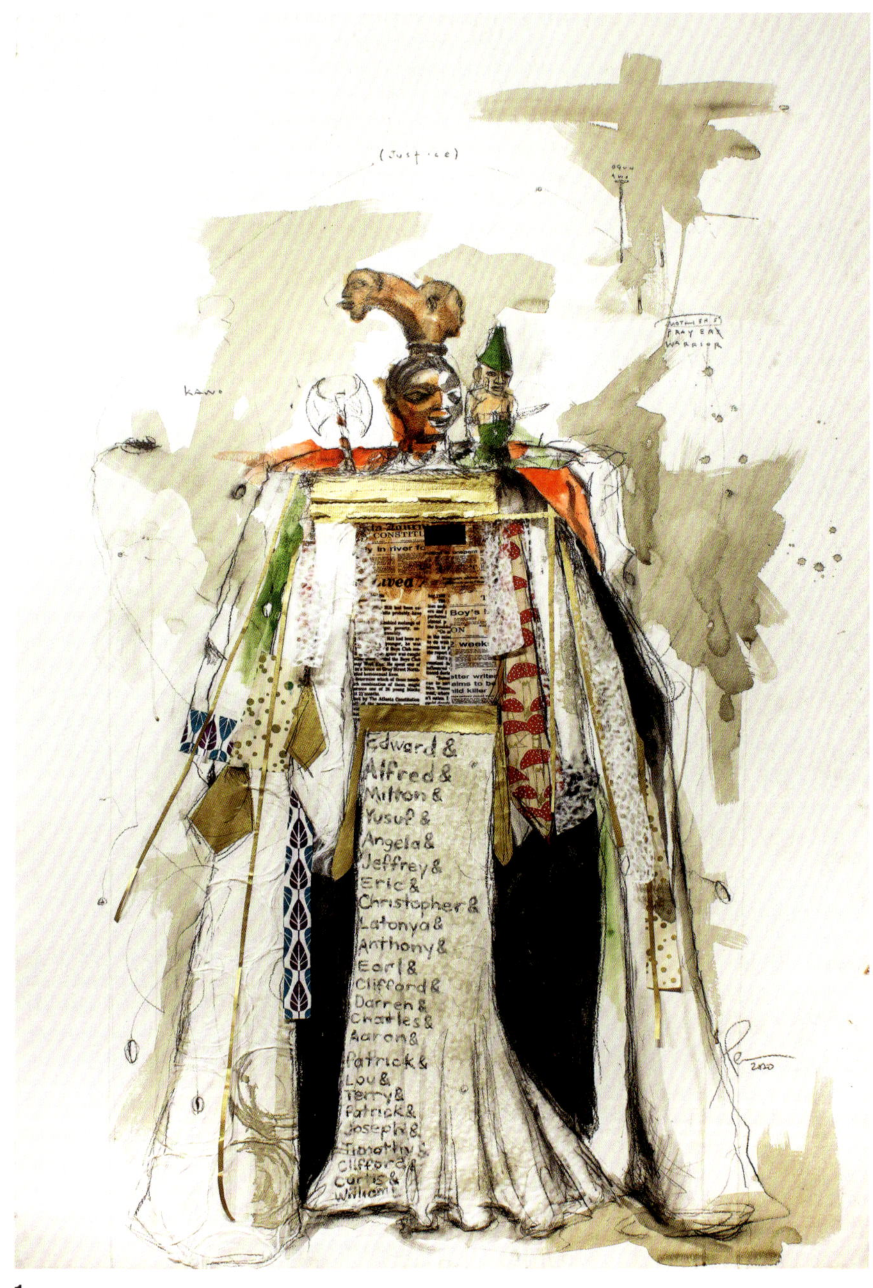

1

FAHAMU PECOU
DRAWINGS

Fahamu Pecou's drawings from the series *Egun Dance* are based on a performance that combined elements of hip-hop dance with Yoruba rituals for ensuring life after death. In the 2016 performance titled *New World Egungun*, the artist commemorated victims of anti-Black violence since the days of Dr. Martin Luther King Jr. He performed in front of Mother Emanuel Church in Charleston, South Carolina, where nine worshippers were shot dead by a white man in 2015; their names were incorporated into the performer's clothing.

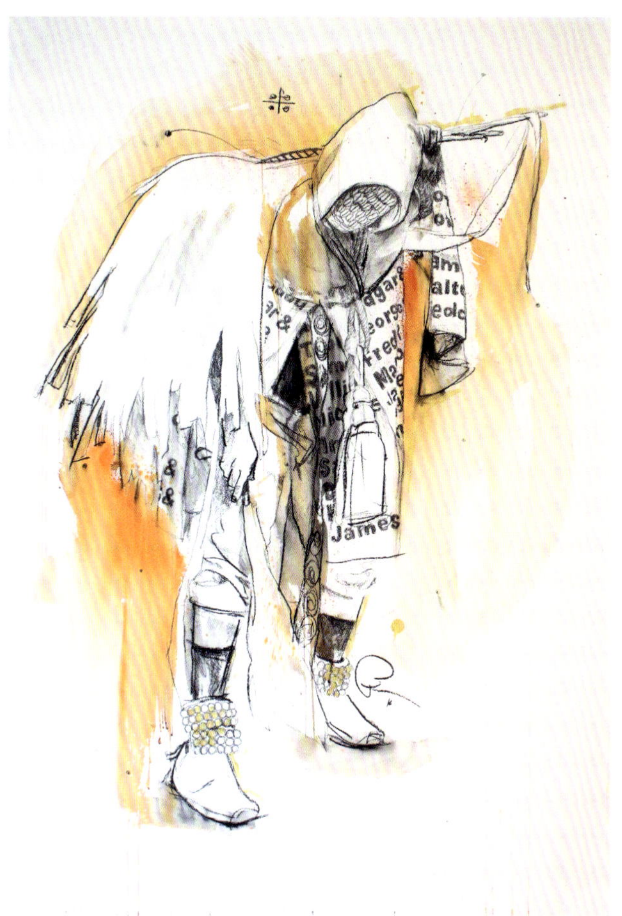

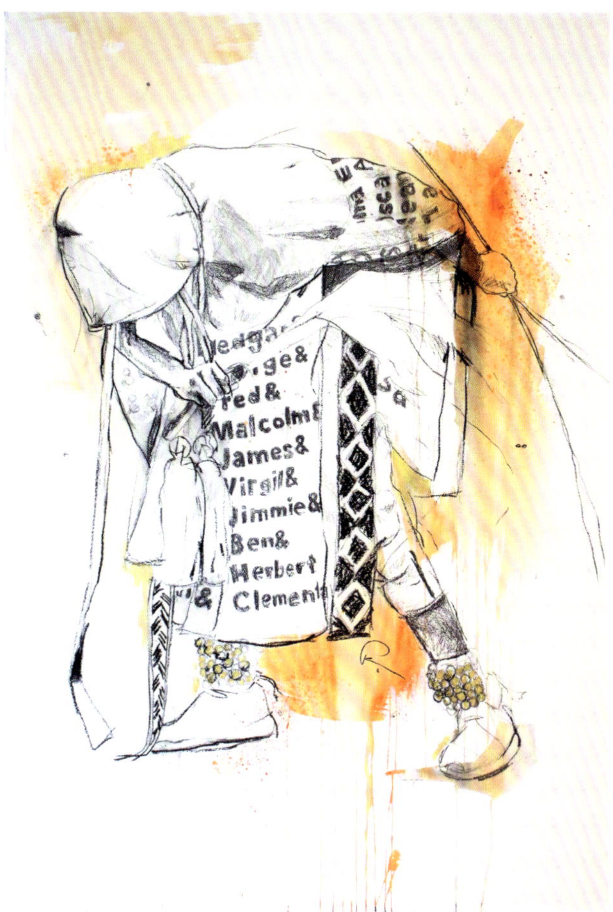

2

3

1   Fahamu Pecou
    Prayer Warrior Egungun, 2020
    Mixed media
    152.4 × 101.6 cm
2   Fahamu Pecou
    Egun Dance 02, 2016
    Graphite and acrylic on paper
    152.4 × 101.6 cm
3   Fahamu Pecou
    Egun Dance 04, 2016
    Graphite and acrylic on paper
    152.4 × 101.6 cm

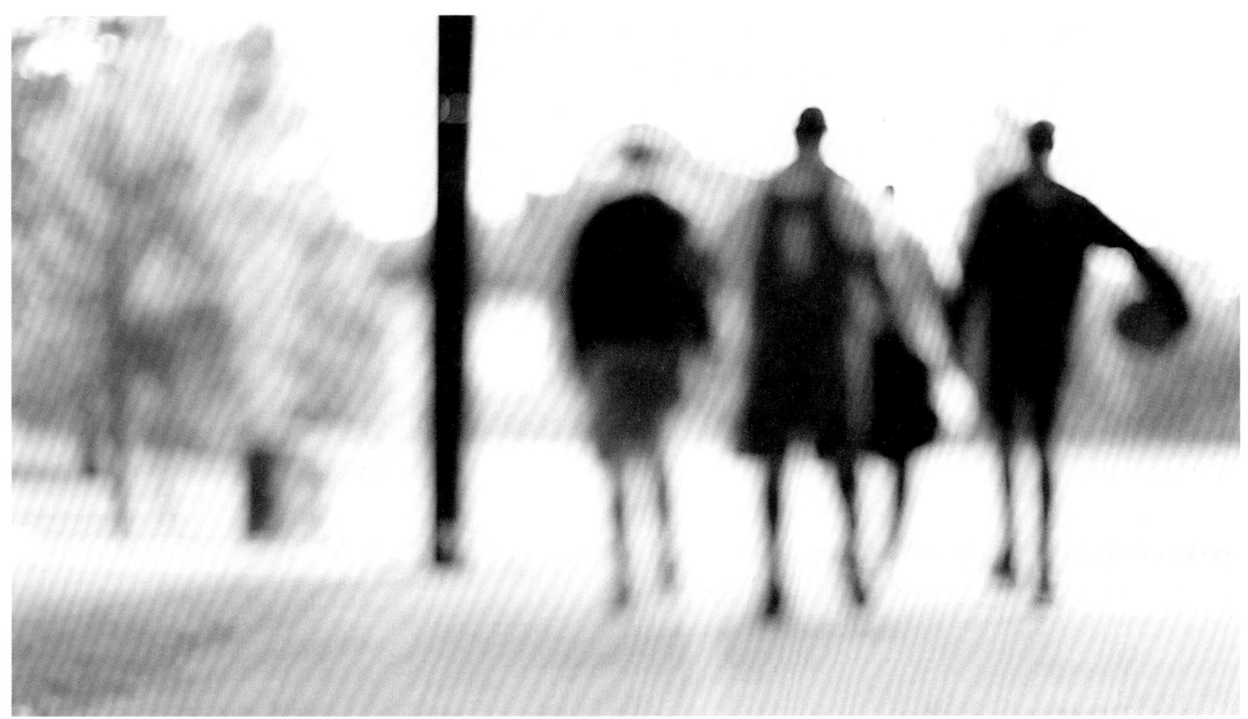

FAHAMU PECOU
EMMETT STILL
2016

The short film *Emmett Still* (fifteen-year-old Emmett
Till was murdered by white men in Mississippi in 1955)
likewise deals with the historical continuity of Black
deaths under conditions of white supremacy. It reflects
on the daily fear instilled in young Black men in the face
of constant murders of Black people at the hands of
violent police or self-appointed "authorities." The film, for
which the artist wrote and performed songs with rapper
Killer Mike and others, integrates excerpts from a
speech by James Baldwin on never-ending white terror.
Emmett Still confronts the racist death toll with the
redemptive power of Yoruba spirituality, hip-hop, and art.

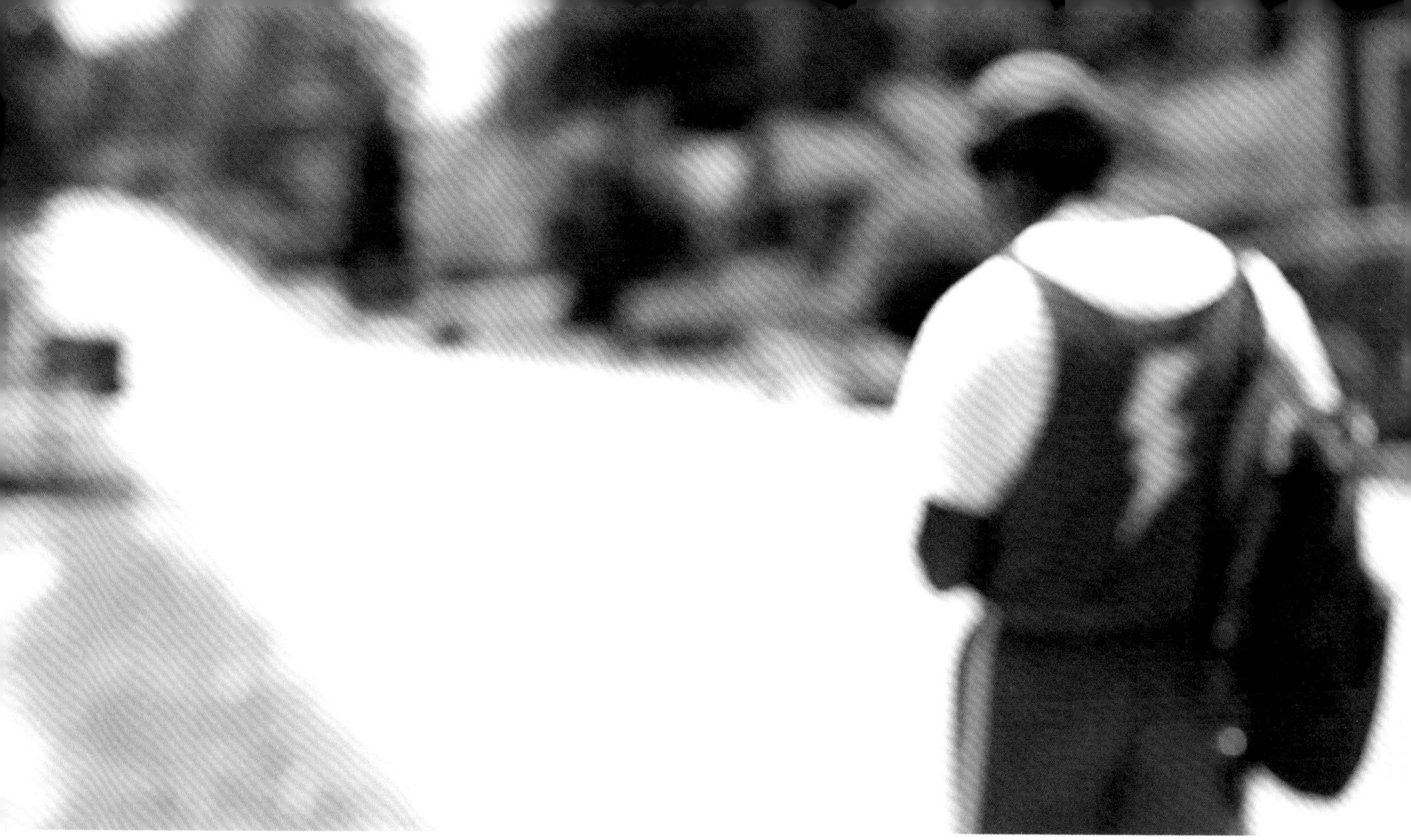

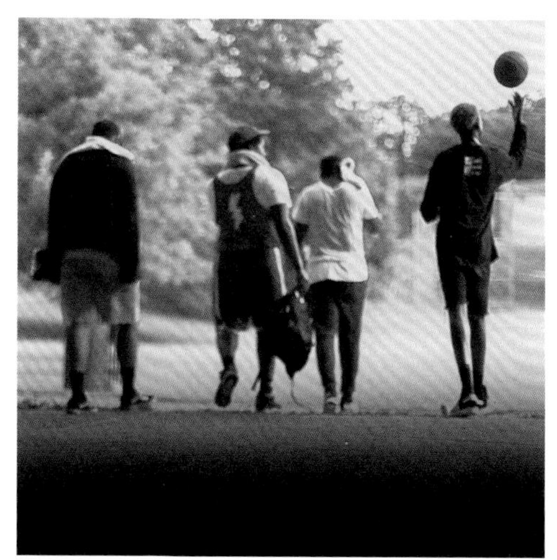

Fahamu Pecou
Emmett Still, 2016
Video, color, sound, 16 min

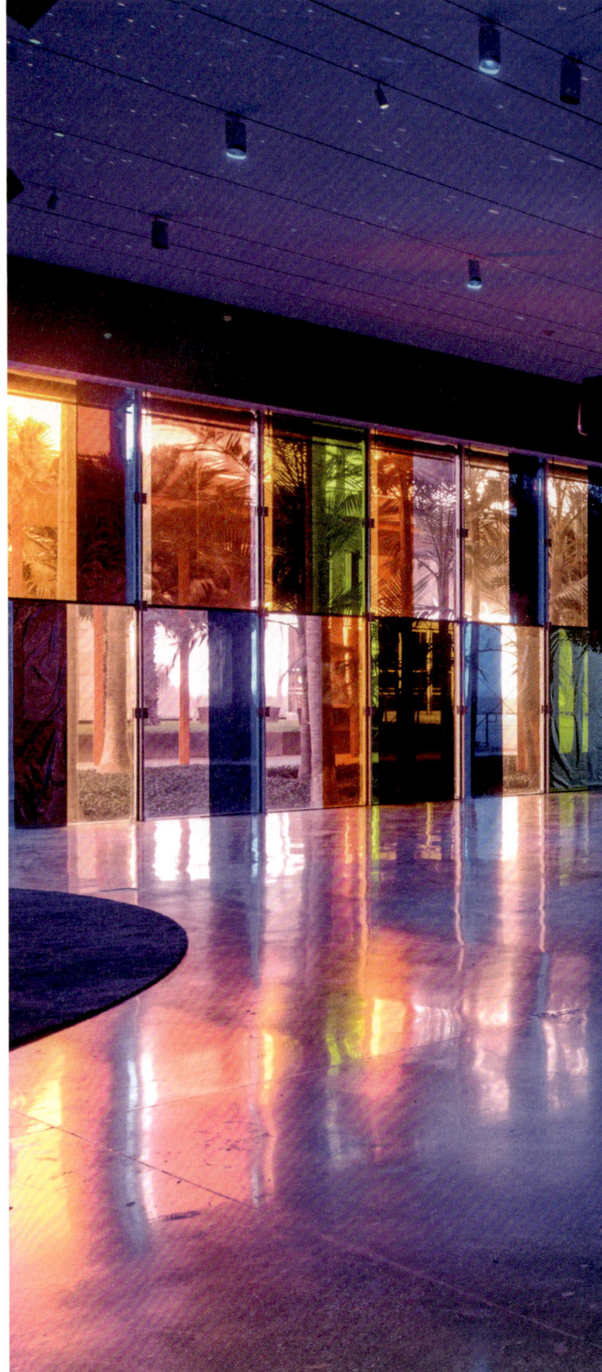

1

CAULEEN SMITH
SOJOURNER
2018

A group of twelve women in colorful robes walk at dawn through the sprawling grounds of the outdoor museum in the California desert created by African American artist Noah Purifoy. Holding up banners, the women listen on transistor radios to Afrofuturist music and spiritual texts by Alice Coltrane, as well as to phrases from the Combahee River Collective's 1977 manifesto against the multiple forms of oppression faced by Black women. The title of the short film refers to Black feminist Sojourner Truth, one of the most famous fighters against slavery in the nineteenth century. *Sojourner* is about the continuation of these struggles in the twentieth century and on into the present, highlighting successful community-building projects promoting liberation from sexist and racist oppression. In the artist's own words, the film revolves around "demonstrations for an abolitionist feminism, radical generosity, and utopian projects." *Sojourner* builds on a complex assortment of allusions that meaningfully connect historical and recent liberation movements—from the abolition of slavery and the early women's movement, to the intersectionally oriented Combahee River Collective of the seventies, to the abolitionist feminism of today—with radical aesthetic practices in the art and music of the nineteen-sixties and -seventies.

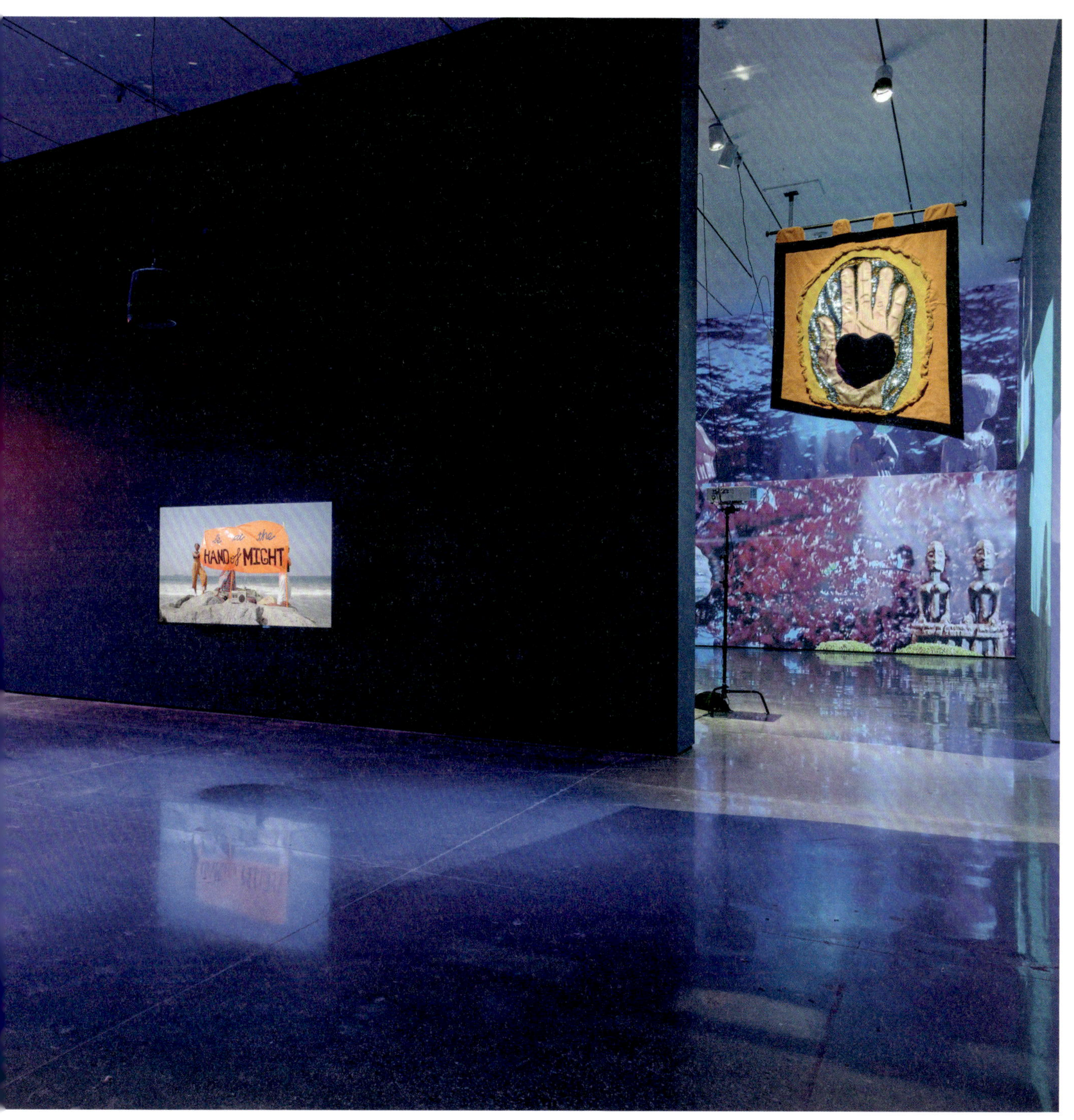

HAND of MIGHT

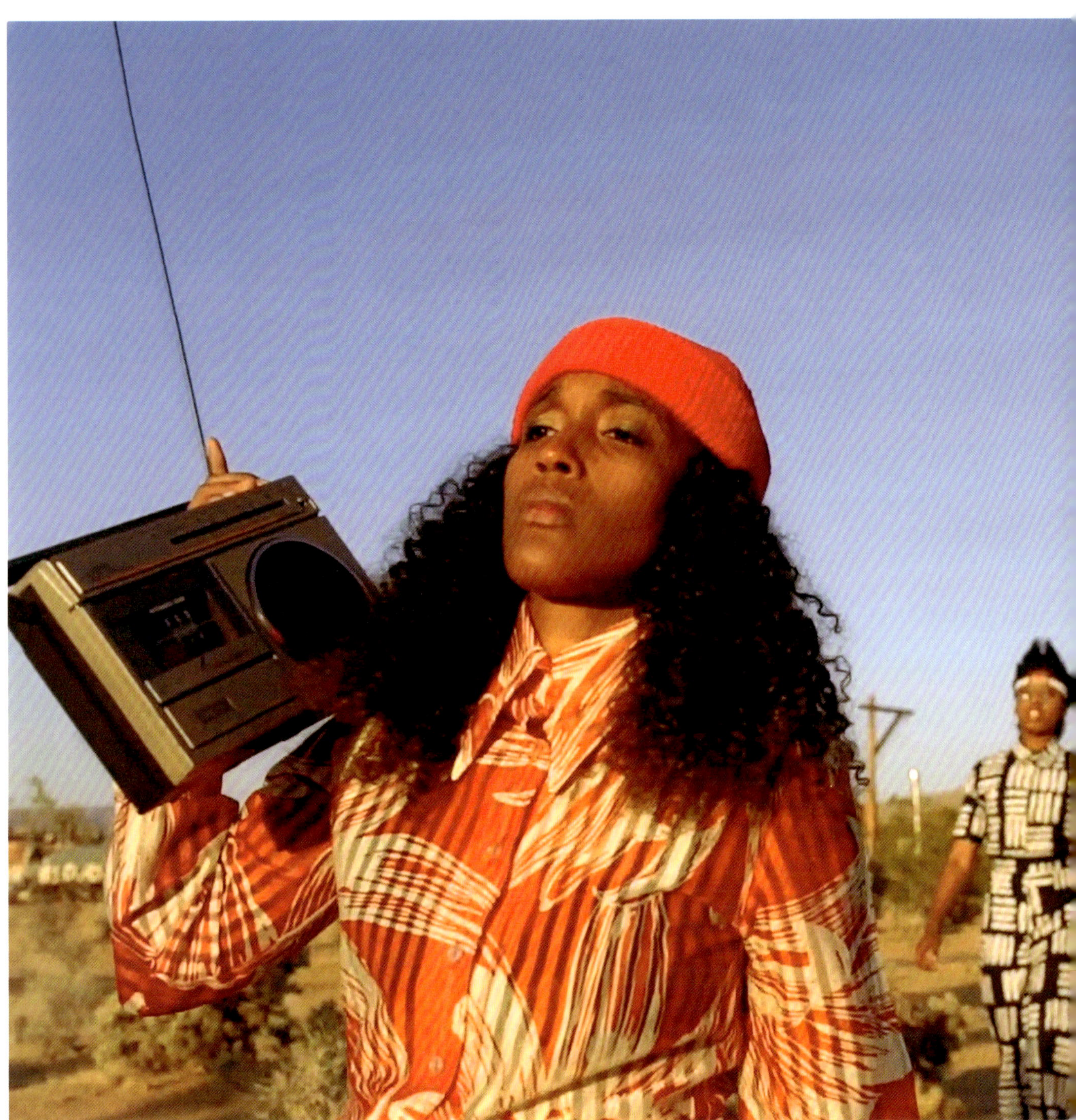

2

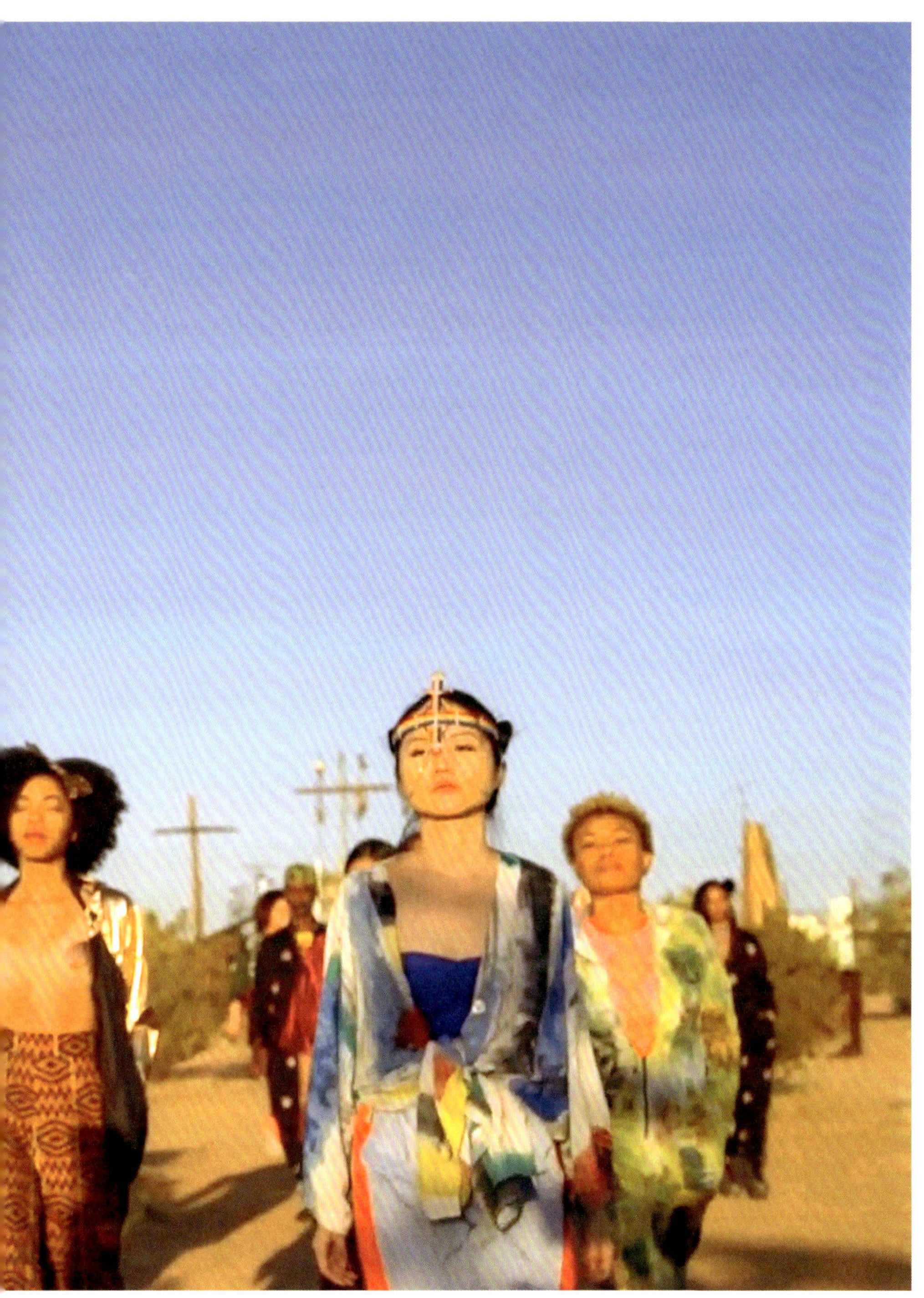

1   Cauleen Smith
     Sojourner, 2018
     **Installation view, *Cauleen Smith: Give It
or Leave It*, Los Angeles County Museum
of Art, 2020–21**
2   Cauleen Smith
     Sojourner, 2018
     Digital video, color, sound, 22:41 min

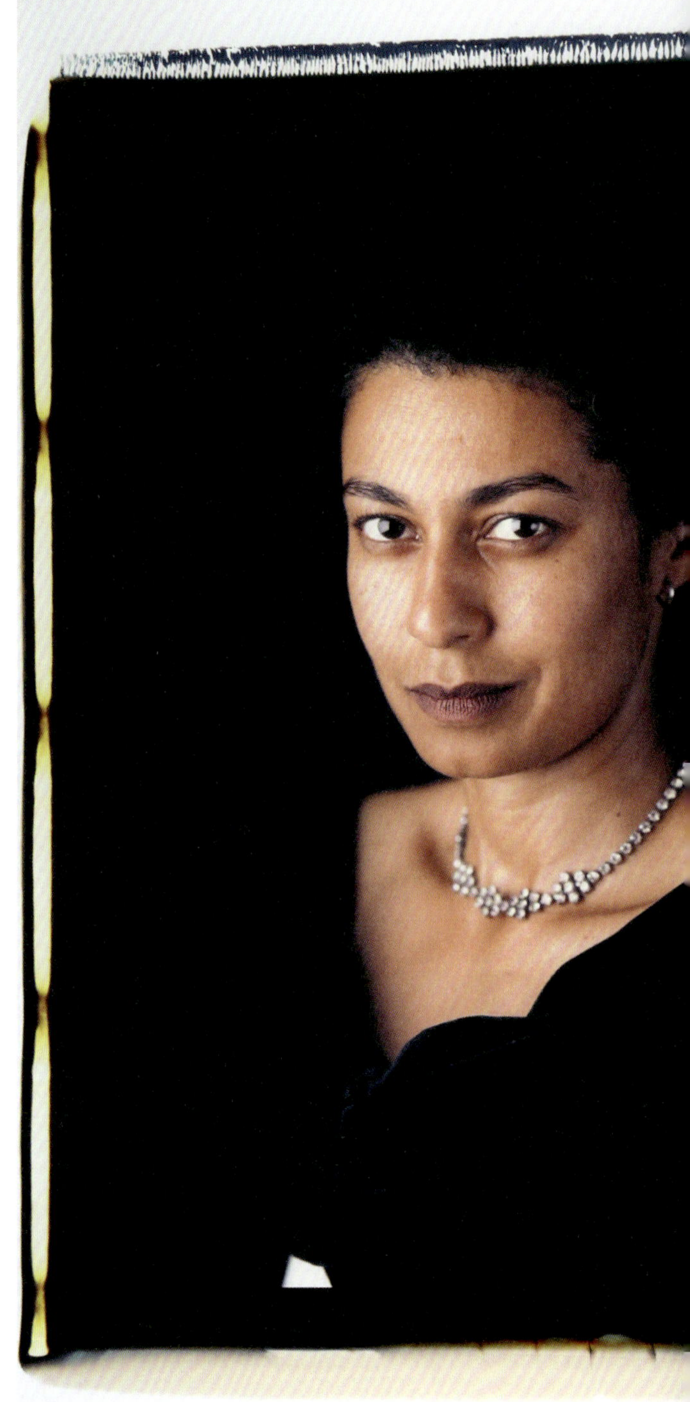

1

MAUD SULTER
LES BIJOUX
2002–06

This series of large Polaroid photos is among the most significant works produced by the Ghanaian-Scottish artist and poet. The title refers to the poem "The Jewels" from the cycle *Les Fleurs du Mal* (1857) by Charles Baudelaire, in which the French poet paints an exotic picture of his Haitian-born lover Jeanne Duval by describing her as clad only in jewels. Duval was also painted by Édouard Manet and photographed by Nadar and is usually cited in Western cultural history as the "muse" of white artists while little mention is made of her own career as a dancer and actress. Intrigued by this figure, Maud Sulter devoted many years of research to trying to gauge the scope of action available to a Black woman within the avant-garde art milieu of her time: "My ongoing visual fascination with Jeanne Duval began in 1988 with a visceral response to a Nadar photograph captioned *Unknown Woman*. There she stared at me willing me to give her a name, an identity, a voice. So for over a decade, I have been image making with her in mind." The photographic search for an alternative way of looking at the personality of her predecessor is reflected in Sulter's self-portraits in the guise of Jeanne Duval, which display a kind of lexicon of gestural and facial expressions evoking the struggle against the restrictions imposed by colonial gender roles. Sulter dons in these images various pieces of jewelry that are charged with stories of slavery and the global colonial economy.

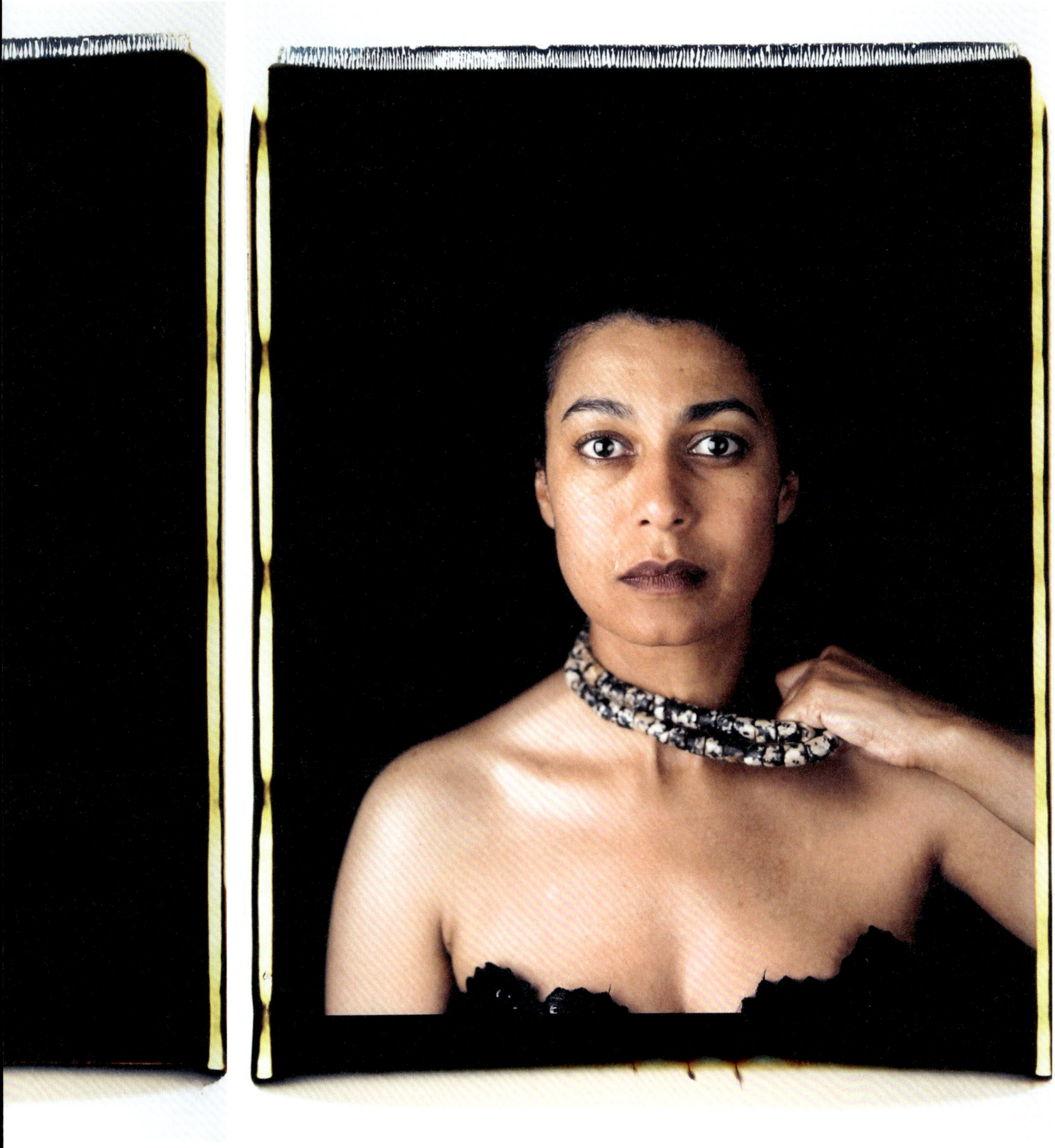

2

Maud Sulter
From the 9-part series *Les Bijoux*,
2002–06, 68.5 × 51.8 cm each

1   *Les Bijoux IX*, 2002–06
2   *Les Bijoux VII*, 2002–06
3   *Les Bijoux I*, 2002–06

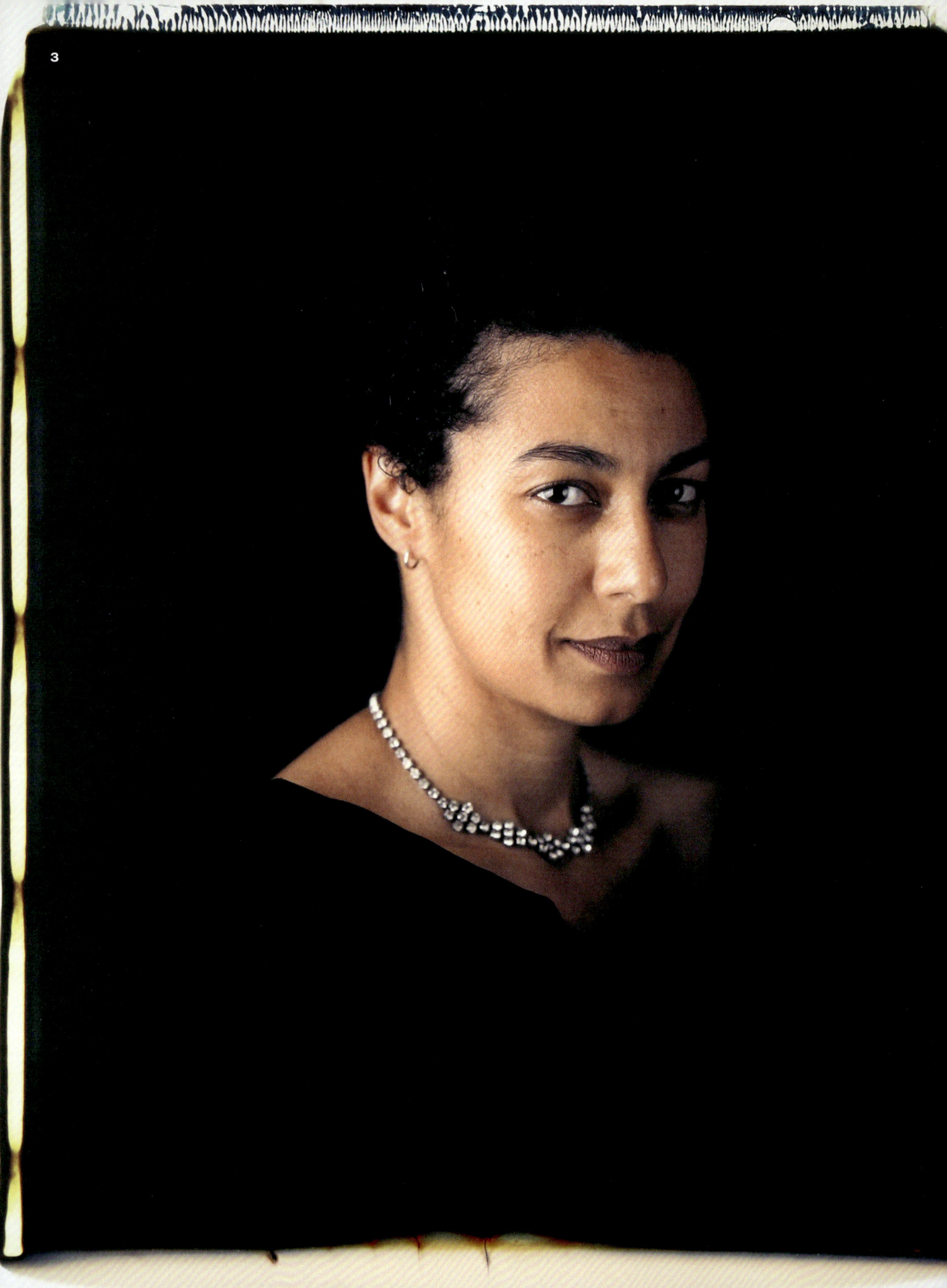

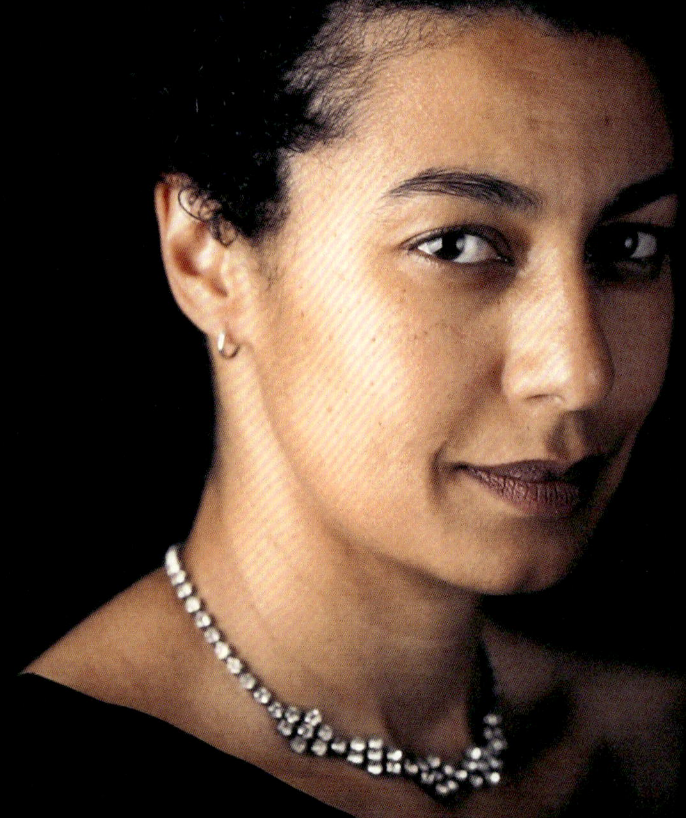

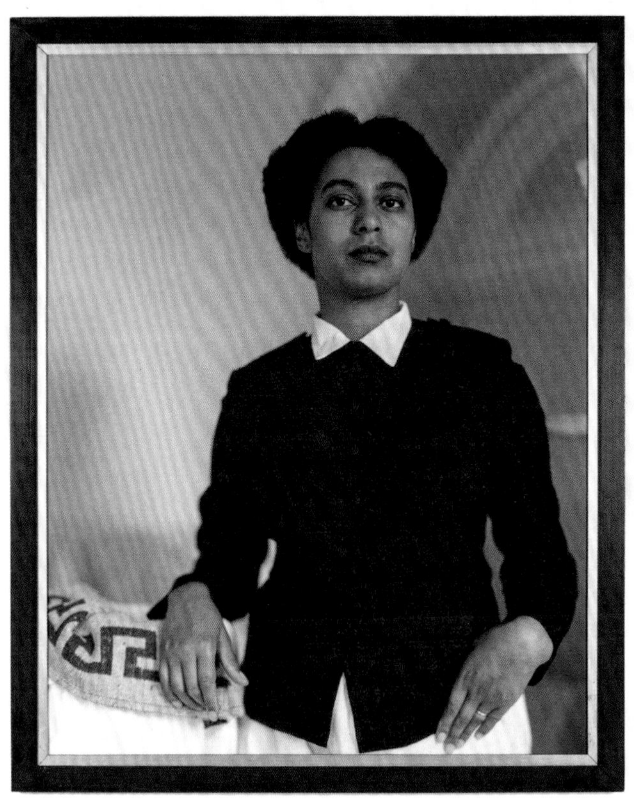

MAUD SULTER
HYSTERIA
1991

Hysteria is an early and significant example of an artwork that demonstrates the importance of Black artists of the past to the struggles of Black artists today. The Ghanaian-Scottish artist Maud Sulter belonged to the generation of the Black British Arts Movement in the nineteen-eighties, which came together in a racist society and an exclusionary art world to critically engage with colonial history. Drawing on her own experiences and aspirations as a Black artist in Britain, Sulter evokes in *Hysteria* the transcultural life and career of Edmonia Lewis, an African American and Native American sculptor who died in 1907 after living many years in Rome, whose work was devoted to the abolition of slavery and to Black liberation politics. Sulter's multipart work, whose title recalls the psychopathological studies carried out by Jean-Martin Charcot, which were influential for Freud's psychoanalysis, consists of marble plaques bearing the names of the protagonists, as well as large-format photographs resembling a storyboard that hark back to the style of nineteenth-century studio photography.

Maud Sulter
Hysteria, 1991
On exhibition with accompanying marble plaque, Street Level Photoworks, Glasgow, 2015
Black-and-white photographic print
148 × 116 cm

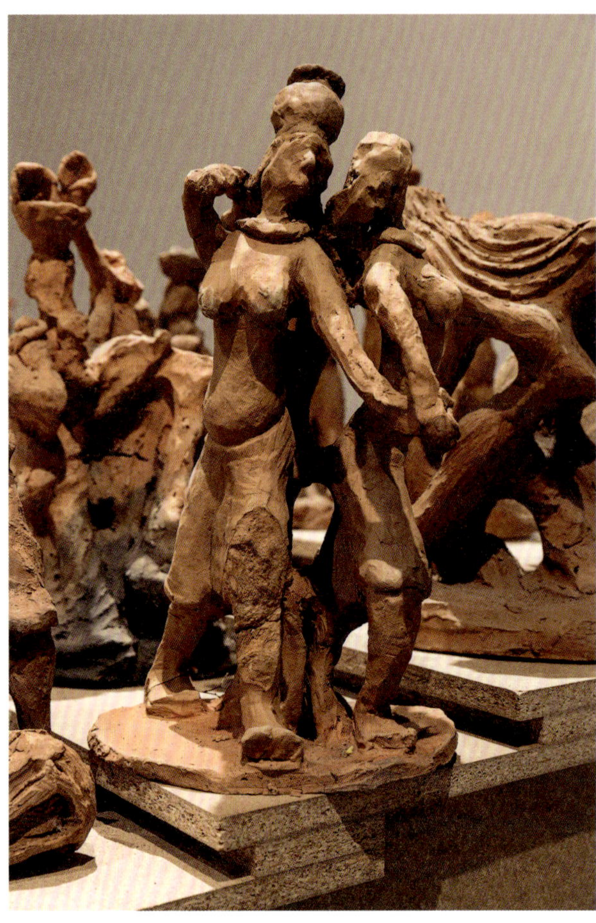

1

VIVAN SUNDARAM

Over the last twenty years of his life, Vivan Sundaram frequently dealt in his work with prominent figures in Indian modernism. From a personal stance of rejecting violence, the politics of exclusion, and the Hindu nationalist movement's narrow view of history, Sundaram focused attention on progressive and cosmopolitan artists from the era of the Indian independence movement. In addition to the painter Amrita Sher-Gil (1913–1941), his aunt, to whom the artist dedicated years of research, publications, and a series of digital photomontages entitled *Re-take of Amrita* (2001–02), the sculptor Ramkinkar Baij (1906–1980) was another important reference point. In the group of works *409 Ramkinkars*, Sundaram reinterpreted several sculptures by the Bengali modernist. Like *Mill Re-Call*, *One and the Many* is part of this complex and consists of 220 terracotta sculptures that Sundaram executed in a cross-generation dialogue with a group of young fellow artists. These pieces take their cue from Ramkinkar's monumental sculptures *Santhal Family* (1938) and *Mill Call* (1956), with which the avant-garde artist honored the political role of subalterns in the Indian struggle for liberation. "I passionately desire a connection with Ramkinkar," wrote Sundaram. "He prods me to make radical choices—as he did in his time, and so valiantly."

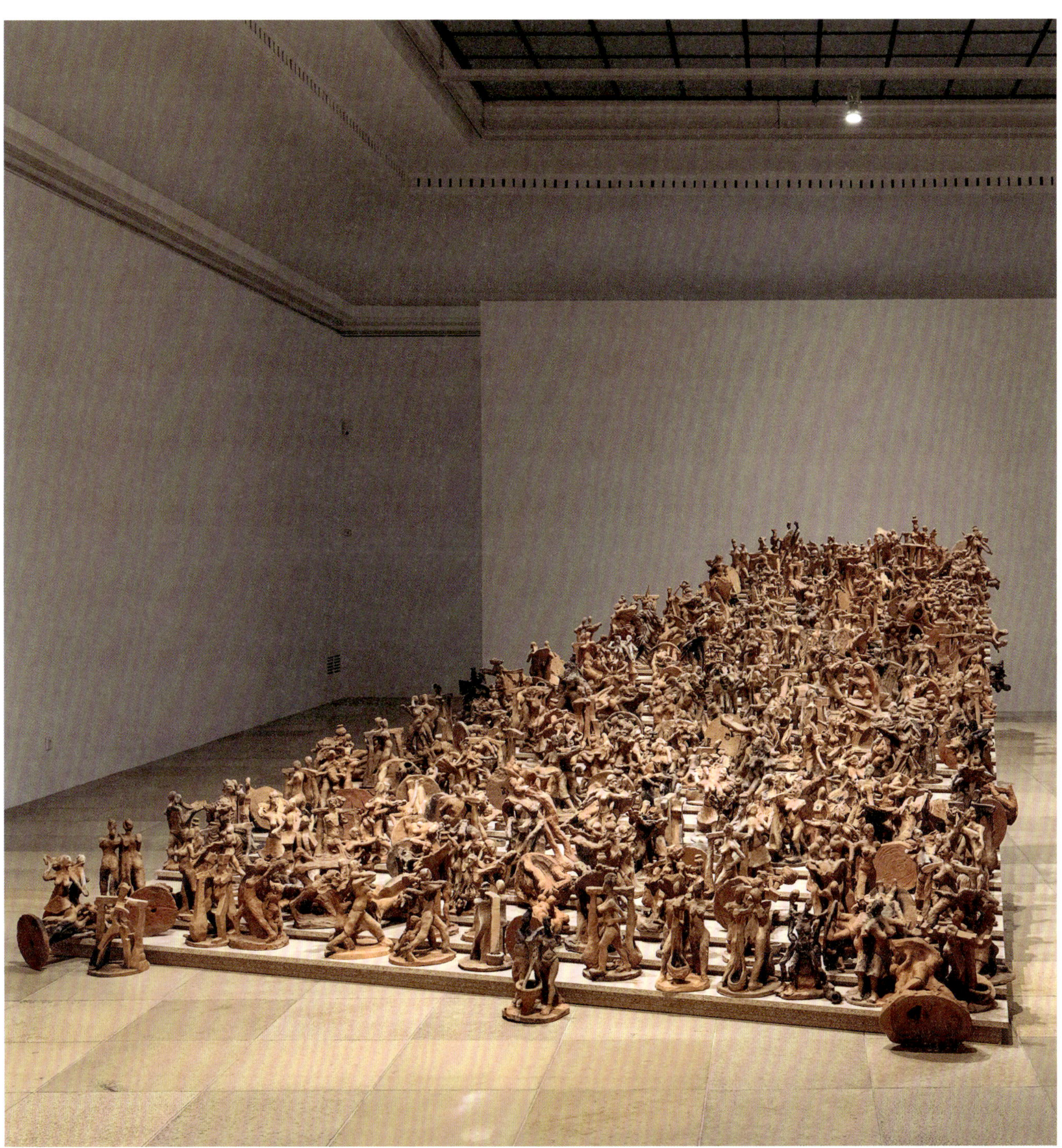

2

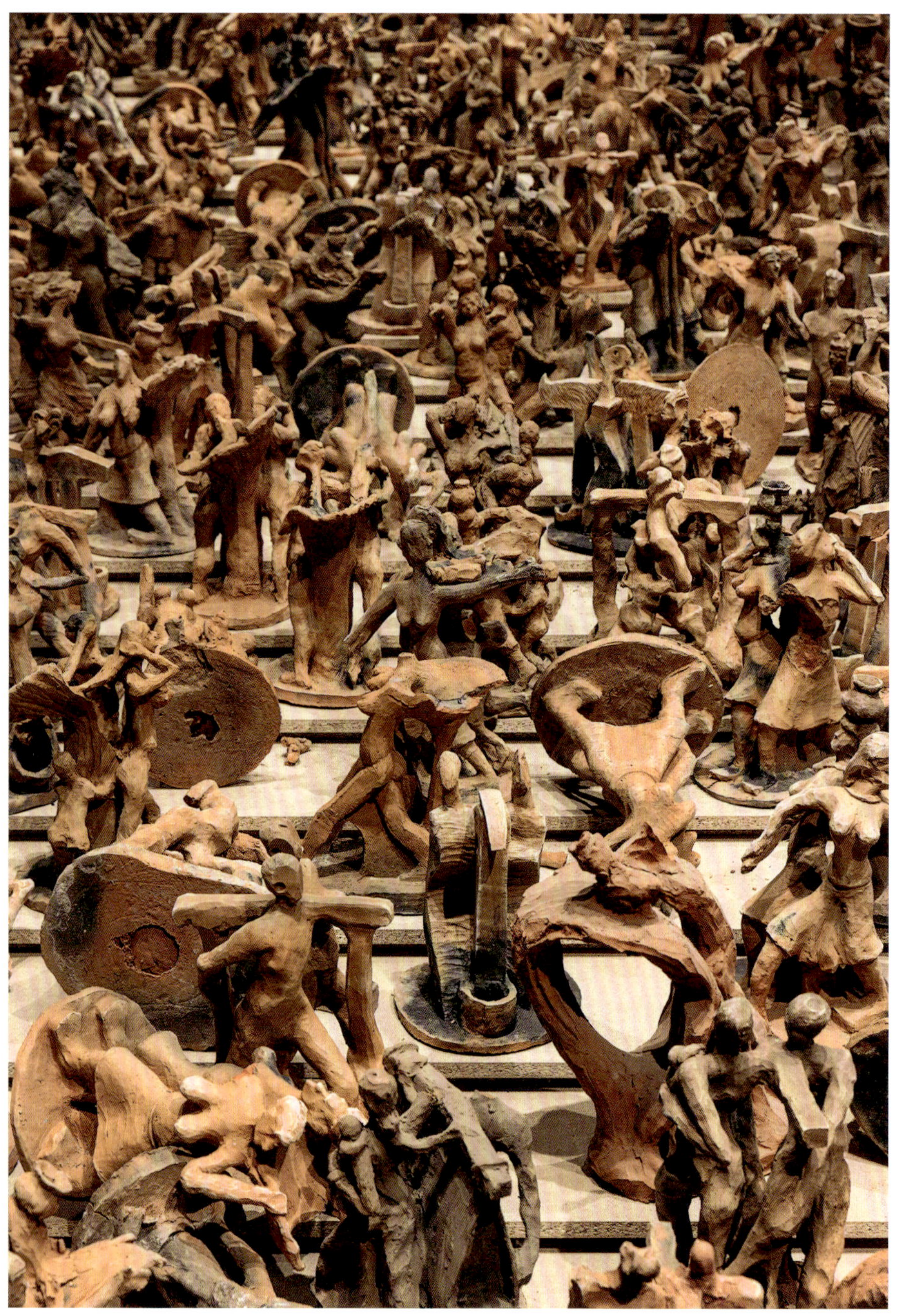

3

1–3 Vivan Sundaram
One and the Many, 2015
Terracotta figurines
Installation view of *Vivan Sundaram:
Disjunctures*, Haus der Kunst, Munich,
2018
4,5 Vivan Sundaram
Mill Re-Call, 2015
Wood, metal, rubber, enamel paint,
electric light
251.5 × 251.5 × 101.6 cm

134

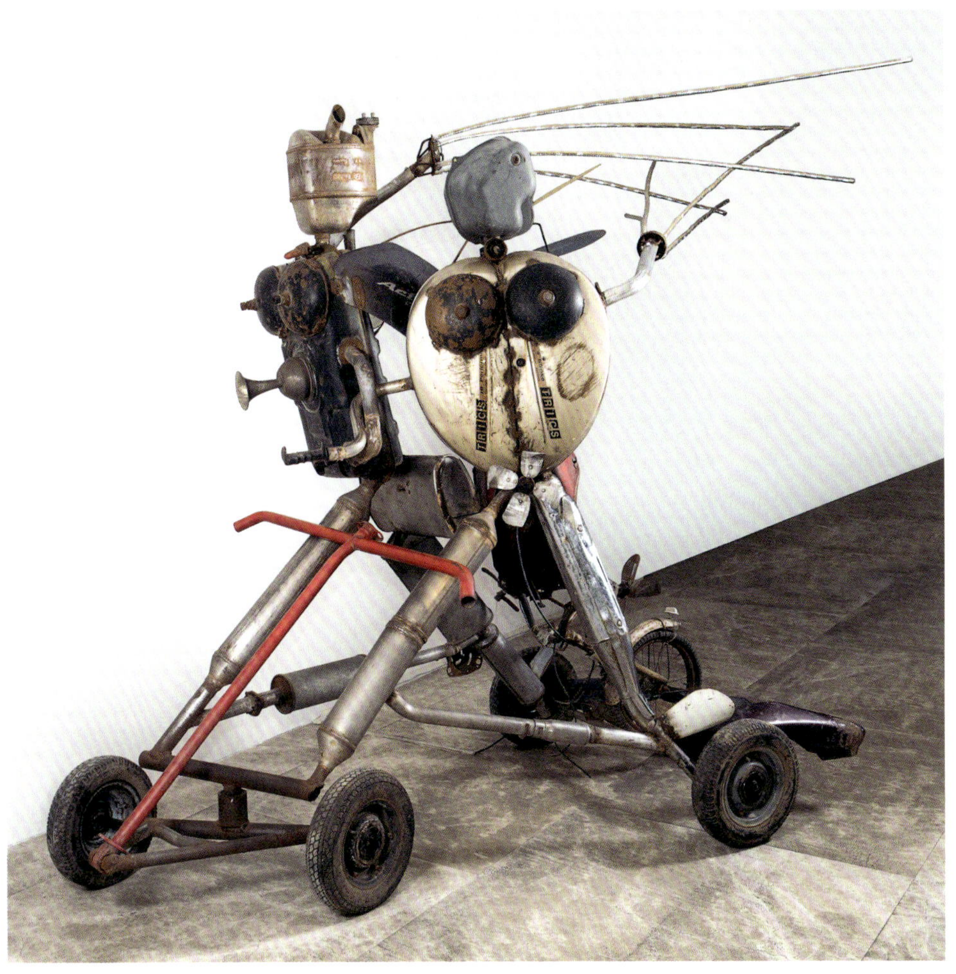

4

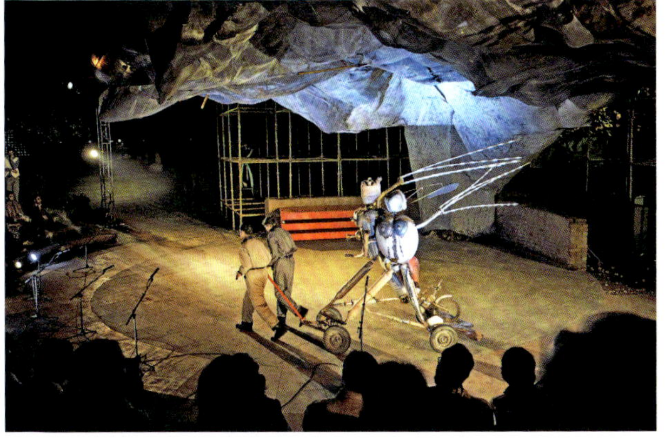

5

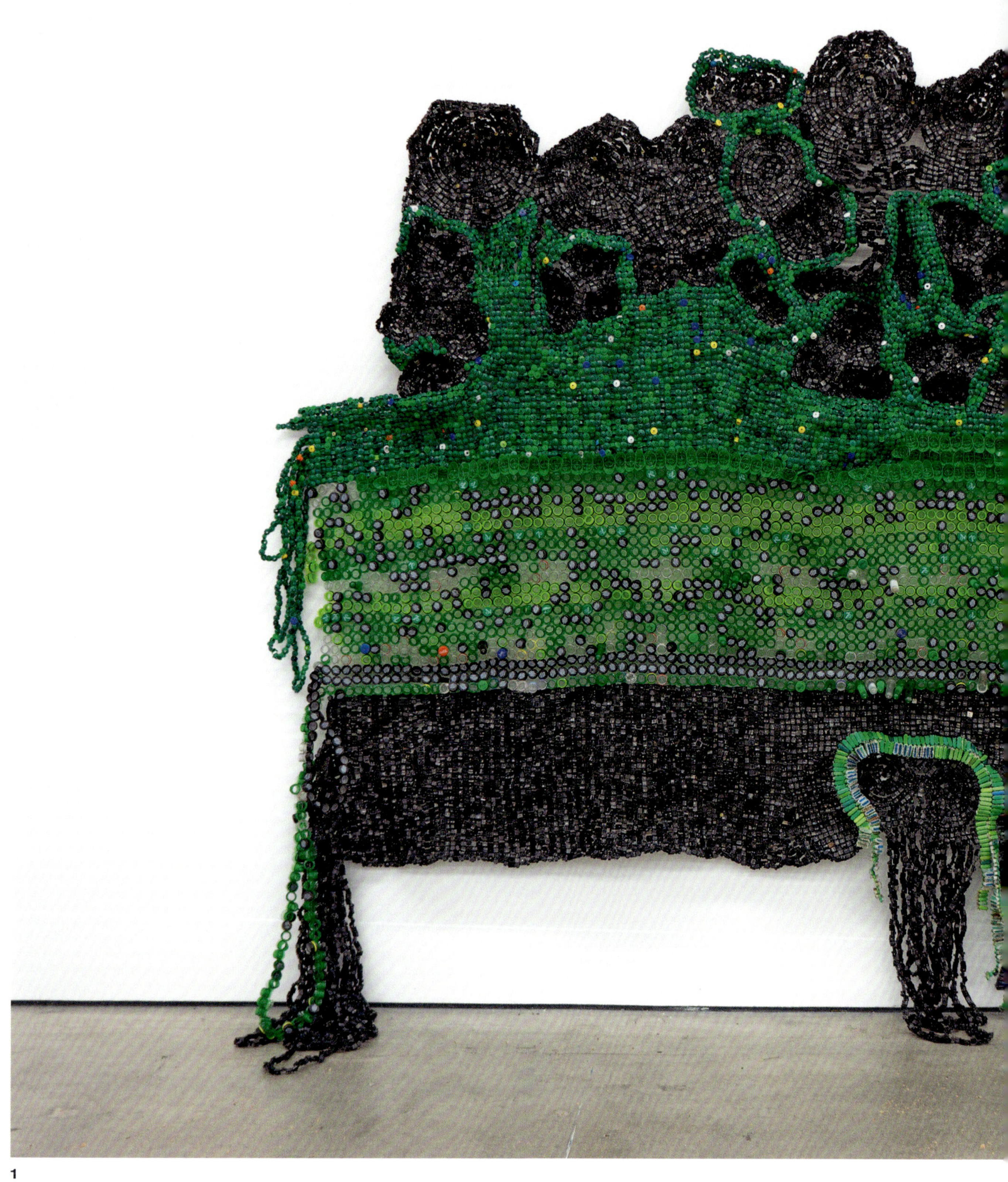

1

136

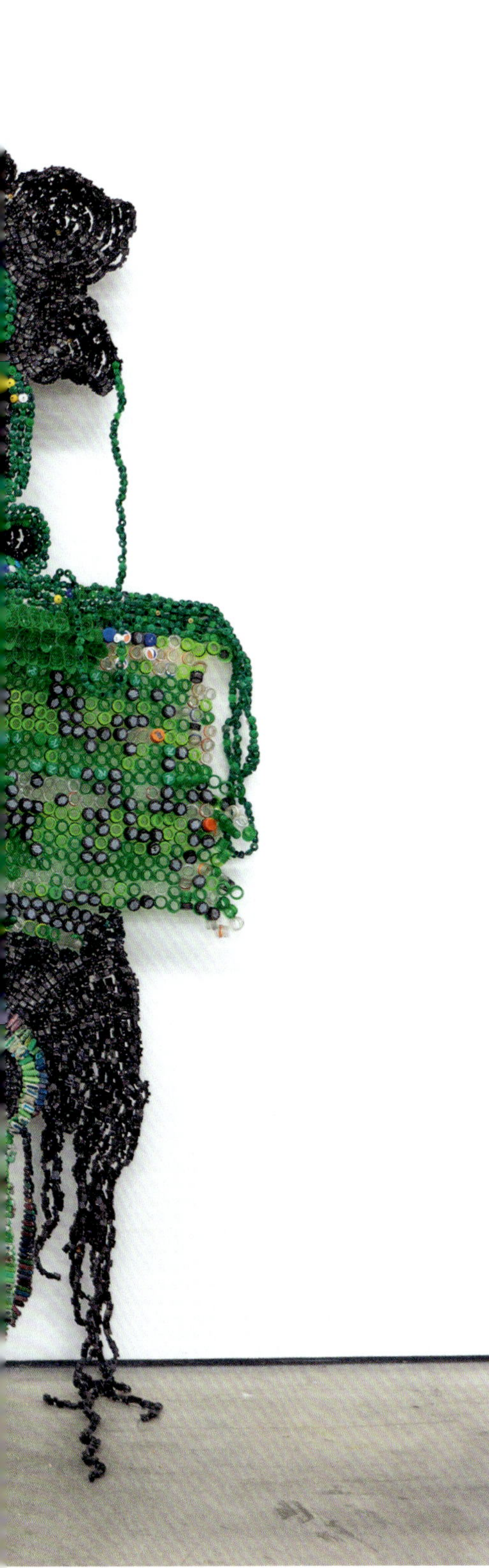

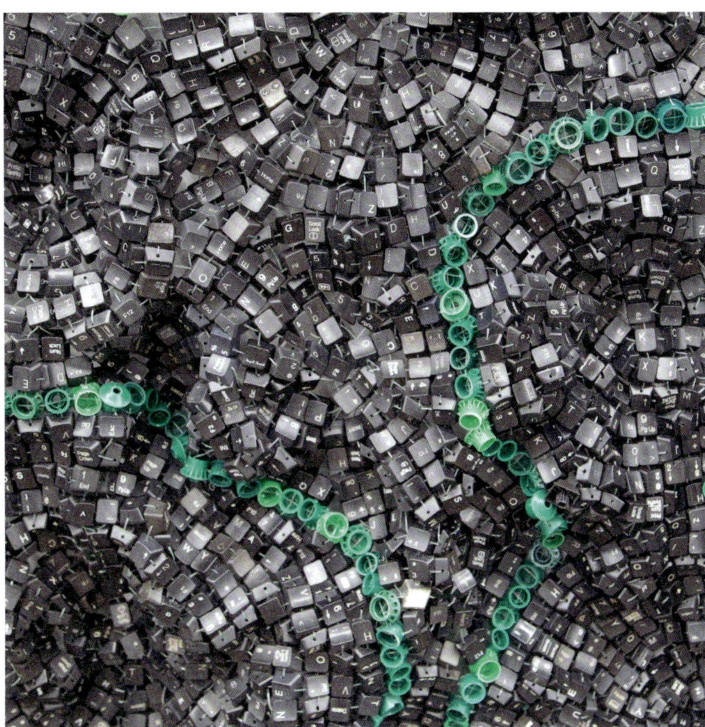

2

MOFFAT TAKADIWA

Moffat Takadiwa makes sculptural images from materials he collects from dumping grounds in Zimbabwe. Using keys from discarded computer keyboards and referencing anti-colonial thinkers such as the Kenyan writer Ngũgĩ wa Thiong'o, who published the influential book *Decolonising the Mind* in 1986, Takadiwa's workshop creates objects that offer a critique of the colonial politics of language and education on the African continent. From these elements of deconstructed European language, the artist develops forms and signs that in turn refer to the aesthetics of almost eradicated local traditions or to musicians such as Thomas Mapfumo, who played an important role in the liberation political struggles in Southern Africa.

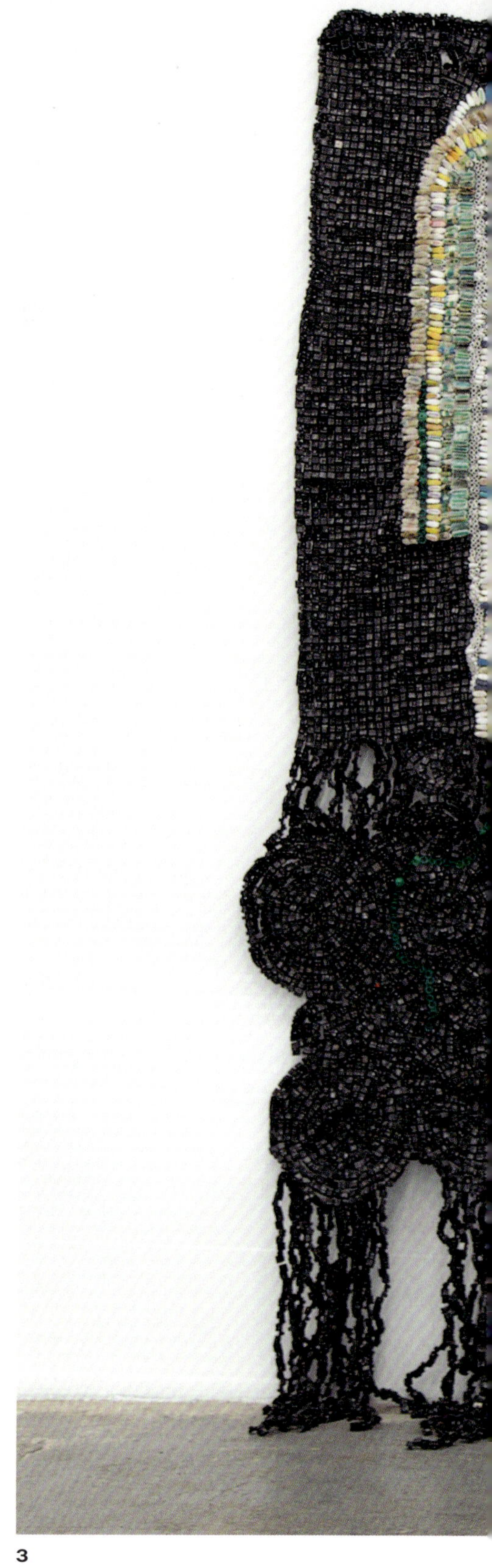

1 Moffat Takadiwa
   The Occupation of Land, 2019
   Found computer keys, toothbrushes,
   plastic bottle tops
   304.8 × 365.7 × 17.8 cm
2 Detail view of *The Occupation of
   Land*, 2019
3 Moffat Takadiwa
   The Afronauts, 2021
   Found bottle caps, computer keys,
   toothbrush heads
   310 × 280 × 15 cm

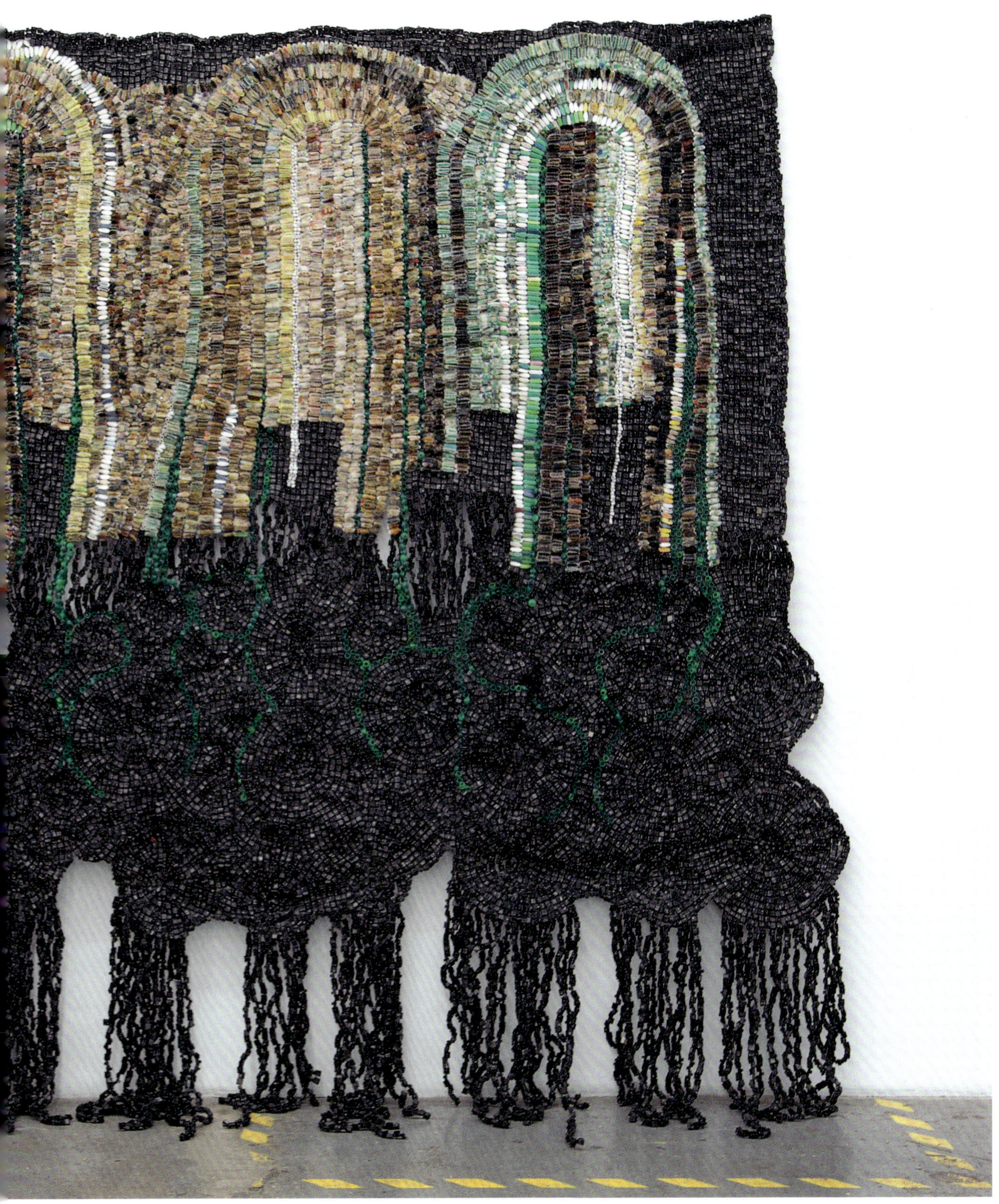

SALONI MATHUR

STRANGE TEMPORALITIES: INDIAN MODERNISM IN CONTEMPORARY ART

Atul Dodiya's striking composition in oil and acrylic depicting a ship at sea in the top left and a mass of onlookers at the bottom right sets up a dynamic set of triangulated sightlines through the interaction between sea, horizon, shore, and crowd. The painting references a historical photograph, that of Mahatma Gandhi's steamship, the S.S. Rajputana, leaving the port of Bombay for London in 1931, where the leader of the Non-Cooperation Movement participated in the second Roundtable Conference to campaign for constitutional reform in British India. Dodiya revisits this archival image by introducing additional elements into the painting, namely the whimsical gold and orange flourishes, and a bird motif that appears to converse with the ship. These graphic forms were derived from abstract swirls and designs that Dodiya found in the paintings and sketchbooks of the great Bengali artist, writer, and social reformer Rabindranath Tagore, a leader of India's cultural renaissance in the early decades of the twentieth century. And they create a kind of sideways dialogue between these two foundational figures of India's modernity and formation as an independent nation— Gandhi and Tagore—that is simultaneously lyrical, chimerical, and disruptive.

Since the nineteen-eighties and -nineties, Dodiya has been producing an almost uncountable number of artworks across many media,

forms, and scales that passionately investigate the figure of Mahatma Gandhi, an icon of Indian nationalism and universal humanism. Gandhi's iconicity can be situated firmly in the space between history and myth, in part due to the martyrdom resulting from his assassination in 1948, only one year after the nation's independence. His image is ubiquitous in the visual culture of India and relentlessly reproduced in photography, cinema, stamps, currency, statues, monuments, and popular forms of media throughout the twentieth and twenty-first centuries.[1] Dodiya has acknowledged a deeply personal relation to this legacy, having emerged from the same birthplace as Gandhi, the Kathiawar region of Gujarat, and having read his texts in the Gujarati language from childhood on. Although Gandhi himself is not depicted in the above-mentioned painting, the artist's inventive reimagining of the scene, with birds circling the departing ship, references one of the many significant historical events to which the anti-colonial leader was attached. Elsewhere in the series, Dodiya depicts Gandhi's famously diminutive body within public spaces, amid crowds of protesters or getting in and out of cars, to construct a dynamic portrait of societal relations that is also unsettled by the presence of shadows, silhouettes, and partial perspectives. While immensely conscious of history, Dodiya's re-presentation of the historic photograph here also disallows any literal

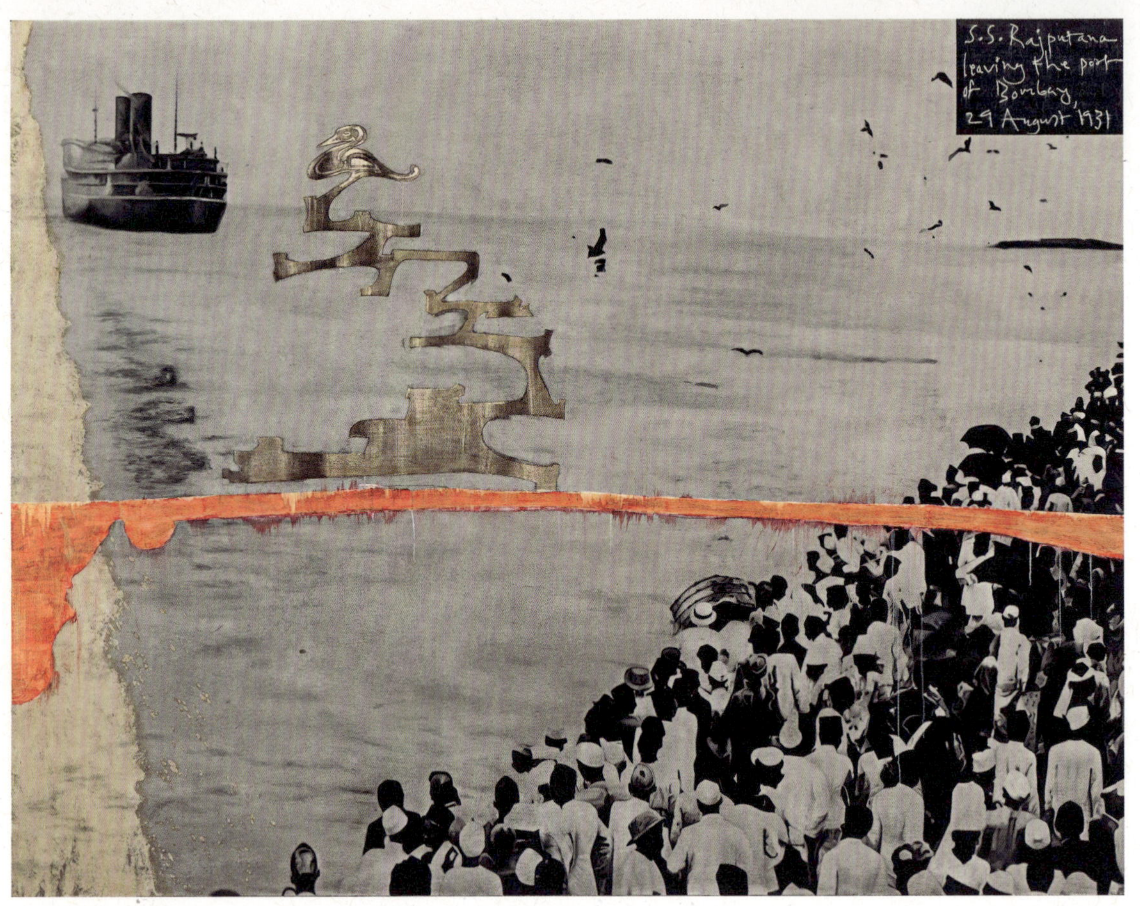

Atul Dodiya
S. S. Rajputana leaving the port of Bombay, 29 August 1931, 2015

or nostalgic portrait of the heroic "Bapu" (or father), a name that attests to Gandhi's paternal force that appeared in the title of the artist's 2008 series, *Re-Imagining Bapu*. Instead, Dodiya's return to such scenes from the archive prioritizes techniques of fragmentation and layering that make way for alternative glances, unfamiliar horizons, liminal sightlines, and oblique ways of seeing.

Dodiya's series of paintings, like the other India-related projects by Vivan Sundaram and The Otolith Group featured in this exhibition, betrays a distinctive kind of historiographic sensibility. Curated by Christian Kravagna, the exhibition *Avant-Garde and Liberation* features contemporary artists who consistently return to the contexts of anti-colonial and anti-racist liberation movements of Asia, Africa, and the Black Atlantic that redefined the world in the twentieth century. Significantly, their modes of investigating this political and aesthetic terrain do not reflect a didactic or linear approach to history, or involve a passive reception of a preexisting tradition. What we witness instead is a self-conscious effort to *actively mine* the decolonial past and its imaginative resources to fuel the needs of the present and future. This insight and its specific operations are not the same as the more banal claim that all artists turn to predecessors and antecedents to gain their inspiration. Nor does the compulsion to return to the most mythic dimensions of India's past—to heroic figures like Gandhi and Tagore, and to legendary sites like Santiniketan—amount to a series of mere utopist projections. On the contrary, Dodiya, Sundaram, and The Otolith Group deploy a range of formal techniques and embrace different mediums, from painting and sculpture to photography and film, to activate a more critical exploration of modernism's entanglements with decolonization in India. Variously positioned as both insiders and outsiders, these artists also differ in their relations of proximity

and distance to the histories with which they engage in familial, regional, and diasporic ways. They nonetheless share a commitment to a practice staged on the geopolitical ground of Indian history, and to a prolonged durational process that works to confront the stability of chronology itself. Ultimately, these investigations are driven by the tension between utopian hopes and the dystopic present that is India today, where the rise of right-wing Hindu nationalism and authoritarian politics has directly threatened the democratic ideals of an earlier era and left the future profoundly uncertain. Their projects thus point to the broader question of the role of art and its radical possibilities within the specific conditions of crises of the postcolonial nation state.

There is an increasing consensus within contemporary art that many significant gestures in the sphere of aesthetics appear to converge under the prefix "re-."[2] These heterogeneous maneuvers, represented by verbs like revisit, reenact, reinstall, or reconstruct, point to a certain intensification of activities involving ideas of repetition and return. Following the lessons of post-structuralism, and the Derridean concept of the "re-mark" in particular—a marking which not only marks but also redefines by marking itself as different from the first—a number of scholars and critics have linked the logic of the "re-" to critical possibilities and radical aesthetic acts.[3] Nicolas Bourriaud has proposed, for instance, that the artist today functions as a "remixer of realities," engaged in modes of recycling and reuse that inaugurate a paradigm of "postproduction" linked to the globalized culture of the digital age.[4] Hal Foster, in his critique of Peter Bürger's influential text *Theory of the Avant-Garde*, has similarly prioritized the elasticity of the return by artists from Europe and America in the nineteen-sixties (the neo-avant-garde) to the artistic movements of the prewar period such as Dada, Surrealism, Futurism, and Constructivism (the historical avant-garde).[5] In the neo-avant-garde's insistent backwards glance to earlier moments of the century, Foster perceives a "strange temporality," as if "lost in stories of twentieth-century art."[6] In the case of India, critic and theorist Geeta Kapur has consistently challenged the enduring hegemony of the avant-garde's exclusively European provenance in such theories and argued for a "partisan" view from the Global South to serve the story of artistic radicalism in much wider geopolitical contexts of the twentieth century.[7]

If Dodiya, Sundaram, and The Otolith Group appear to embody the "strange temporality" identified by Foster, then the unique character of their different projects also helps broaden the field of artistic modernism by multiplying its coordinates on the world historical stage. The experimental film *O Horizon* (2018) **(pp. 114–117)**, by the London-based Otolith Group, a collaboration between the artists Anjalika Sagar and Kodwo Eshun, is an excellent case in point. The Otolith Group are by now well known for their innovative "essay films" that blend both fictional and documentary modes while dissolving the boundaries between them.[8] This eighty-one-minute experimental film is concerned with daily life at Visva-Bharati University, the site of Tagore's experiments in education, which he founded in Santiniketan, a rural setting outside of Calcutta between 1919 and 1921, at the same time that Gandhi launched his Non-Cooperation Movement. Significantly, Kala Bhavana, the art school at the center of Tagore's vision, was also established the same year as the Bauhaus in Weimar, Germany, and, like the Bauhaus, it was conceived in response to the conservative legacy of the nineteenth-century art academy.[9] Both institutions sought to create a sense of community and purpose within a deeply intellectual framework, both rejected the separation between fine art and craft, and both sought to carry their utopian ideals outward into society at large. And

yet, Santiniketan's rural setting, with its vast stretches of barren land, earthy groves of palm trees, and scattering of small villages, could not seem further removed from the sleek architectural landscapes of the Bauhaus, with their radiant cube-like buildings designed by Walter Gropius and Mies van der Rohe. Nonetheless, the Bauhaus's modern industrialist sensibility and Santiniketan's primeval one would each exert a powerful influence on the successive generations of twentieth-century artists who flocked to their environs.

O Horizon does not take up this comparative moment in the global history of modernism, which has been examined elsewhere by curators and scholars in a well-researched exhibition and book project.[10] Instead, the film takes the form of an extended meditation, both visual and aural, of Tagore's ecologically oriented pedagogy, which emphasized a holistic, spiritual, and philosophical relation between learning and the natural environment. The camera captures the earthly beauty of the Santiniketan campus, its airy architecture and majestic banyan trees, and its outdoor classes held under the canopies of those trees, a crucial aspect of Tagore's vision for decolonizing education. The viewer encounters contemporary students training in dance, poetry, and classical music alongside the study of soil science and geology. The film pays an especially affectionate homage to Visva-Bharati's famous legacy of outdoor sculptures and murals by Indian modernists such as Nandalal Bose, Benode Behari Mukherjee, Ramkinkar Baij, and K. G. Subramanyan. At once poetic and analytical, historical and subjective, the resulting meditation is consistent with other projects by The Otolith Group that have returned to the aspirational struggles of twentieth-century Black and Third World movements for social justice. It also highlights what art historian Partha Mitter has described as Tagore's "environmental primitivism," symbolized by his romantic investments in the Santhal tribal community, the long-standing indigenous inhabitants of this rural part of West Bengal.[11]

The complex temporality that informs *O Horizon* is evident in the opening sequence of the film. The footage begins with a recital of "The Year 1400," a Bengali poem written by Tagore in 1896, in which the poet imagines his words being received a century later ("Today, in a hundred years …"). Invoking the idea of time travel, this thought experiment is one of several ways that *O Horizon* as a cinematic text manages to collapse past, present, and future into the immediacy of the here and now. Elsewhere, the image of Santiniketan as a pure, rural paradise is undercut by a forest fire, toxic plumes of smoke, the industrial commotion of a railway being laid, and the faces of students seen through the eerie glow of their cell phones at night. The portrayal of local Santhal tribeswomen wearing peculiar, other-worldly metallic masks while dancing to the rhythmic beat of *dhol* drumming is surely one of the film's most memorable scenes. Somehow riveting, poetic, and entirely enigmatic, the segment embraces forms of speculation and fantasy to reject the overdetermined history of primitivist imagery attached to the figure of the Santhal woman. If this long history of modernist projection onto the gendered tribal subject left her static, unchanging, and "stuck in time," then The Otolith Group manage to dissolve that terrible fixity by way of disruptive displacements and fantastical effects. Using the complex structure of film as a medium to enact such visual and temporal disjunctions, the artists present this legendary site of modernism in India through the dynamic framework of a century of change.

The medium of film, with its editing procedures of the jump cut or retake, also informs and inspires Vivan Sundaram's powerful *Re-take of Amrita* project from 2001–02. A more intimate and familial engagement with the past, the series is comprised of digital photomontages related to Sundaram's maternal aunt, India's pioneering modernist painter Amrita Sher-Gil.[12] In the series, the myths and legends enveloping (the biracial and bisexual) Sher-Gil as a foundational figure of modernism are subjected to unique forms of subterfuge made available to the artist through computer technologies. For Sundaram, the digital era enables a great deal: "You can shift to the playful, the provocative; you can lie to tell a truth. … There is a constant double-take or, in cinema terms, 'a re-take' of the shot," he explains.[13] Thus the technique of revisitation is used to "multiply points of entry and exit" and to enter the intricate entanglements of the Sher-Gil family and their cosmopolitan life journeys through the privileged social milieus of Budapest, Simla, Paris, and Lahore.[14] As I have argued elsewhere, Sundaram's "retake" project is best understood as both a visual argument and a theorized intervention and is perhaps the most iconic result of the artist's multifaceted engagements interrogating the mythic structures surrounding Sher-Gil.[15] The absence of an actual relationship to Amrita, who died before he was born, allows for a proliferation of fictive scenarios and highly creative imaginative acts, even as they expose the artist's unique burdens related to ancestral relations and the personal archive of an exceptional family past.

The hermeneutic method of the "retake" is also apparent in Sundaram's sculptural installation *One and the Many* (pp. 132–134), comprised of the multitude of terra-cotta figures. The assemblage is but one component of a much larger project involving an immersive theater performance with live actors that was concerned loosely with the work of the legendary Bengali modernist Ramkinkar Baij (1906–1980). Baij was a unique figure in twentieth-century Indian art: a painter, sculptor, and (less well-known) theater artist, he was connected to

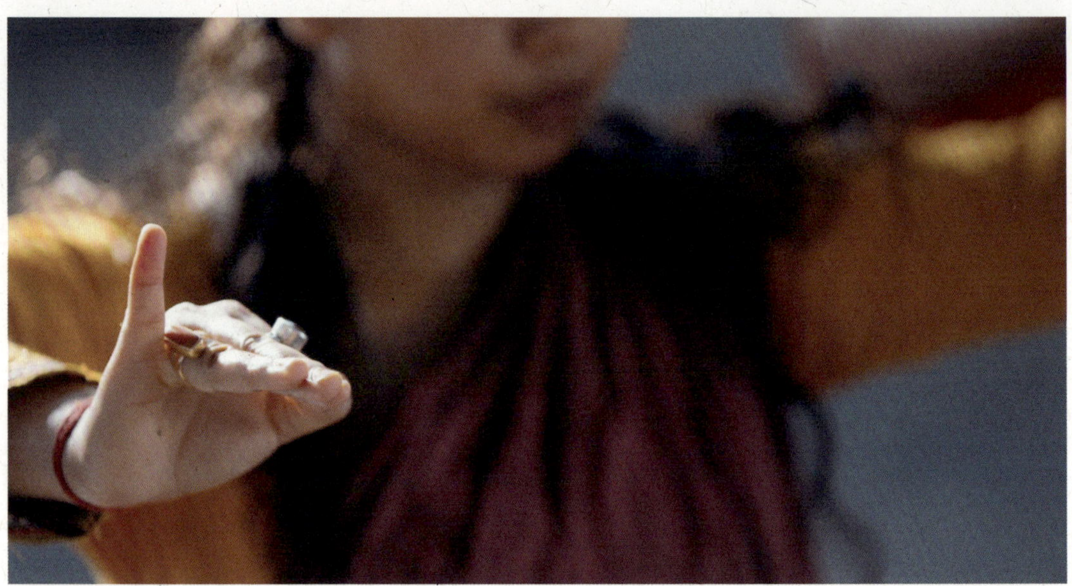

The Otolith Group
O Horizon, 2018

the esteemed institution of Santiniketan for most of his life. However, Baij's own humble background—he came from a relatively poor village family in the nearby Bankura district of West Bengal—along with his flexible experiments with form and genre, and his decisive orientation towards peasants and workers point to an ambivalent relation to the high intellectual context of Tagore, and it imbued his work with a subversive and iconoclastic edge. Drawing inspiration from Baij, Sundaram's return to this modernist pioneer took the form of an ambitious collaboration that involved two years of preparation with Anuradha Kapur, theater practitioner and former director of the National School of Drama in India, and three additional theater specialists and scholars.[16] The result was a two-and-a-half-hour theatrical experiment, held at the IGNCA (Indira Gandhi National Center for the Arts) in Delhi, comprising approximately ten nightly performances in the spring of 2015.

This complex, multilingual, and non-linear show was "conceptualised on a grand and bold scale" by Sundaram, according to one reviewer,[17] involving elaborate tableaus, props, and sound and lighting, both inside and outside of the gallery space, culminating in a one hour open-air performance. The project *409 Ramkinkars* derived its title from the 400 pieces of sculpture produced by Sundaram (plus the nine letters in Ramkinkar's name), which included recreations of such iconic works by Baij as *Santhal Family* (1938) and *Mill Call* (1956) (p. 148), depicting tribal and worker figures respectively. Sundaram's version of the latter, *Mill Re-Call* (p. 135), is a mobile industrial stage prop on wheels made from old manufacturing, scooter, and motor-car parts, deliberately *unlike* Baij's immoveable, open-air sculpture.[18] At the center of the project was the small army of terra-cotta figures, which Sundaram titled *One and the Many* (pp. 132–134), an installation which points in both form and title to the tensions and transpositions between the individual and the collective that was a recurrent theme in Baij's work.

The art historian Parul Dave Mukherji has noted the many layers of complexity in this project, in which Sundaram's sculptural assemblages explicitly reference and reinterpret Baij's work without any pretense to replicating its tradi-

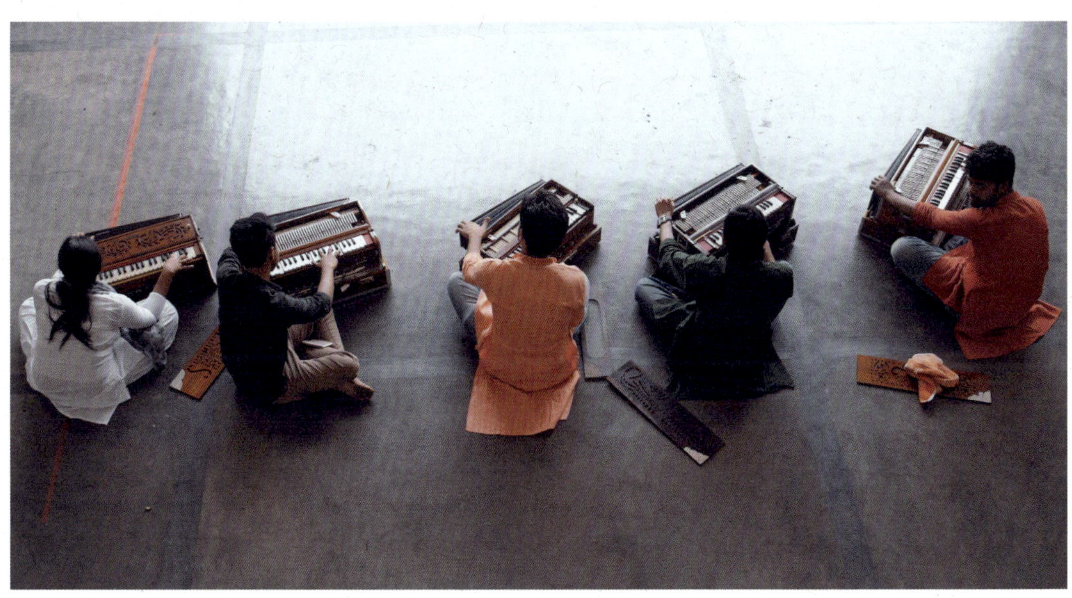

The Otolith Group
O Horizon, 2018

tional forms. Here, as she has stated, we witness a familiar archival impulse in which the contemporary is staged through "a detour to the past" and reanimated "around a figure that acts as a peg for a range of experiences from the cerebral to the sensual, for the now."[19] In other words, the artist's "recall" of Baij purposefully evokes the earlier "retake" of his legendary aunt, Amrita Sher-Gil, effecting some of the same temporal-historical disjunctions witnessed in that earlier project. In fact, *409 Ramkinkars* gathers together many techniques, gestures, and preoccupations apparent throughout Sundaram's artistic career that I have analyzed in detail elsewhere: a compulsion towards history and archives, towards repurposed materials and multimedia assemblages, and towards collaborative projects and relational engagements.[20] Simultaneously pointing backward and forward in time, inward to an individual figure and outward onto a vast spectrum of repeating issues and themes, *409 Ramkinkars* was both a powerful collaboration and a kind of elliptical, polyphonic, and reverberative occasion, whose structure and meaning will continue to emerge in the afterlife of its multiple texts.

As the examples of Sundaram, Dodiya, and The Otolith Group convey, the modes and methods of revisiting India's modern past take many different forms in contemporary art. Deploying film, photography, sculpture, and painting, these artists display a deep historical consciousness that involves mining the resources of the past from the vantage point of the uncertainties of the present. Their self-conscious reinscriptions of twentieth-century history in India help to challenge the space between history and myth, in part by confronting the sanctified ground of the latter with more radical kinds of imaginary acts. These artists refuse the master narratives of the nation state in favor of micro-narratives, fragmentary forms, elliptical gestures, and anachronistic acts. They reanimate history to energize the present, and offer tactical interventions that alter ways of seeing. Finally, they do not passively inherit an aesthetic tradition presumed to preexist as the "decolonial avant-garde." They actively seek the experimental agency of the past and reactivate this agency for a more socially just future.

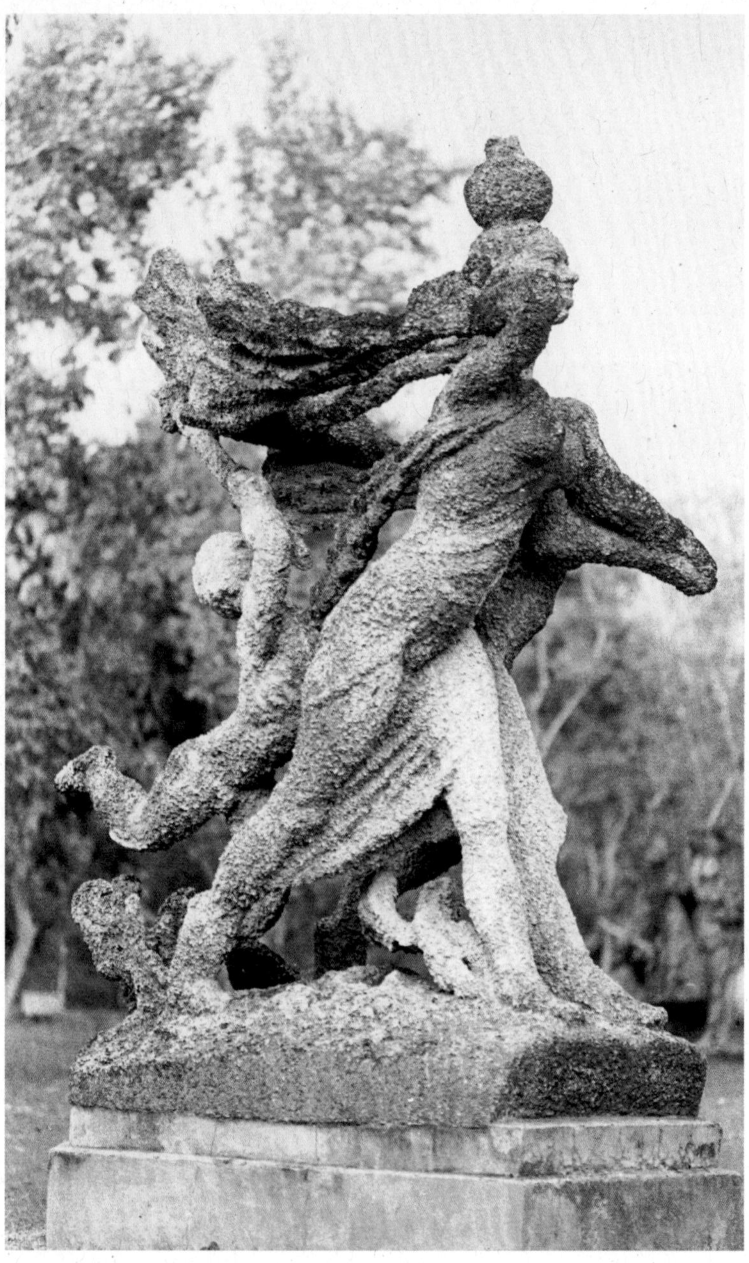

Ramkinkar Baij, *Mill Call*, 1956
Photograph by artist Jyoti Bhatt in 1974

1   Sumathi Ramaswamy, *Gandhi in the Gallery: The Art of Disobedience* (New Delhi: Roli Books, 2020); Gayatri Sinha, "The Afterlives of Images: The Contested Legacies of Gandhi in Art and Popular Culture," *South Asian Studies* 29, no. 1, 2013, pp. 111–129.

2   Martha Buskirk, Amelia Jones, and Caroline Jones, "The Year in 'Re-'," *Artforum* 52, no. 4 (December 2013).

3   Jacques Derrida, "The Double Session," in *Dissemination* (Chicago: University of Chicago Press, 1981).

4   Nicolas Bourriaud, *Postproduction* (New York: Lukas and Sternberg, 2002), p. 44.

5   Hal Foster, *The Return of the Real: The Avant-Garde at the End of the Century* (Cambridge, MA: MIT Press, 1996); see also Peter Bürger, *Theory of the Avant-Garde* (Minneapolis: University of Minnesota Press, 1984).

6   Foster, p. x.

7   Geeta Kapur, *When Was Modernism: Essays on Contemporary Cultural Practice in India* (New Delhi: Tulika Books, 2001); Kapur, "Proposition Avant-Garde: A View from the South," *Art Journal* 77, no. 1 (Spring 2018), pp. 87–89; Saloni Mathur, "Ends and Means: A Conversation with Geeta Kapur," *October* 171 (Winter 2020), pp. 115–138.

8   See T. J. Demos, *The Migrant Image: The Art and Politics of Documentary during Global Crisis* (Durham, NC: Duke University Press, 2013).

9   Regina Bittner and Kathrin Rhomberg, eds., *The Bauhaus in Calcutta: An Encounter of the Cosmopolitan Avant-Garde* (Ostfildern: Hatje-Cantz, 2013).

10 Ibid.

11 Partha Mitter, *The Triumph of Modernism: India's Artists and the Avant-Garde, 1922–1947* (London: Reaktion Books, 2007), p. 78.

12 Sher-Gil's unusual biography has been elaborated in detail elsewhere. See the Tate Modern exhibition catalogue *Amrita Sher-Gil: An Indian Artist Family of the Twentieth Century* (London and Munich: Schirmer/Mosel, 2007); Yasodhara Dalmia, *Amrita Sher-Gil: A Life* (New Delhi: Penguin, 2006); Vivan Sundaram, ed., *Amrita Sher-Gil: A Self-Portrait in Letters and Writings*, 2 vols. (New Delhi: Tulika Books, 2010); and *Umrao Singh Sher-Gil: His Misery and his Manuscript*, with texts by Vivan Sundaram and Deepak Ananth (New Delhi: Photoink, 2008).

13 Vivan Sundaram, "Recycling Photographs," in James Elkins, ed., *Photography Theory* (London: Routledge, 2007), p. 338.

14 Vivan Sundaram, *Re-take of Amrita: Digital Photomontages* (New Delhi: Tulika Books, 2001), p. 5.

15 Saloni Mathur, *A Fragile Inheritance: Radical Stakes in Contemporary Indian Art* (Durham, NC: Duke University Press, 2019).

16 They were Santanu Bose, Rimli Bhattacharya, and Aditee Biswas, all part of the core team.

17 Soumitra Das, "A Grand Spectacle," *The Telegraph* (Calcutta), April 26, 2015.

18 Meera Menezes, "Interview with Vivan Sundaram on the Making of *409 Ramkinkars*," Critical Collective, April 14, 2015, accessed June 6, 2023, https://criticalcollective.in/ArtistConversationInner3.aspx?Aid=273

19 Parul Dave Mukherji, "4092015," Critical Collective, April 14, 2015, accessed June 6, 2023, https://criticalcollective.in/ArtistInner2.aspx?Aid=41&Eid=994

20 Mathur, *A Fragile Inheritance*.

LINA RAMADAN

A PAST CENTERED TODAY CENTERED TOMORROW: MOMENTS OF RETURN IN THE WORK OF YTO BARRADA, MOHAMED BOUROUISSA, AND IMAN ISSA

Testimonies of the past rely on history, memory, and substantial evidence in order to be recognized in the present. Peripheral stories are not peripheral by definition; dominant structures lay out narratives with fixed convictions for them. The term marginal is charged with meanings of the minor, the unwanted, and the outside of something. It is one culture in this context that renounces the other. Language, and the inherit structural power that it emerges from, is challenged in the visual linguistics of North African artists Yto Barrada, Mohamed Bourouissa, and Iman Issa.[1] Language within forms of contemporary art is stripped from assigned meanings through the destabilization of underlying power. Form, representation, and historical references are all brought to life in the form of a diasporic revolution shaped by avant-garde philosophies—most importantly, local philosophies drawn from a necessity to invent new methods of articulation.

The reawakening of the supposedly dead, in a form of whispering—the literal action of low sound and breath command—unsettles the listening process. The historical return is chaotic, and its features are unfamiliar. Reappearance spirals between the tragic, comical, and utter madness.[2] It's indeed a paradoxical presence in an era that is ostensibly approaching post-ism.[3] Mohamed Bourouissa asks, how can recovery take place if what caused the injury keeps returning? The colonized body, be it

land, people, culture, and so forth, reconstructs a presence of absence in order to heal. Edward Said speculates "what happens *after* the ending, what it is like to live past one's time and place, how survival after the aftermath becomes an esoteric and certainly an exotic situation for the poet and his people."[4] The dead in Said's words are the living. The living in Bourouissa's artworks are the multigenerational confronted with traumatic legacies.

THE WHISPERING OF GHOSTS

The unequal nature of return arrives in the form of trauma and extended structures of violence on diasporic figures. Mohamed Bourouissa explains what it means to be sixth generation colonized, giving voice to the collective, giving image to the individual. At the center of his sculptural installation *The Whispering of Ghosts* (2018) (pp. 66–67) is a film that addresses the legacy of trauma created by over a century of colonization. It features an interview with Bourlem Mohamed, a patient of the Blida-Joinville Psychiatric Hospital, during the war of independence in Algeria (1954–62), under a French colonial operation. Charged with symbolic references, the film sets off with a digital face of one of the figures who designed the hospital and who is less written about in an attempt by Bourouissa to personify elements of colonial cruelty, thus creating a closer-to-reality image of the oppressor in the cyber age.[5] The flying petals or dashes of blood that appear in the film are "shifters" trumpeting the arrival of *madness* through the chanting of the young Algerian lady. Historically, colonial empires perceived the belief of "supernatural" and spirits' existence, such as the *djinn*, as a medical mental condition embedded within the indigenous. A phenomenon to be controlled and cured. The chanting, or *zaghrouta*, is performed during celebrations as well as a way to mourn the dead whose body has been sacrificed in the protection of indigenous land. The opposing states are echoed in Bourlem's laughter, a paradoxical expression opening the door to the past.

The hospital, which is located in Bourouissa's hometown in Blida, operated within apartheid architecture that separated French and Algerian patients. This segregation was brought to light by Frantz Fanon, who served as a doctor in Blida for three years (1953–56) and resigned in protest over the racial cruelty of the targeted medical treatments.[6] Fanon utilized his involvement in the Algerian struggle against the uprooting of natives from their lands using social therapy based on cultural understanding of the patients. The psychiatry methods followed in the hospital before Fanon's intervention incorporated "curing" sessions based on the exclusion of race, gender, and religion embodied with systematic colonial isolation. At their core, those structures were erasing the patients' identities, creating additional mental disorders. Bourouissa pushes the boundary of the meanings we make of this historical evidence and revisits the difficult past through multidimensional images of the people involved. Fanon actively observed the ill-treatment of patients and the overcrowding of the Algerian part of the hospital. Several aspects of the patients' daily existence, including culture, were not taken into consideration, as he describes in his resignation letter, and later in published books.[7] Fanon understood that healing can only be started when patients are recognized by

their identities attached to ancestral rootedness. He created a gardening system as part of the healing therapy, which has proven to be effective in the improvement of their mental state. Bourouissa recreates a similar structure within an artistic framework situated in a museum and public spaces. This is to create inclusive environments, where the echoing voices of the past and today's triggers speak not in conversation but in confrontation to the many affected polarities.

Bourlem was struggling mentally during a brutal period in Algeria and was admitted there around 1965 (following the armed conflict that resulted in a million of deaths). Maintaining gardening activities was his main way of healing. His body remains an important witness that survives into the present. It carries this weight of memories and turbulent present, yet major healing came from Fanon's influence. Karima Lazali, a psychoanalyst in postwar Algeria, makes a contemporary scholarly contribution in an attempt to illustrate the internal wars that people struggled with. Her medical practice, taking place between France and Algeria, examines the effect of colonization on people from both ends rather than the effect of external war, which is often overlooked in psychiatry. She looks at historic terror as an inner conflict. In her recent book, *Colonial Trauma* (2021), Lazali refers to an oppressive method used during colonial Algeria which denies the existence of "burial sites," be they for the dead or the living memory. Mourning is confused with an absence of presence, and Lazali points to this being a result of a systematic tool that blurs the role of oppressors.[8] The missing bodies make the evidence difficult to contain. She asks, "Who killed whom?" and,

While the narrative and memory of the first war are forgotten, bodies remain marked by this catastrophe. Did what escaped memory find refuge in the body? In the colonial

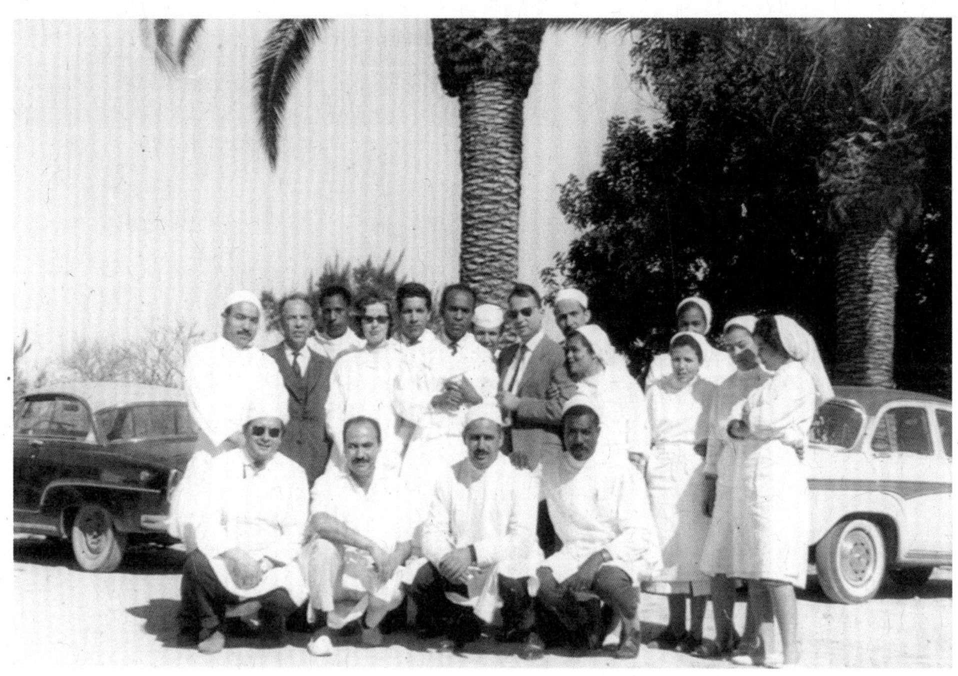

Frantz Fanon and his medical team at the Blida-Joinville Psychiatric Hospital in Algeria

context, memory is in a paradoxical state of confusion, caught between erasure and the impossibility of forgetting. What to do with the memory of these bodies torn to pieces? How to facilitate their entry into a healthy oblivion? We will see how mutilated bodies and disappearance still belong to a practice of non-forgetting in Algeria today.[9]

Bourouissa invents new methods to speak about memory by bringing all positions, including the contradictory, together. The film is presented in fragments ignited in video footage from 2001 of a football match showing clashes after the loss of the Algerian national team against the French in a friendly match. "Madness" comes back through the symbolic defeat.

PROXIES, WITH A LIFE OF THEIR OWN

The Surrealist art of nineteen-thirties Cairo and a photograph of an iconic poet resting in the middle of a sandy track are two possible imageries that could appear when referring to Georges Henein (1914–1973). A renowned writer and activist, Henein is known for co-founding the Art et Liberté group in Egypt, a movement that promoted itself as an intellectual necessity to counter rising fascism in the years following the First World War. Iman Issa brings to light his ideas, which have shaped the transcultural arts and the literary world for a century. Yet, Issa reformulates other possibilities of these image significations of how icons can be remembered. Completed in 2021 using digital (3D) printing, her abstract sculpture titled *Self-Portrait (Self as Georges Henein)* **(p. 94)** emancipates itself from any potential figuration; the visual is impaired and split into two parts: one carrying text, the other structure. Abstraction is given a life of its own.

The overarching series *Proxies, with a Life of Their Own* commemorates late nineteenth- and twentieth-century cultural figures such as Ananda K. Coomaraswamy, Taha Hussein, Doria Shafik, and Georges Henein, among others. All are advocates for freedom and independence during nation-building and anti-colonial struggles.[10] The series presents modern black and white bust-like sculptures, appearing as capsules to be carried into the future. The proxies do not stand alone but are rather accompanied by texts with individual descriptions assigned by the artist. They convey fractional meaning but lie at the edge of a riddle waiting to be solved. This shifting role of the artwork within labels is promoted by Issa, giving it agency as a commentator, as a grand hyper-awareness of the position the work holds in a museum space. This raises questions of cultural knowledge and reliability. At the same time, within the unity of the portraits, there's an agency presented through significant carved lines and keywords. This unification does not denounce the past shapes but rather attempts to articulate a possible independent visual ground. As a result, ultimate neutrality is erased.

The traditional definition of the representation of the self could be as "a portrait of oneself done by oneself."[11] However, in the case of Issa's artistic occupation, the depiction emerges through the representation of an external self—to be precise, a new independent self, one departing from the artist. Identity within this formula is together doubled and subtracted from the original. Nonetheless, neither the artist (the painter/creator) nor the subject (historic figure) is concerned with the divergence between the "I" and the "other." The "othering," as far as the context is concerned, refuses to distinguish itself outside of a midpoint as a new construct.[12] The additional "new" self, which is appointed by Issa, lies within the center and goes against a hegemony of a preassigned form. In simpler words, Issa follows an abstract form that reveals segments of identity. This consequently draws the viewer closer to the subject but also contrasts against conventional interpretations of what the sculpture communicates. This is an ongoing approach that Issa produces within a framework of space vs. form, where they are not in conflict with one another but are not able to exist without each other. Kaelen Wilson-Goldie writes on Issa's spatial

division and non-isolation method, "True to themselves, they are conveyed through positions, relations, and associations. They communicate as shifters: your east is my west, or perhaps my center. Again and again, Issa's work refuses pat divisions between form and content, self and other, art and life, public and private, abstraction and figuration."[13] This differentiation that Wilson-Goldie describes in Issa's work lies within the tensions of *traditional* museological object understanding and autonomy of representation. Moreover, it challenges practices applied today by critically using history as a fundamental basis to understand the present in almost a Foucauldian approach.[14]

There's also a rather violent element that goes into Issa's abstraction of popular figures and "retro-understanding" of history. The viewer does not see words that match what one expects to see and feel. Erasure is a necessary act of violence here, in an abstract form, removing what uniquely signifies revolutionary thinkers (or those who made a tangible change). All of these figures seem identical when Issa revisits museological fundamentals. What does it mean to give something meaning? In her essay "Abstraction," Iman Issa says,

One can imagine an artwork offering knowledge about the state of its referent that relates little to an artist's emotional state or subjective inclinations—an artwork that lays a claim to the world no less substantial than a scientific claim to the world. It is an art that, although not science, similarly to science refuses to reside merely in the "I" of its maker, even if this "I" is who partly brought it about.[15]

Her artistic approach is political in that it is rarely seen from one medium not relying on singular facts produced and that it is continuously departing, modifying, expanding, and growing over time. Issa's preoccupation with

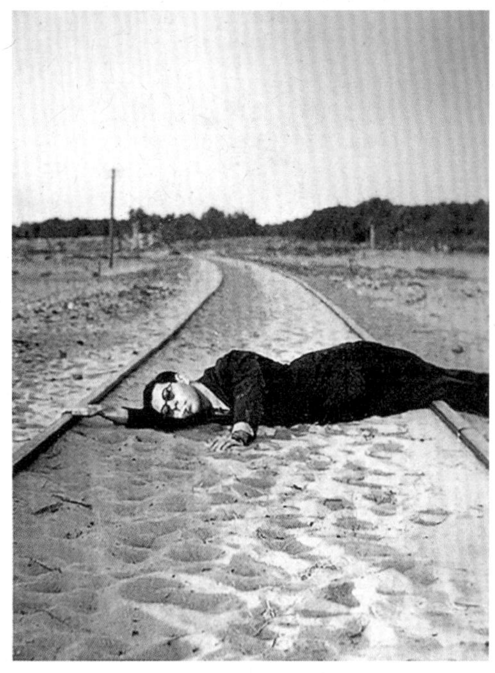

Image of Georges Henein
by Boula Henein

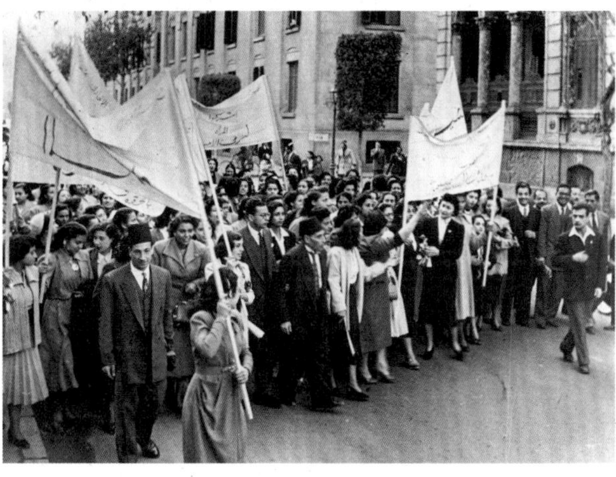

Doria Shafik leading a feminist procession in Cairo,
June 11, 1953

the destabilization of museological displays started from an early period working at the campus museum of the American University in Cairo while studying philosophy and political science. It sparked an inquiry that appears in the work asking how knowledge is made, accumulated, and translated into practice. How language via form is conveyed in a political space.

NOUGAT CROSS SECTION FLAVOR SAMPLER

Yto Barrada's works lead a practice with a distinctive feminist mediation on art education and the history of production. Through the use of colorful scales, scientific visualization, and humor that presents a world reconstructed, her work transforms into potential sites of resistance. At the same time, Barrada's continual search for the right technique is crucial in determining the final medium used. Like that of Issa's, it incorporates components of museological and anthropological investigations which provide a timeless parameter that guides the work. This approach is rarely seen in a singular form. It traces historical phenomena that were sometimes forgotten or made to be forgotten, only to be brought back in a playful take into the challenging present. This simultaneously reveals a double, vulnerable side to humans when discussing unchained complex realities. The core of this innovation highlights how knowledge is transmitted, examining trajectories and failures of history. Barrada alters the material form and asks, what is the proper method for discussing a subject while being conscious of transferred powers?

The direct reference to the personal ancestry and land lineage of Morocco often takes shape as an underlying origin of form, whether it is the use of local dyes, cultural materials, or lexicon. The word "nougat," for instance, appears in her artworks in different ways, transitioning from a scientific anecdote that studies fossils in Morocco to themes of domesticity, learning systems, and colonial legacy.[16] In *Untitled (Nougat Cross Section Flavor Sampler)* (2016) **(p. 65)**, a sculpture made up of six stacked confectionary bars placed in a museum-like vitrine could be read as a replacement of the scientific investigation into cultural studies and museological interpretation.[17] Looking closer, the glass that contains the sculpture resembles market windows that could be seen in the multiethnic Naschmarkt of Vienna, for instance, or at a stand in a local bazaar and which within living memory carry a biological lifespan. Time is measured with food that is designed to be digested for a generative circle. This nutritious circle has been interrupted by long periods of struggle and cultural disturbance and stands as a symbol of such.

Nonetheless *Nougat* becomes a testimony, a recipe transmitted from one generation to another, among post-independence women. Curator Laura Barlow draws a comparison between Barrada's sculptural work and that of Lebanese avant-garde artist Saloua Raouda Choucair, who similarly led a life that included all components of art and architecture as well as civil community engagement within her practice.[18] She writes,

> Barrada's references align international modernism as a larger associative system, with artists like Bettina Grossman and Saloua Raouda Choucair appearing as muses. The practices of self-education and living and learning by doing explored by these artists are crucial threads in the subversive empowerment and agency of women as leaders of experimental society; and in the making of art that tests the limits of knowledge and existence.[19]

In the fifties, Anissa Rawda Najjar, a renowned feminist figure and sister of Saloua, ran a craft workshop called Jamiat Inaash Al Ussrah (Village Welfare Society) in Lebanon. The workshops were joined by Saloua to assist the village women with designs, crafts, and the documentation of activities. Both Barrada and Choucair contributed to the social, cultural, and civil life of their cities through the trans-

mission of knowledge through art. Choucair created a vast number of modules to imagine her city functioning in a self-sufficient and sustainable way. And in addition to Barrada's contribution to her hometown, Tangier, she recently created an initiative called The Mothership, a residency space and garden that grows plants for natural dyes used in artworks, and Cinema Rif (Cinémathèque de Tanger), a house cinema and a cultural project established in 2006, which all operate within eco-feminist philosophies.[20]

While continuing this lineage, the film *Tree Identification for Beginners* (2017) centers on Barrada's mother, Mounira Bouzid El Alami, the main narrator of a trip she took to the United States as part of Operation Crossroads Africa in 1966, joined by several voice-overs.[21] Together with the invited young African activists and students, she participated in what was meant to be a cultural exchange in the "hope that grantees will return convinced that the US is a vital society worthy of sympathy," as stated by the organizers. The film presents a stop-motion animation of Montessori toys featuring verbs like "reinform," and adjectives such as "oblong," "linear," and "obcordate."[22] The narration unfolds the underlining motifs by both the participants and organizers encouraging them to consider the country's values and the viewpoint put forth at a time when the US was fighting in Vietnam while locally people were continuing a civil rights movement against racial violence and discrimination. El Alami, who had been politically engaged with the Pan-African and international solidarity activities throughout her years of study abroad, elaborately regaled manysided stories. Upon her return from the trip, an anti-imperialist group whom she stayed with in Paris ended their friendship since they believed she was supporting US politics. The film's staging, which is at times satirical, employs Barrada's techniques of bringing history and its

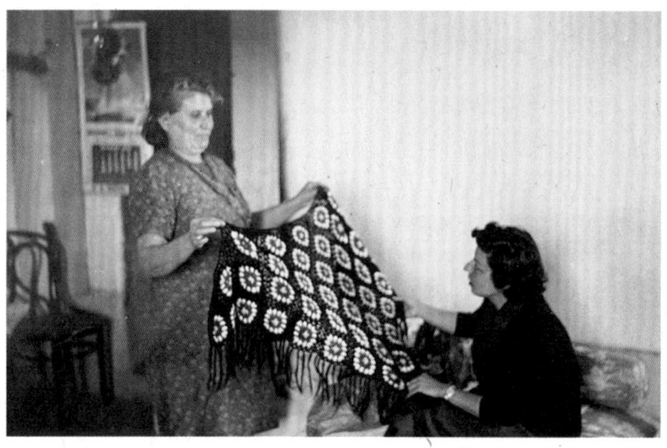

Saloua Raouda Choucair supporting Jamiat Inaash Al Ussrah (Village Welfare Society), co-founded by women's rights activist Anissa Rawda Najjar

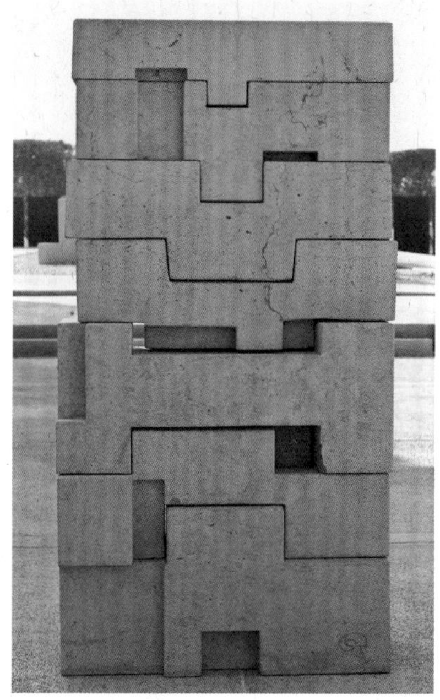

Saloua Raouda Choucair
Poem, 1966
Sculpture, stone, 92 × 102 × 51 cm

contradictions to life through primary learning methods and storytelling.

The entanglements of generational knowledge in post-independence Morocco and means of expression find their way into Barrada's art history interrogation as well. She includes elements of Moroccan avant-garde modernist painters Mohamed Melehi, Farid Belkahia, and Mohamed Chebaa, who were all indirect subjects in her series *After Stella*, created in 2018. The textile series looks at Frank Stella's fluorescent paintings known as the Morocco series (1964–65), depicting Morocco's cities. At the same time, the work connotes the motifs used in the nineteen-sixties paintings by these artists, who together formed the Casablanca Art School, which celebrated the abstraction of African and Arab art. Melehi in particular developed a series inspired by Hard-edge during a fellowship he undertook at Columbia University in New York.[23] This experience of color and motifs came about through his participation

in a mural work at the campus of Minneapolis Institute of Arts (1963).[24] All of these visual approaches create pairs to already existing testimonies, while Barrada interrogates hidden histories backed by living witnesses and is shifting gazes and methods of making art today.

In thinking about the entanglements that artists Yto Barrada, Mohamed Bourouissa, and Iman Issa engage with, from questioning cultural legacies to contemporary neocolonial relations, it is important to emphasize how their work reclaims language within their construct of mediums. This experimentation enables the filling of absent language that they propose in their work in order to offer material clarity on "the history of the present," as well as enabling the reconciliation of paradoxes that forms bring, and will continue to bring. The return (as indicated in the introduction) is not concerned with a fixed period; rather, it is concerned with the past and future emancipating themselves from a systematic order of events.

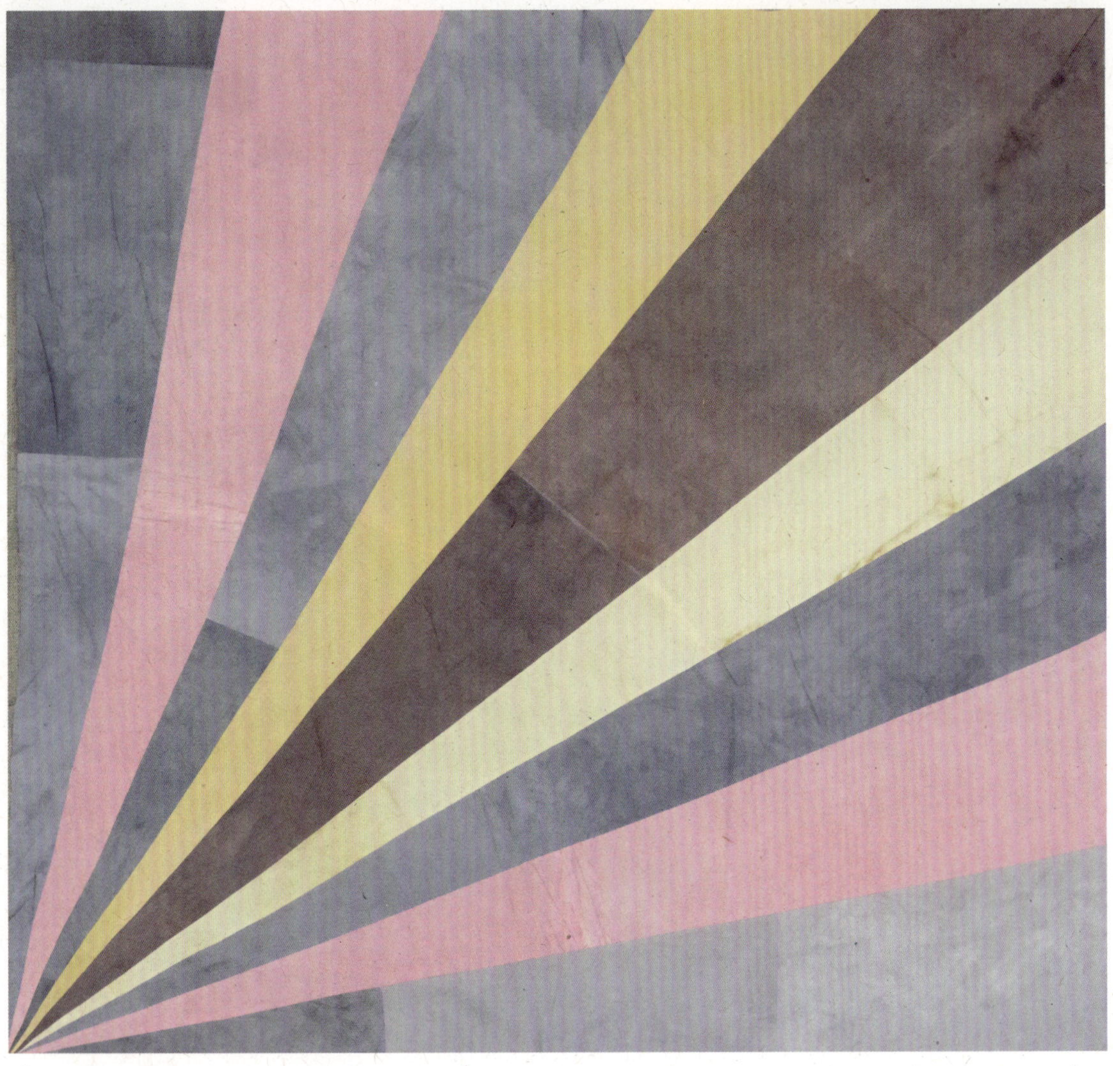

Yto Barrada
Untitled (After Stella Melilla II), 2019
Cotton and natural dyes on burlap, 149 × 153 cm

1   See Etel Adnan, "To Write in a Foreign Language," in *Unheard Words*, ed. Barbara Potter-Fasting and Mineke Schipper (London: Allison & Busby, 1985). Adnan speaks about the political aspect of language and how it amplifies itself when one's inner identity clashes with the employment of foreign language during times of conflict.

2   For more on the relations of tragedy and madness, see Jacques Derrida, *Specters of Marx: The State of the Debt, the Work of Mourning, and the New International* (New York: Routledge, 1994).

3   The term "postcolonial" does not mean the end of colonial oppression today; it refers to the study of the aftermath and ongoing impact of colonialism. So by processes of its end I mean revisiting the history and language used to articulate the struggle and function today. For more, see Julie Drew, "Cultural Composition: Stuart Hall on Ethnicity and the Discursive Turn," *JAC: A Journal of Composition Theory* 18, no. 2, 1998, p. 189.

3   Edward W. Said, "On Mahmoud Darwish," *Grand Street* 48 (Winter 1994), p. 115.

5   Bourouissa creates a remake of the face of psychiatrist Antoine Porot (1876–1965), a professor and one of the founders of the Blida-Joinville Psychiatric Hospital. He co-theorized psychiatric approaches under the School of Algiers that attempted to medically impose superiority over what they believed to be "primitive" cultures.

6   Frantz Fanon is one of the most influential philosophical and psychiatric figures of the twentieth century. In Algeria he was a member of the Algerian National Liberation Front alongside his psychiatric career. This period inspired one of the most significant books on anti-colonialism and pathological cases within medical institutions, namely his *The Wretched of the Earth* (New York: Grove Press, 1968), which is well-read amid the social and political global struggles today.

7   See "Letter to the Resident Minister (1956)" in Frantz Fanon, *Toward the African Revolution*, transl. Haakon Chevalier (New York: Grove Press, 1967), pp. 52–54. In the letter, Fanon writes, "If psychiatry is the medical technique that aims to enable man no longer to be a stranger to his environment, I owe it to myself to affirm that the Arab, permanently an alien in his own country, lives in a state of absolute depersonalization. What is the status of Algeria? A systematized de-humanization. … The decision I have reached is that I cannot continue to bear a responsibility at no matter what cost, on the false pretext that there is nothing else to be done."

8   See chapters 3 and 4 in Karima Lazali, *Colonial Trauma: A Study of the Psychic and Political Consequences of Colonial Oppression in Algeria*, Critical South series (Cambridge, UK: Polity Press, 2021), esp. pp. 62–101.

9   Ibid., p. 69.

10 Sri Lanka and India were under British colonial rule, and North Africa was undergoing severe liberation fights.

11 See the definition of self-portrait at https://www.merriam-webster.com/dictionary/self-portrait.

12 For more, read Shehla Burney, "Chapter One: Orientalism: The Making of the Other," *Counterpoints* 417, *PEDAGOGY of the Other: Edward Said, Postcolonial Theory, and Strategies for Critique* (2012), pp. 23–39.

13 Kaelen Wilson-Goldie, "Proxies, with a Life of Their Own," Rodeo Gallery, 2022, accessed February 10, 2023, https://www.rodeo-gallery.com/exhibitions/proxies-with-a-life-of-their-own-london/.

14 For more, see Michel Foucault's concept of genealogy in *Discipline and Punish: The Birth of the Prison* (New York: Vintage Books, 1977).

15 Iman Issa, "Abstraction," in *Parapolitics: Cultural Freedom and the Cold War*, ed. Anselm Franke, Nida Ghouse, Paz Guevara, and Antonia Majaca (Berlin: Sternburg Press & Haus der Kulturen der Welt, 2021), p. 77.

16 Barrada created this project as part of a study of fossils in Morocco. She visited an abandoned natural history museum and stumbled upon lithological charts made by local geologists. The data collected was originally noted down by hand based on observations. The color codes transformed the scientific information into natural dye experiments. For more, see https://www.sfeir-semler.com/galleryartists/yto-barrada/work?page=3.

17 Nougat is a Mediterranean dessert that consists of dense layers of sugar or honey paste with eggs, hazelnut, and almonds. Its origin can be traced to tenth-century Baghdad.

18 Laura Barlow, "In Good Practice", in *My Very Educated Mother Just Served Us Nougat*, ed. Laura Barlow and Wadha Al Aqeedi (Cinisello Balsamo: Silvana Editoriale, 2021), p. 21.

19 Ibid.

20 For more on the Mothership initiative in Tangier, read the 2021 interview of Yto Barrada in conversation with artist and educator Valerio Rocco Orlando, "Collective Mentorship," *South of Imagination*, accessed May 23, 2023, https://southofimagination.org/conversation/collective-mentorship-yto-barrada-and-the-mothership/.

21 Operation Crossroads Africa is a governmental volunteer organization that funds educational travel and cultural exchange. The voice-over included political activists such as Stokely Carmichael.

22 A Montessori toy is an informal educational tool for young children based on self-learning to develop the building of knowledge through creative processes.

23 These experiences fostered exchanges between post-painterly and Hard-edge artists to engage with geometric abstraction and information theories. Additionally, it was at the core of avant-garde experimentation that Melehi called for freedom and established several de-colonial journals and festivals.

24 See "Mohamed Melehi in conversation with Morad Montazami," *Third Text Online*, 2021, accessed May 17, 2023, http://www.thirdtext.org/domains/thirdtext.com/local/media/images/medium/Mohamed_Melehi_in_conversation_with_Morad_Montazami_PDF_1.pdf.

* Exteriorization means rendering things or events visible, concrete, and giving a name to them. The crisis we are experiencing today is a crisis of exteriorization—there is much talk about different levels of crisis, but there is no proper name for what it actually is. Exteriorization, understood in this sense, is a visualization of externality, and art is one of the most important techniques for making elements of the outside world visible by means of objects. Exteriorization is, furthermore, closely related to the concept of technicity (perception, speech, visualization, and so on), which helps to avoid the confusing notion of "subjectivity."

ZEIGAM AZIZOV

THE CHANGING SHAPE OF TIME: THE CRISIS OF EXTERIORIZATION AND THE CHRONOTOPE

This text addresses the question of time in relation to the idea of liberation. The notion that modernism, which gave rise to the comprehension of time as liberation, should not be obliterated as a misunderstanding of this problem but needs to be supplemented by new ideas. These ideas derive from the current process of decolonization demands to revise the question of time. The process of decolonization also has its beginning in the work of Frederick Douglass, who despite his critique of Enlightenment's individualism appreciated its orientation towards freedom.[1] Decolonization continues the demand for exteriorization,* since in our times most questions related to liberation are recognized yet they are not completely exteriorized. It is due to the fear of the recognition of indeterminacy which produces the crisis of exteriorization. I will address only one aspect of this crisis, which resides in indeterminacy and the dialogical nature of art as the passage of time where liberation can take place.

"Apart from time there is one other means to bring about important change—force," said the eighteenth-century German physicist and writer Lichtenberg, concluding that if time works too slowly, the force will do it faster.[2] We are in the age of understanding and recognizing this pattern in the exteriorization crisis taking place on different levels. This crisis is inseparable from the question of time since "time has always put the notion of truth into crisis."[3]

It is not a situation of restraint but is instead one of proliferation without boundaries and of excessive accumulation. The crisis of exteriorization is also accompanied by the deepening conflict of autonomy with automation. The roots of this crisis stem from the industrialization, which includes colonialism, which started in the late eighteenth century, and the ensuing intensification of automation. Within the paradigm of exteriorization, automation takes place when time is spatialized by technologies. Gadgets and devices, controlling time are in excess, whereas aesthetic exteriorization is in decline and is reduced to familiar representations. Automation should be understood—in connection to autonomy—as time-space compression and the *conscious* recognition of time alongside the unconscious imitation. This time-space compression, which holds together sensibility and intelligibility as an experience, is called "the chronotope" (from the Greek *chronos*, time, and *topos*, place) by Bakhtin, and it is a phenomenon that I will discuss below in more detail. The chronotope, as the event of the connection between autonomous and internally not finalized consciousness is the possibility of assembling. This conflict between automatic spatialization and the autonomous consciousness of time-space compression opens up another way of assembling in order to provide a different understanding of the real. This "real" is a fiction as a production of time, which produces further exteriorizations. These exteriorizations amount to a spatiotemporal actuality consisting of fuzzy objects, objects that are not fully determined. The reality of the world is absolutely non-determined and our knowledge of the world is always partial.

The real, understood as the spatiotemporal actuality, is "an impasse of formalization."[4] The only way of giving shape to time is exteriorization, which is stimulated by a lack, or the excess, produced by the crisis. The impossibility of the real is meant to evoke the notion that although the actuality exists, we are not happy with this actuality, because what is exteriorized today by automation disorientates this actuality and brings even more confusion. This confusion is due to the loss of exteriorization's meaning in relation to the actuality. The real resides in time, and the boundaries of time made by earlier exteriorizations are lost. This loss also leads to a constant indeterminacy, and yet, since time is never determined, it is either pre-determined or over-determined, and this indeterminacy produces the further constellation of sets of fuzzy objects. These objects cannot be reduced to laws of change but exist with their own internal dynamic outside of precision and perfection. What is changing is "the shape of time"[5] exteriorized in objects. These objects contain traces of time as signs, and the force of assembling these signs temporarily shapes time.

From this angle, I would like to stress the question of time and its emergence in modernism through the deterministic approach of Immanuel Kant that paradoxically has led to an understanding of time as a non-linear entity by his critics. Kant's determinism, which has been criticized ever since its initial exposition and which also opened up the way to the non-deterministic approach, and its relevance, is strongly felt in today's thought and images as a different concept of time. The difference that emerged here gave rise to an intercultural dialogue consisting of refuting Kant's definition of comprehension. Kant insisted that because any comprehension is determined by experience, it is impossible to comprehend what is outside of one's experience, as well as that which has not been given by intuition. This determinacy as the exclusion of the exterior world has to be understood as the breaking point in modern philosophical thought. The main point of my argument is that the exclusion of the exterior from the experience of temporality itself is the condition of the possibility of exteriorization. Any exclusion is repressing the potential of inclusion, which persists as the missing indeterminate dimension of time, which resides in the aforementioned fuzzy objects. In Western philosophy, "time" is questioned from early on, sometimes as a "known unknown,"[6] and mostly understood in relation to the exterior world. Nevertheless, this short text addresses the current crisis of exteriorization and the critique of modernism heavily influenced by Kantian philosophy. Ergo, Kant!

Kant's cosmological argument of whether the universe had a beginning in time or not is crucial to the entire project of critical philosophy in connection with his call of dare to be free: "Have courage to use your own understanding!" "Sapere Aude!"[7] It emerged after the awakening from the "dogmatic slumber"[8] he had undergone, triggered by Hume's skepticism. Hume argued that exterior reality cannot be fully grasped by the human mind, since the mind itself is not capable of perceiving the world fully and cannot represent the exterior world in its entity. On the one hand, Kant followed Descartes's view of knowledge based on representation; on the other hand, he followed Hume's skepticism. Kant understood Hume's view of indeterminacy very well; nevertheless, he decided to go on to find a solution for this problem by adopting the Newtonian understanding of space-time as intuition. Space and time as a form of external reality exist as intuition, but understanding comes through experience, and from experience knowledge emerges. "There can be no doubt that all our knowledge begins with experience," says the opening line of Kant's First Critique.[9] Kant adopted the Newtonian vision of time as a universal variable in equations describing time as nature in motion, the idea derived from Aristotle's claim that time is the measure of motion. Kant came to the conclusion that intuition (time and space) is a substance which gives rise to experience. The question that emerged was how one can grasp the truth of seeing things as they are, if either the subject or the truth changes. Kant understood time as it resides in the very form of sensibility and thus not as a property of objects of the world. Therefore, time can be manipulated and categorized as an imperative just as much as the sensible can be categorized, rather than being accepted in its irreducibility and indeterminacy. What is missing from Kant's doctrine is the question of what I call the missing dimension of time: the fictional "origin." There is no such a thing as the origin, be it intuition or experience; there is only process and contingent circulation of fuzzy objects of time.

Because Kant restricted his research to the limits of human reason, he completely forgot about time as a main feature of the world outside of reason, and this radical refusal turned his philosophy into an inward-looking discipline. Before going on to explore this problem, a brief historical excursion is needed to see what has emerged following this vision. The culture of industrialized modernity, which started during the prominence of Kantian philosophy, has "naturally" reflected its limits; modernism is both an enormous progression in having invented novelties in relation to oneself, yet it is an equally enormous regression regarding others and the outside world. Historically, there are some conditions which also have to be taken into account. The Industrial Revolution engendered a vast array of technologies that have brought about fundamental changes to our understanding of time. The classical approach, which concluded that time is just movement in space seemed obsolete and unconvincing. The question of time started to receive a new shape, touching upon such variations as temporality, speed, and velocity, with the persistence of both automation and autonomy. Subsequently, scientific and artistic attitudes dramatically altered and gave rise to a rapid classification of the knowledge of things and a completely new use of images. While witnessing these changes, Marx liked to repeat the Shakespearean sentiment "The time is out of joint."[10] This meant to evoke two novelties: that time is, first, disjoined and, second, out of joy, which was an unprecedented event disrupting those who practiced slow and ascetic lifestyles. Stiegler characterizes this time as follows:

An ordinary person of two centuries ago could expect to die in the bed in which he had been born. He lived on a virtually changeless diet, eaten from a bowl that would have passed on to his grandchildren. Through seasons, years, generations, his surroundings, possessions, and daily routines were close to identical. The world appeared to be absolutely stable, change was such an exception that it seemed to be an illusion.[11]

Terms like "the change" and "the new" entered into the vocabulary of modernism, announcing the work of modern art as "the transient, the fleeting, the contingent."[12] The nineteenth century saw events that led to many changes; these changes continue to affect us today: the shift to the capitalist formation, the triumph of colonialism, the striking domination of technologies. These historical disruptions became a theme of modern paintings, like crowds rushing in the streets depicted in Impressionist paintings and the image of steam engines as in Turner's work; such themes have dominated art.

It is not surprising that the notion of "entropy" was developed at this conjecture. Philosophy of this time was very much influenced by Kant. Through this influence, the question of time became more crucial than ever before. The impulsive energy of modernism "forced" time to accelerate, simultaneously excluding its multiple dimensions together with its subjects.

Kant's followers started their critique from this particular point. For example, among the followers of Kant there was the poet and playwright Heinrich von Kleist, also a philosopher and mathematician, who in his text on speaking insisted that thought comes into existence while speaking, where speech is a form of the exteriorization of time.[13] Speech as a technique of exteriorization brings into existence secrecy, speed, and affect, "and in Kleist the secret is no longer a content held within the form of interiority; rather, it becomes a form, identified with the form of exteriority that is always external to itself."[14] The technique of exteriorization precedes the internal thought and later becomes the condition of transforming thought, where thought is the dialogue between the exterior and the interior. The dialogue further exteriorizes the intrinsic relationship between time and images without any closure. The dialogue occurs in time, because it is only time that can tell in which conjuncture we are. The conjuncture is the passage of time and the possibility of articulation.[15] This articulation doesn't separate the intuition from the experience in a way as it doesn't separate time from space. It was the main idea challenging Kant's view of "time-space" as an intuition separated from the experience, and this critique was made by Mikhail Bakhtin. This was also the view of the neo-Kantian philosopher Hermann Cohen, whose work had a huge influence on Bakhtin. Bakhtin accepted Cohen's view while rejecting his notion of "an all-encompassing oneness, or Allheit."[16] Bakhtin instead insisted on the recognition of experience itself as a

time-space compression, a chronotope. The chronotope doesn't exclude intuition and also doesn't strictly separate intuition from experience but offers a view of the compression, which amounts to articulation. Bakhtin regarded time and space as forms of the most immediate reality rather than transcendental pre-conditions of experience. Kant was right in saying that time is evident in the experience, but he was not clear by excluding what is not experienced by the self simply as a matter of the transcendental. Bakhtin also understood that any experience has its limits and has to be understood not only as chronological but also as dialogical, polyphonic. Bakhtin's dialogue evokes the conversation of what is experienced with what is not experienced—what is outside of experience—the dialogue which alters the experience, making it experience of neither the self nor the other. The experience is dialogical, multiple, and never-ending, not finalized consciousness; it is indeterminate. For his theory of "dialogism" it is the relationship between the exterior world and the interior world that created the dialogue while moving away from the essentialism of the substance and understanding of time as an intrinsic relationship between images and thought. From this point, my own theorizing of the question of the lack of the real in time, and the question of assemblage as the shape of time, is developed.[17]

The chronotope or "the fourth dimension of space" problematizes signs not simply as semiotic elements but also as remnants of time. Combining Einstein's theory of relativity with neo-Kantian critique, Bakhtin demonstrated that the notion of dialogue as a heteroglossia produces multiple meanings which emerge from signs, which may in fact lose their meanings as remnants of time, varying depending on the context. Einstein, like Kant, was also influenced by Hume. But differently from Kant, he took more seriously Hume's idea that time is a fiction; it is a construct, and identity is in the notion of time, or duration and has to be understood "through a supposed variation of time."[18] Einstein's famous thought experiment about the observer and train is derived from his interest in Hume's challenge. For Einstein, this challenge is his own critical rejection of Newton's claims about simultaneity.[19] His positing the priority not of things but of relations among things is the historical event which demonstrated that the relation between time and space are not static, isolated objects but active, simultaneous events.

Bakhtin reverted Einstein's famous thought experiment of the observer looking at two lightning bolts simultaneously hitting a train into the observer looking at the observer. It is the case when one observer can see things behind another observer who cannot see them. Although they both are participating in the same event, that event is different for each of them. Their places are different only because their bodies occupy different positions in exterior space, and also because they regard the world and each other from different centers in "cognitive time/space."[20] In this cognitive space all perception unfolds. Bakhtin insisted on the combination of time and space and their inseparability, even if we are always forced to separate things. The problem is that if we need to separate things for the reason of analyzing, we should not forget to connect them again, albeit differently. This difference includes the connection between intuition and experience. The chronotope as the time-space compression is itself already experience, and, differently from Kantian understanding, experience doesn't derive from the intuition as the basis of space and time but is the very beginning of understanding, since it already contains the intuition. If further difference occurs by repetition, it is because the repetition unfolds the difference, which is compressed in the chronotope and not visible until the dialogue makes

exteriorization possible. The dialogue is the exteriorization of this experience through signs, which contain the traces of time, and therefore any experience is already residing in the difference produced by signs, which exists as "signs taken for wonders."[21] Time floats in the exterior world, but after the internalization it needs to be exteriorized again. *Exteriorization–interiorization–exteriorization* is the process made possible by signs produced by time.

The chronotope underlines the contingent nature of the world, which is reflected in images. In images, time exists as a pure convention, and its laws don't coincide with the laws of real time. There is no distinction between "conventional" and "real" as two different times because time in real life is no less organized than it is in images. The chronotope is grounded simultaneously at all levels, including those of real time and images of time. The chronotope is a fictional constitution of time, and time is a fiction, whereas we experience time in the real world or in images. There is no purely chronological sequence inside or outside of the artwork. Bakhtin's interest in the theory of relativity's postulation of the inseparability of time and events has to be understood from this angle of contingency.

Time is non-linear; it is trans-historical and "transmodern."[22] Time is exteriorized in the dialogue, and the dialogue translates time into the image. This image is the assemblage, is extra-temporal, and is an effect of both time and space. This is the condition of the irreducibility, which resides in signs of time and is assembled as the image of time. The image of time creates the passage of time, a form of exteriority, external to itself. A dialogical passing through this passage is the only time one can experience. Liberation, including but not exclusively decolonization, is one such dialogical experience.

1   Frederick Douglass, *Narrative of the Life of Frederick Douglass, an American Slave, Written by Himself* (New York: Norton, 1997).

2   Georg Christoph Lichtenberg quoted in Johannes Fabian, *Time and the Other: How Anthropology Makes Its Object* (New York: Columbia University Press, 1983), p. 1.

3   Gilles Deleuze, *Cinema 2: The Time-Image* (London: Continuum, 2005), p. 126.

4   Jacques Lacan, *Seminars XX* (New York: State University of New York Press, 1994).

5   George Kubler, *The Shape of Time* (New Haven: Yale University Press, 2008).

6   "What is time then? If nobody asks me, I know; but if I were desirous to explain it to one that should ask me, plainly I do not know." Saint Augustine, *Confessions* (New York: Penguin Books, 1961), XI, 14, p. 264.

7   Immanuel Kant, "What is Enlightenment" (1784), accessed January 12, 2023, https://www.nypl.org/sites/default/files/kant_whatisenlightenment.pdf.

8   Immanuel Kant, *Prolegomena to Any Future Metaphysics* (Indianapolis/New York: The Bobbs-Merrill Company, 1950), p. 8.

9   Immanuel Kant, *Critique of Pure Reason* (London: Macmillan, 1976), p. 41.

10 Ernesto Laclau, "The Time Is out of Joint," *Diacritics* 25, no. 2 (Summer 1995), p. 85.

11 Bernard Stiegler, *Technics and Time 2: Disorientation* (Stanford: Stanford University Press, 2009), p. 1.

12 Charles Baudelaire, *The Painter of Modern Life* (London: Penguin Books, 2010), p. 17.

13 Heinrich von Kleist, "Über die allmähliche Verfertigung der Gedanken beim Reden" (1805–06), accessed January 12, 2023, https://pure.mpg.de/rest/items/item_2352284_4/component/file_2352283/content.

14 Gilles Deleuze and Félix Guattari, *Nomadology: The War Machine* (New York: Semiotext (e), 1986), p. 9.

15 Stuart Hall, "On Articulation and Postmodernism," in David Morley and Kuan-Hsing Chen, eds., *Stuart Hall: Critical Dialogues in Cultural Studies* (London: Routledge, 1996), pp. 131–151.

16 Michael Holquist, *Dialogism: Bakhtin and His World* (London: Routledge, 1990), p. 6.

17 Zeigam Azizov, *The Time of the Image* (Cologne: Herbert von Halem, 2020).

18 David Hume, *A Treatise of Human Nature* (Oxford: The Clarendon Press, 1978), p. 253.

19 Albert Einstein, "The Electrodynamics of Moving Bodies" (1905), accessed January 12, 2023, https://users.physics.ox.ac.uk/~rtaylor/teaching/specrel.pdf.

20 Holquist, p. 22.

21 Homi K. Bhabha, *The Location of Culture* (London: Routledge, 1994), p. 145.

22 Christian Kravagna, *Transmodern: An Art History of Contact, 1920–60* (Manchester: Manchester University Press, 2022).

APPENDIX

NANA ADUSEI-POKU is Assistant Professor in the History of Art and African American Studies Department at Yale University, New Haven. She was the curator of the exhibition *Black Melancholia* at CCS Bard Galleries, New York, USA (2022) and also curated the event *Performances of No-thingness* at the Akademie der Künste Berlin, Germany (2018). Adusei-Poku is the editor of the book *Reshaping the Field: Art of the African Diasporas on Display* (2022). Her monograph *Taking Stakes in the Unknown: Tracing Post-Black Art* (2021) contextualizes the term "Post-Black" in its socio-historical and cultural contexts. She is currently working on her second monograph, which deepens and expands the theme "Black Melancholia."

ZEIGAM AZIZOV is a British philosopher and artist living and working in London, UK. His work addresses questions of time, image, and technics through the narrative procedures of globalization in relation to the languages of migration, media, and the new mimesis. He has exhibited his work worldwide, including most recently at the Biennale di Venezia at the Azerbaijan pavilion (2011, 2019) and Utopia Station (2003), as well at Tate Modern, London (2006), Haus der Kunst, Munich (2004), Grazer Kunstverein, Graz (2002), and TN Probe, Tokyo, Japan (2001), among others. His recent and forthcoming publications include *The Time of the Image* (Herbert von Halem Verlag, 2020), *Noomimesis: A Political Economy of the Meaning-less Sign* (Brill, 2024), and *Realism [without] the Real* (forthcoming).

CHRISTIAN KRAVAGNA is an art historian and Professor of Postcolonial Studies at the Academy of Fine Arts Vienna. From 2005 to 2014 he was artistic director (with Hedwig Saxenhuber) of Kunstraum Lakeside in Klagenfurt. He is the author of the books *Transmodern: An Art History of Contact, 1920–60* (Manchester University Press, 2022) and (with Cornelia Kogoj) *Das amerikanische Museum: Sklaverei, Schwarze Geschichte und der Kampf um Gerechtigkeit in Museen der Südstaaten* (Mandelbaurm Verlag, 2019). He is also editor of the books *Privileg Blick: Kritik der visuellen Kultur* (Id-Verlag, 1997), *Agenda: Perspektiven kritischer Kunst* (Folio, 2000), and *The Museum as Arena: Artists on Institutional Critique* (König, 2001), and (with Model House Research Group) co-editor of *Transcultural Modernisms* (Sternberg Press, 2013).

SALONI MATHUR received her PhD in Cultural Anthropology from the New School for Social Research in New York and is currently a professor in the Art History Department at the University of California, Los Angeles. Her areas of interest include the visual cultures of modern and contemporary South Asia and the South Asian diaspora, colonial studies and postcolonial criticism, and museum studies in a global framework. She is author and editor/co-editor of five books, including most recently *A Fragile Inheritance: Radical Stakes in Contemporary Indian Art* (Duke University Press, 2019). The latter is available online as part of an open access initiative at the following link: https://library.oapen.org/handle/20.500.12657/22291

LINA RAMADAN is a curator and writer specializing in contemporary and modern art. Her research focuses on postcolonial MENA (Middle East and North Africa), women artists, and literary productions. From 2016 to 2022 Ramadan served as a curator at Mathaf: Arab Museum of Modern Art in Doha. She is the recipient of the 421 Curatorial Development Program (2023–24). Ramadan holds a master's degree from University College London (2016) and a bachelor's degree in English Literature from Qatar University (2014). Her recent curated exhibitions include *Taysir Batniji: No Condition Is Permanent* (2022–23) and, as assistant curator, *Kader Attia: On Silence* (2021), *Raqs Media Collective: Still More World* (2019), and *Revolution Generations: Artists from the Arab Art* (2018), among others. Ramadan has contributed to various publications, including *Farid Belkahia: For a New Modernity* (Centre Pompidou & Mathaf, 2021), *Madness of the Anthropocene* (421 Abdu Dhabi, 2024), *Yemen Art Now* (Romooz Foundation, 2023), and "Modern Art in Qatar," in *Modern Art in the Arabian Peninsula* (American University of Cairo, 2024). She is currently pursuing a PhD in Art and Cultural Studies at the Academy of Fine Arts Vienna.

MATHIEU KLEYEBE ABONNENC
born 1977 in Cayenne, French Guiana
lives and works in Sète, France

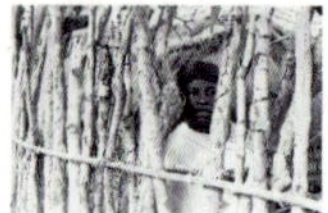

Foreword to Guns for Banta, 2009–11

Installation: set of photographs taken by Suzanne Lipinska during the shooting of Sarah Maldoror's movie *Guns for Banta*, 1970; analogue slide projection, transferred to digital, 25:40 min; stack of posters, designed by deValence, 160 × 120 cm each

Dimensions variable

Courtesy Mathieu Kleyebe Abonnenc and Galerie Marcelle Alix, Paris

---

OMAR BA
born 1977 in Dakar, Senegal
lives and works in Dakar, Senegal

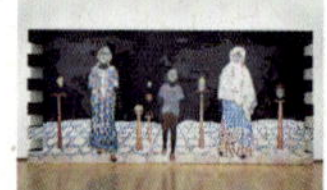

Clin d'œil à Cheikh Anta Diop – Un continent à la recherche de son histoire, 2017

Oil, pencil, acrylic, ink, gouache on corrugated card

330 × 718 × 40 cm

Courtesy Omar Ba and Galerie Templon,
New York / Paris / Brussels

RADCLIFFE BAILEY
born 1968 in Bridgeton, USA
died 2023 in Atlanta, USA

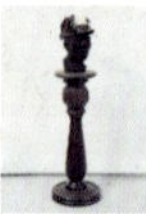

Untitled, 2010
Glitter, felt, feather, wood
125 × 35.5 × 28 cm
Courtesy Radcliffe Bailey and Jack Shainman Gallery, New York

---

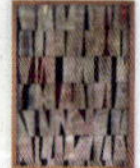

Mahalia, 2021
Mixed media including flock and acrylic paint components mounted on board, with window tint elements adhered to glazing
193 × 139 × 15.2 cm
Courtesy Radcliffe Bailey and Jack Shainman Gallery, New York

---

YTO BARRADA
born 1971 in Paris, France
lives and works between Tangier, Morocco; and New York, USA

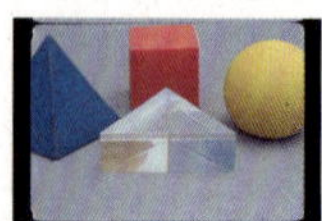

Tree Identification for Beginners, 2017
16 mm film, transferred to digital, color, sound
36 min
mumok – Museum moderner Kunst Stiftung Ludwig Wien, on loan from the Austrian Ludwig Foundation, since 2021

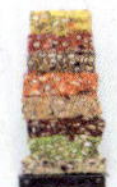

Untitled (Nougat Cross Section Flavor Sampler), 2016
Moroccan sweets, varnish
5 sculptures: 1: 28.7 × 15 × 3.5 cm, 2: 28.4 × 14.5 × 3.6 cm,
3: 28.9 × 15 × 4.4 cm, 4: 28 × 14.5 × 4.4 cm, 5: 28 × 15 × 4 cm
Courtesy Yto Barrada and Sfeir-Semler Gallery,
Beirut / Hamburg

MOHAMED BOUROUISSA

born 1978 in Blida, Algeria
lives and works in Gennevilliers, France

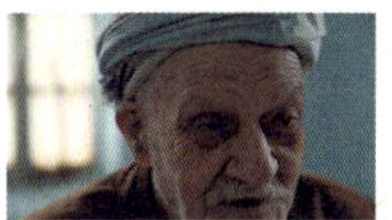

The Whispering of Ghosts, 2018
Video installation: wooden structure, video: color, sound, 13:15 min
Dimensions variable
Courtesy Mohamed Bourouissa and Mennour, Paris

DIEDRICK BRACKENS

born 1989 in Mexia, USA
lives and works in Los Angeles, USA

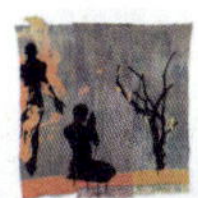

infernal garden, 2022
Woven cotton and acrylic yarn
264.2 × 251.5 cm
Courtesy Diedrick Brackens and Jack Shainman Gallery
New York

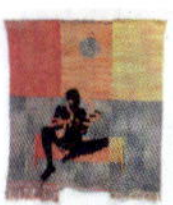

ingredients for lovers, 2022
Woven cotton and acrylic yarn
216 × 193 cm
Collection of Miyoung Lee and Neil Simpkins

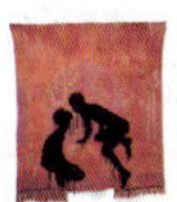

taste honey for nerves, 2021
Woven cotton and acrylic yarn, charms
228.6 × 205.7 cm
Courtesy Collection Lonti Ebers, New York

SERGE ATTUKWEI CLOTTEY

born 1985 in Accra, Ghana
lives and works in Accra, Ghana

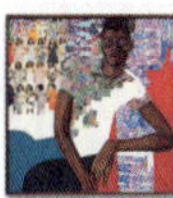

James Baldwin, 2020–21
Oil paint, paper posters, and duct tape on cork board
127 × 124.5 cm
Courtesy Serge Attukwei Clottey and Simchowitz Gallery,
Los Angeles

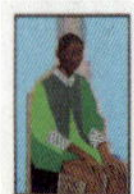

The Orphan, 2020–21
Oil paint and duct tape on cork board
193 × 124.5 cm
Courtesy Serge Attukwei Clottey and Simchowitz Gallery, Los Angeles

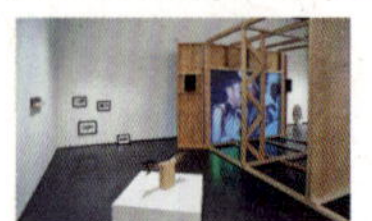

Yellow Sweater, 2020–21
Oil paint and duct tape on cork board
160 × 124.5 cm
Courtesy Serge Attukwei Clottey and Simchowitz Gallery, Los Angeles

WILLIAM CORDOVA
born 1969 in Lima, Peru
lives and works in Lima, Peru; Miami and New York, USA

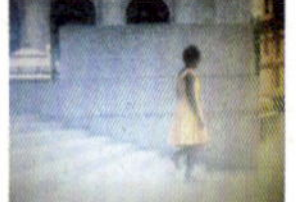

this one's 4U (pa' nosotros), 2008–15
Installation: wooden structure, screen, video
Image: *Tupac Shakur: Thug Angel* by Peter Spirer, 2002, 92 min;
Sound: *Tupac Amaru* by Federico Garcia Hurtado, 1984, 92 min
Dimensions variable
Courtesy william cordova and Livia Benavides 80M2, Lima, Peru

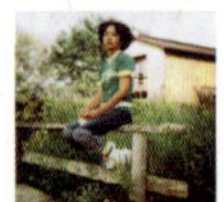

Sacsayhuaman (Stand Up Next 2 A Mountain), 2006–08
Digital video, filmed by the artist from Super 8 mm:
color, sound
1:10 min
Courtesy william cordova and Sikkema Jenkins & Co, New York

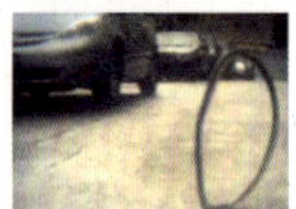

Badussy (or machu picchu after dark), 2003
Digital video, filmed by the artist from Super 8 mm film:
color, sound
2:30 min
Courtesy william cordova and Sikkema Jenkins & Co, New York

18° 6' 11.87" N, 94° 2' 24.69" W (de cero a la infinidad), 2009
Digital video, filmed by the artist from Super 8 mm film:
color, sound
0:30 min
Courtesy william cordova and Sikkema Jenkins & Co, New York

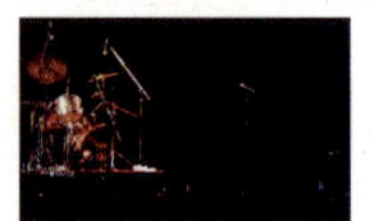

2 cents, 2005
Digital video, filmed by the artist from ¾-inch video:
color, sound
4 min
Courtesy william cordova and Sikkema Jenkins & Co, New York

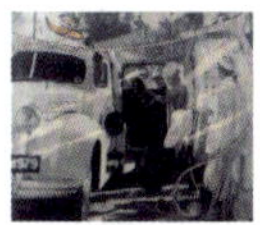

ATUL DODIYA

born in 1959, Mumbai, India
lives and works in Mumbai, India

Mahatma Gandhi entering G D Birla's Packard, 2016–18
Oil on canvas
182.1 × 212.6 cm
Courtesy Kiran Nadar Museum of Art, New Delhi

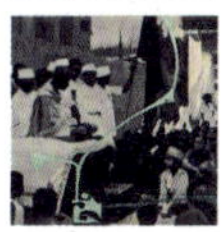

Volunteers at the Congress House – August 1931, 2014
Oil, acrylic with marble dust and oil-stick on canvas
183 × 183 cm
Courtesy Shirin and Kurush Jungalwala Collection, Mumbai

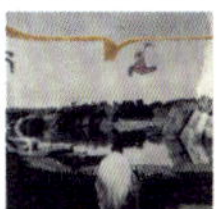

Visit to the marble rocks at Jabalpur 1941, 2016
Oil on canvas
183 × 183 cm
Courtesy private collection, Switzerland

ROBERT GABRIS

born 1988 in Hnúšťa-Likier, Slovakia
lives and works in Vienna, Austria

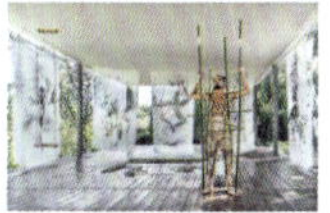

Insectopia, 2020

Performance and installation: 10 insects "autoprints": black
ink on white, transparent silk panels, 150 × 100 cm each;
2 swings: bamboo sticks and white bondage ropes; 6 masks:
bamboo sticks, pink cord; performance artifacts on transparent paper with black body print, 120 × 90 cm; 2 videos of
the performance (*Insectopia* by Ela Bialkowska / OKNOstudio,
2020: color, sound, 13:33 min; *Insectology in My Body* by David
Pujadas Bosch and Christiane Peschek, 2021, color, sound,
5:36 min)
Dimensions variable
Courtesy Robert Gabris

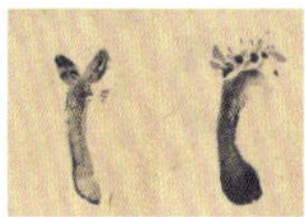

Insectology in My Body, 2020
7 "autoprints": black ink and fine liner 0.25 mm on brown paper
Framed 29 × 41 cm each
Courtesy private collection, Vienna, and Judit Reszegi, Budapest

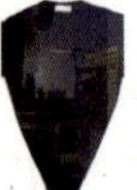

JOJO GRONOSTAY
born 1988 in Hamburg, Germany
lives and works in Vienna, Austria

Avant-Garde City, 2023
Video installation with three 75-inch display cubes: plywood
and acrylic; video: color, sound (soundpiece by Sami Mandee),
6 min (loop)
Courtesy Jojo Gronostay

LESLIE HEWITT
born 1977 in New York, USA
lives and works in Houston, USA

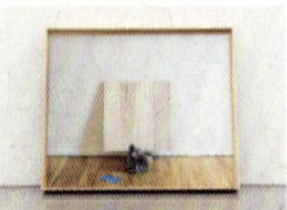

Untitled (Double Entendre), 2019
Digital C-print in custom elm frame
133 × 158 × 18 cm
Courtesy Leslie Hewitt and Perrotin

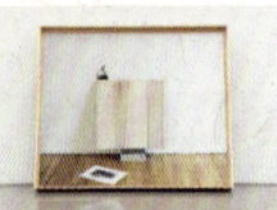

Untitled (Dreambook or Axis of the Ellipse), 2019
Digital C-print in custom elm frame
133 × 158 × 18 cm
Courtesy Leslie Hewitt and Perrotin

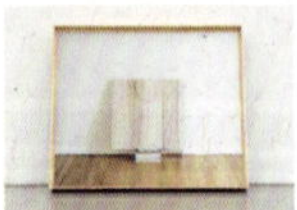

Untitled (The Notion of Labor), 2019
Digital C-print in custom elm frame
133 × 158 × 18 cm
Courtesy Leslie Hewitt and Perrotin

IMAN ISSA
born 1979 in Cairo, Egypt
lives and works in Vienna, Austria; and Berlin, Germany

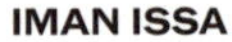

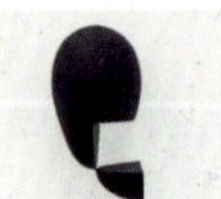

Self-Portrait (Self as Ananda K. Coomaraswamy), 2022
3D print, acrylic, epoxy, paint, metal poles
53 × 34 × 43 cm
Text panel under glass, 7 × 12 cm
Courtesy of Rodeo, London / Piraeus

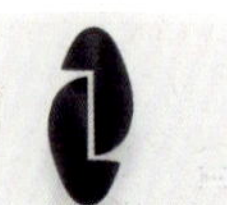

Self-Portrait (Self as Doria Shafik), 2020
3D print, acrylic, epoxy, paint, metal poles
60 × 33.5 × 43.5 cm
Text panel under glass, 7 × 12 cm
Courtesy of Rodeo, London / Piraeus

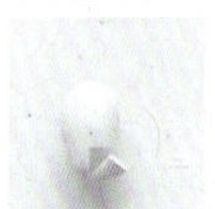

Self-Portrait (Self as Georges Henein), 2021
3D print, paint, epoxy, paint, metal poles
48 × 33 × 43 cm
Text panel under glass, 7 × 12 cm
Courtesy of Rodeo, London / Piraeus

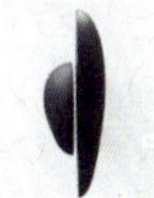

Self-Portrait (Self as Taha Hussein), 2020
3D prints, acrylic, epoxy, paint, metal poles
90 × 32.5 × 42.5 cm
Text panel under glass, 7 × 12 cm
Courtesy of Rodeo, London / Piraeus

JANINE JEMBERE
born 1985 in Magdeburg, Germany
lives and works in Vienna, Austria

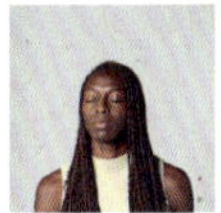

Channelling (Vienna), 2023
10-part series: C-prints
20 × 20 cm each
Courtesy Janine Jembere

PATRICIA KAERSENHOUT
born 1966 in Den Helder, Netherlands
lives and works in Amsterdam, Netherlands

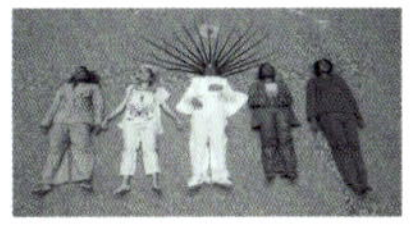

Le retour des femmes colibris, 2022
Film: black-and-white, sound
18:23 min
Courtesy patricia kaersenhout and Bonnefanten, Maastricht

BELINDA KAZEEM-KAMIŃSKI
born 1980 in Vienna, Austria
lives and works in Vienna, Austria

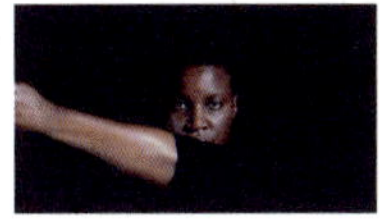

Untitled, K. T. C. I., 2022
Video: color, sound
5 min (loop)
Courtesy Belinda Kazeem-Kamiński and Wonnerth Dejaco

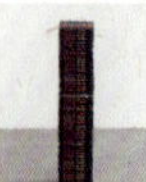

ZOE LEONARD
born 1961 in New York, USA
lives and works in New York, USA

Tipping Point, 2016
Installation: stack of 53 books (James Baldwin, *The Fire Next Time*, first edition, New York: Dial Press, 1963)
100 × 15 × 20 cm
Courtesy Artworkers Retirement Society

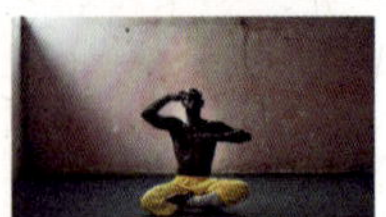

VINCENT MEESSEN
born 1971 in Baltimore, USA
lives and works in Brussels, Belgium

Juste un mouvement. The Sun Will Always Rise, 2020
Video installation: color, sound
110 min
Courtesy Vincent Meessen and NORMAL asbl

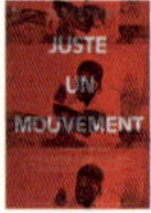

Juste un mouvement, 2021
Poster: print on paper
Graphic design: Speculoos
Courtesy Vincent Meessen and Speculoos

THE OTOLITH GROUP
founded in London in 2002 by Anjalika Sagar, born 1968 in London, United Kingdom, lives and works in London, United Kingdom and Kodwo Eshun, born 1967 in London, United Kingdom, lives and works in London, United Kingdom

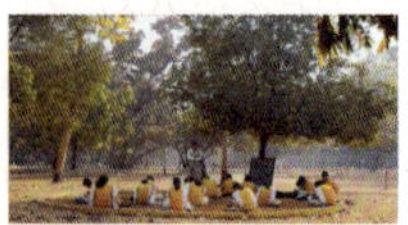

O Horizon, 2018
Video installation: color, sound
81 min
Courtesy The Otolith Group

FAHAMU PECOU
born 1975 in New York, USA
lives and works in Atlanta, USA

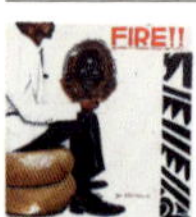

Return to My Native…, 2012
Acrylic on canvas
152 × 130 cm
Courtesy Fahamu Pecou and Backslash Gallery, Paris

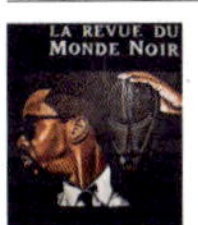

A.W.N. (Artist with Negritude), 2012
Acrylic on canvas
178 × 147 cm
Courtesy private collection, Switzerland

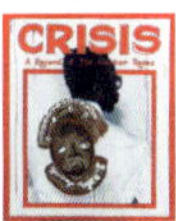

Corps perdu, l'âme se retrouve, 2012
Acrylic on canvas
178 × 148 cm
Courtesy Fahamu Pecou and Backslash Gallery, Paris

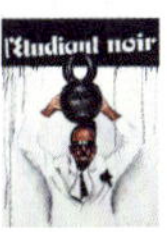

Real NEGUS do Real Things, 2012
Acrylic on canvas
178 × 137 cm
Courtesy Elena Markwalder

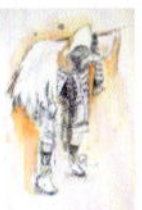

Egun Dance 02, 2016
Graphite and acrylic on paper
152.4 × 101.6 cm
Courtesy Fahamu Pecou

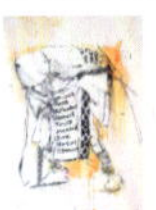

Egun Dance 04, 2016
Graphite and acrylic on paper
152.4 × 101.6 cm
Lent by the Michael C. Carlos Museum
Anonymous gift

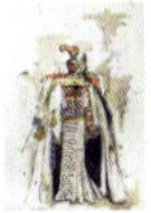

Prayer Warrior Egungun, 2020
Mixed media
152.4 × 101.6 cm
Courtesy Fahamu Pecou

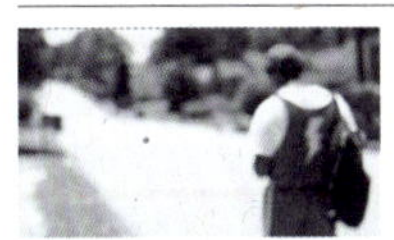

Emmet Still, 2016
Video: color, sound
16 min
Courtesy Fahamu Pecou and Backslash Gallery, Paris

CAULEEN SMITH
born 1967 in Riverside, USA
lives and works in Los Angeles, USA

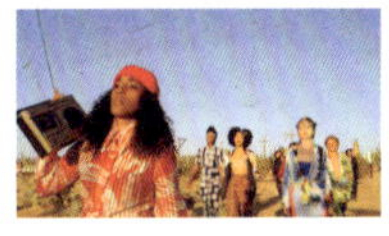

Sojourner, 2018
Video installation: color, sound
22:41 min
Courtesy Cauleen Smith and Morán Morán,
Los Angeles / Mexico City

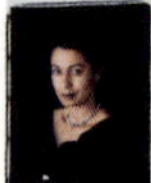

MAUD SULTER
born 1960 in Glasgow, Scotland
died 2008 in Dumfries, Scotland

Les Bijoux, 2002–06
9-part series: large-format Polaroid
68.5 × 51.8 cm each
Courtesy The Estate of Maud Sulter

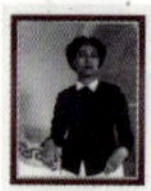

Hysteria, 1991
Documentation materials
Courtesy The Estate of Maud Sulter

VIVAN SUNDARAM
born 1943 in Shimla, India
died 2023 in New Delhi, India

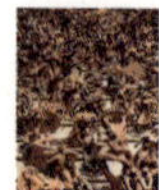

One and the Many, 2015
Installation: 220 terracotta figurines
Dimensions variable
Edition 2/2
mumok – Museum moderner Kunst Stiftung Ludwig Wien,
donation courtesy Geeta Kapur, 2024

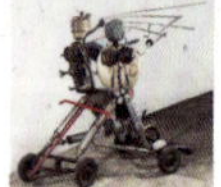

Mill Re-Call, 2015
Wood, metal, rubber, enamel paint, electric light
251.5 × 251.5 × 101.6 cm
Courtesy Kiran Nadar Museum of Art, New Delhi

MOFFAT TAKADIWA
born 1983 in Karoi, Zimbabwe
lives and works in Harare, Zimbabwe

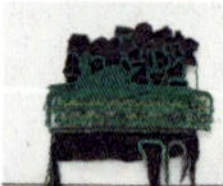

The Occupation of Land, 2019
Found computer keys, toothbrushes,
plastic bottle tops
304.8 × 365.7 × 17.8 cm
Courtesy Moffat Takadiwa and Nicodim Gallery

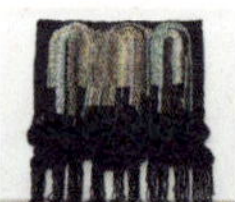

The Afronauts, 2021
Found computer keys, plastic bottle tops,
toothbrush heads
310 × 280 × 15 cm
Courtesy Moffat Takadiwa and Nicodim Gallery

COLOPHON

**MUMOK – MUSEUM MODERNER KUNST
STIFTUNG LUDWIG WIEN**

General Director
Karola Kraus

Managing Director
Cornelia Lamprechter

Assistants to the Director
Sandra Adam, Simone Arnold

Board and Fundraising, Sponsoring
Karin Kirste (Head)
Cornelia Stellwag-Carion

**Assistance Personnel and
Internal Communication**
Julia Grandmontagne

**Head of Special Projects and
Quality Management**
Robert Reitbauer

Curators
Manuela Ammer, Marianne Dobner,
Heike Eipeldauer, Naoko Kaltschmidt,
Matthias Michalka, Franz Thalmair

Head of Exhibition Management
Birgit Schretzmayr

Exhibition Organization
Natascha Boojar, Claudia Dohr,
Elena Guerrero, Chiara Juchem,
Lisa Schwarz (Maternity Leave),
Dagmar Steyrer

Publications
Ines Gebetsroither, Nina Krick,
Manuel Millautz

Head of Collection
Marie-Therese Hochwartner

Registrars and Depot Management
Lisa Sträter (Head), Nicole Bauer,
Anna Kudla, Alexandra Pinter,
Katarina Savora, Suska Tunks (Registrars),
Franklin Castanien (Art Handling),
Max Halstead (Art Handling, Depot and
Site Management)

Conservation
Christina Hierl (Head), Andrea Kappes,
Kathrine Ruppen, Andreas Schweger,
Karin Steiner

Digital Collection and Archives
Marie-Therese Hochwartner (Head),
Claudia Freiberger (Curator Digital
Collections), Hannah Imhoff (Digital
Collections), Benedikt Hochwartner
(Curator Creative Learning), Nora Linser
(Data Curator), Christina Schaaf-Fundneider
(Strategy and Innovation)

Library
Simone Moser (Head), Martha Horvarth

Photography
Leni Deinhardstein-Myers (Head)
Stella Roth

**Head of Finances,
Deputy to the Managing Director**
Laura Hamid (Maternity Leave)

Accounting and Controlling
Simon Novotny, Sonja Scherz

Personnel Administration and Accounting
Andrea Cee, Charlotte Schwarz

Controlling and Internal Revision
Laura Hamid (Maternity Leave)

**Head of Marketing,
Communication, and Sales**
Martina Kuso

Marketing
Elisabeth Dopsch, Isabella Pedevilla,
Malina Schartmüller, Lisa Sycha

Public Relations
Katharina Murschetz (Head)
Katharina Kober

Events and Rentals
Victoria Mascha, Thomas Tröger

Shop and Ticketing
Mario Greller (Head), Lisa Chittilappilly,
Gerald Heltschel, Pia Renk, Stefan Simos

Head of Art Education
Marie-Therese Hochwartner

Organizational Head of Art Education
Julia Hürner

**Strategic Community
and Educational Management**
Lena Arends

**Assistants to the
Art Education Department**
Maria Huber, Lea Tiernan

Art Education Team
Lena Arends, Jakob Diallo, Annika Friedrich,
Astrid Frieser, Florentina Gara, Stefanie
Graf, Marisa Emma Heyn, Ivan Jurica
(Educational Leave), Michaela Molnar, Mikki
Muhr, Patrick Puls (Educational Leave),
Carlotta Rothenstein

**Head of Technical Department and
Operations**
Oliver Kern

**Inhouse and Exhibition Technicians,
Facility Management**
Tina Fabijanic (Head), Wolfgang Moser,
Gregor Neuwirth, Andreas Petz,
Helmut Raidl, Sylwester Syndoman

IT
Thorsten Rüben (Head), Reinhard Mader,
Alexander Sacher, Rudolf Sacher (IT),
Anselm Pavlik (Event Technology and Digital
Formats), Leopold Weiß (Apprentice)

**Head of Museum Guards and
Security Office**
Rubin Zistler

Security Office
Werner Appel, Rosa Falzarano,
Marcin Grudzien, Kateryna Hrynenko,
Gernot Enrique Korinek, Jan Petersen,
Alexandra Tscherne, Daniel Yilmaz

**Technical Administration and Assistance
to the Head of Inhouse and Exhibition
Technicians, Facility Management**
Barbara Panny

**Technical Administration and Assistance
to the Head of Security Centre and
Supervision**
Danijel Woynar

Thanks to all Museum Guards

EXHIBITION

***Avant-Garde and Liberation.
Contemporary Art and
Decolonial Modernism***
June 7 to September 22, 2024

Exhibition Curators
Christian Kravagna (Guest Curator)
Matthias Michalka (Co-Curator)

Head of Exhibition Management
Birgit Schretzmayr

Exhibition Organization
Claudia Dohr

Exhibition Architecture
Wilfried Kühn, Wassily Walter

**Head of Technical Department and
Operations**
Oliver Kern

Exhibition Installation
Tina Fabijanic (Head), Wolfgang Moser,
Gregor Neuwirth, Andreas Petz,
Helmut Raidl, Sylwester Syndoman,
with must. museum standards

Audiovisual Technician
Michael Krupica

Conservation
Christina Hierl (Head), Andrea Kappes,
Kathrine Ruppen, Andreas Schweger,
Karin Steiner, Sophia Vogler

Fundraising and Sponsoring
Karin Kirste (Head)
Cornelia Stellwag-Carion

Marketing, Communication, and Sales
Martina Kuso (Head of Department),
Katharina Murschetz (Head of Press),
Katharina Kober (Press), Elisabeth Dopsch
(Social Media), Isabella Pedevilla (Digital
Marketing), Malina Schartmüller (Marketing
Cooperations), Lisa Sycha (Print Production)

Art Education
Marie-Therese Hochwartner (Head of
Department), Julia Hürner (Head of Art
Education), Maria Huber (Assistant),
Benedikt Hochwartner (Curator Creative
Learning), Lena Arends (Strategic
Community and Educational Management),
Jakob Diallo, Annika Friedrich, Astrid Frieser,
Florentina Gara, Stefanie Graf, Marisa Heyn,
Michaela Molnar, Mikki Muhr, Carlotta
Rothenstein (Art Education Team)

**Head of Museum Guards and
Security Office**
Rubin Zistler

Exhibition Sponsors

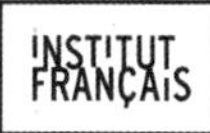

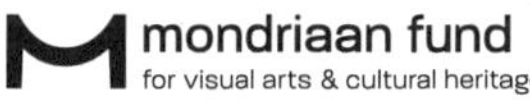

mondriaan fund
for visual arts & cultural heritage

A...kademie der
bildenden Künste Wien
Academy of Fine Arts Vienna

Media Partners

DER STANDARD

FALTER

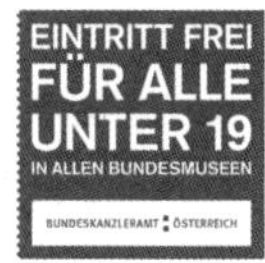
Ö1 CLUB

Free admission under 19

CATALOGUE

This catalogue is published in conjunction
with the exhibition

***Avant-Garde and Liberation.
Contemporary Art and
Decolonial Modernism***
June 7 to September 22, 2024

Edited by
Christian Kravagna

and mumok – Museum moderner Kunst
Stiftung Ludwig Wien
Museumsplatz 1
1070 Wien
T: +43 (0) 1 525 00-0
F: +43 (0) 1 525 00-1300
www.mumok.at

ISBN
978-3-903446-11-3

Managing Editors
Ines Gebetsroither, Nina Krick

Editorial Staff
Ines Gebetsroither, Christian Kravagna,
Nina Krick, Matthias Michalka

Texts
Nana Adusei-Poku, Zeigam Azisov,
Karola Kraus, Christian Kravagna,
Saloni Mathur, Matthias Michalka,
Lina Ramadan

Work Descriptions
Christian Kravagna

English Copy Editor
Wendy Brouwer

English Translation
Jennifer Taylor (Preface, Kravagna essay,
work descriptions)

Graphic Design
Clemens Jahn, Berlin

Lithography
Pixelstorm, Vienna

Typefaces
ROM (ABC Dinamo)
Signifier (Klim Type Foundry)

Papers
Invercote G 260 g/m², Circle Offset
white 110 g/m², Garda Pat Bianka 135 g/m²

Printed by
Gugler GmbH, 3390 Melk/Donau

Print Run
850

© 2024 Museum moderner Kunst Stiftung
Ludwig Wien, Verlag der Buchhandlung
Walther und Franz König, Cologne, the
artists, authors, graphic designers, photographers, and their assignees.

The Deutsche Nationalbibliothek lists this
publication in the Deutsche Nationalbiblio-
grafie; detailed bibliographic data are available on the Internet at http://dnb.ddb.de.
No part of this book may be reproduced in
any form or by any electronic or mechanical
means without prior permission from the
copyright holders.

Printed in Austria
All Rights Reserved

Distribution
Published by Verlag der Buchhandlung
Walther und Franz König, Cologne, Germany

ISBN 978-3-7533-0611-7

Buchhandlung Walther und Franz König,
Cologne
Ehrenstraße 4
50672 Köln
Germany
T: +49 (0) 221 205 96-53
F: +49 (0) 221 205 96-60
verlag@buchhandlung-walther-koenig.de

UK & Ireland:
Cornerhouse Publications
2 Tony Wilson Place
Manchester, M15 4FN
United Kingdom
T: +44 (0) 161 212 34 66
F: +44 (0) 161 236 90 79
publications@cornerhouse.org

Outside Europe:
D.A.P. | Distributed Art Publishers, Inc.
75 Broad Street, Suite 630
New York, NY 10004
United States of America
T: +1 (0) 212 627 19 99
F: +1 (0) 212 627 94 84
eleshowitz@dapinc.com

A German edition (ISBN 978-3-7533-
0610-0) is also published by Verlag der
Buchhandlung Walther König